Rediscovering Voluntary Action

The Beat of a Different Drum

Colin Rochester
Birkbeck, University of London, UK

palgrave
macmillan

© Colin Rochester 2013

All rights reserved. No reproduction, copy or transmission of this publication may be made without written permission.

No portion of this publication may be reproduced, copied or transmitted save with written permission or in accordance with the provisions of the Copyright, Designs and Patents Act 1988, or under the terms of any licence permitting limited copying issued by the Copyright Licensing Agency, Saffron House, 6–10 Kirby Street, London EC1N 8TS.

Any person who does any unauthorized act in relation to this publication may be liable to criminal prosecution and civil claims for damages.

The author has asserted his right to be identified as the author of this work in accordance with the Copyright, Designs and Patents Act 1988.

First published 2013 by
PALGRAVE MACMILLAN

Palgrave Macmillan in the UK is an imprint of Macmillan Publishers Limited, registered in England, company number 785998, of Houndmills, Basingstoke, Hampshire RG21 6XS.

Palgrave Macmillan in the US is a division of St Martin's Press LLC, 175 Fifth Avenue, New York, NY 10010.

Palgrave Macmillan is the global academic imprint of the above companies and has companies and representatives throughout the world.

Palgrave® and Macmillan® are registered trademarks in the United States, the United Kingdom, Europe and other countries.

ISBN 978–1–137–02944–7 hardback
ISBN 978–1–137–02945–4 paperback

This book is printed on paper suitable for recycling and made from fully managed and sustained forest sources. Logging, pulping and manufacturing processes are expected to conform to the environmental regulations of the country of origin.

A catalogue record for this book is available from the British Library.

A catalog record for this book is available from the Library of Congress.

Contents

List of Figures and Tables   vii

Acknowledgements   viii

List of Abbreviations   x

1 Introduction: Why the Theory and Practice of Voluntary
   Action Need Rethinking   1

Part I The Context

2 Revisiting the Roots of Voluntary Action   15

3 The Invention of the Voluntary Sector and its
   Consequences   36

4 The Invention of Voluntary Work and its Consequences   53

Part II Pressures and Influences

5 A Perilous Partnership? Voluntary Action and the State   69

6 Selling Out? Voluntary Action and the Market   85

7 The Hegemony of the Bureaucratic Model   99

8 The Pressure from Within   112

Part III Alternative Perspectives

9 Governance, Ownership and Control   133

10 What Is Voluntary Action For?   147

11 The Fallacies of Managerialism   161

12 Towards a 'Round Earth' Map of Volunteering   176

13 Dissenting Voices: The Case of the National Coalition for
    Independent Action   189

Part IV Conclusions and Implications

14 The Paradox of Sectorisation 205

15 Towards an Alternative Paradigm 216

16 The Implications of Rethinking Voluntary Action 231

References 245

Index 258

Figures and Tables

Figures

7.1 The traditional ABC model   101
7.2 The Billis 'worlds' theory   107
12.1 A three perspectives model   181

Tables

15.1 The conventional organisational model   221
16.1 A sector typology   236

Acknowledgements

I could not have written this book without the education I have received at the hands of many people – far too many to acknowledge properly – during the 45 years I have worked with volunteers and voluntary organisations. In my early years, as a practitioner, I benefitted from working with a series of inspiring colleagues – in the Workers' Educational Association (WEA), at Cambridge House and Talbot Settlement and in the wider networks of the British Association of Settlements and Social Action Centre (BASSAC) and the voluntary sector in Southwark. In my second career as a researcher and teacher I have had the great good fortune to work with colleagues at the London School of Economics (LSE) Centre for Voluntary Organisation, at Roehampton University and with the Institute for Volunteering Research as well as in three associations of researchers – the Association for Research on Voluntary Action (ARVAC); the Voluntary Sector Studies Network (VSSN); and the Voluntary Action History Society (VAHS). And my thinking has been shaped by fruitful encounters with a series of students who have taught me more than I managed to teach them – in WEA classes and in postgraduate courses at the LSE and at Roehampton.

I hope the many who remain unmentioned by name will not mind if I single out a smaller number of people who have made more specific contributions to the development of the book. In the first place, my intellectual debt to David Billis will be clear to the reader and I count myself very fortunate indeed to have enjoyed his support and encouragement as teacher, colleague, mentor and friend. If David has provided me with the means of writing the book, others have given me valuable assistance in converting a vague aspiration into the finished article. I received a great deal of initial encouragement from Jurgen Grotz, who prodded me until I had developed the original outline for the work and provided me with an early platform for sharing some of my ideas at an ARVAC event. I am grateful to Andy Benson and Penny Waterhouse for their enthusiastic support and, with other members of NCIA, for their contribution to the series of seminars at Roehampton University where I clarified and tested my thinking. I should also like to thank the other friends and colleagues who took part in these critical discussions. I am very much indebted to my former colleagues at Roehampton,

Steven Howlett and Bill Rushbrooke, who, as well as providing general encouragement and support, have helped in very specific and practical ways. Steven took on the lion's share of organising the seminar series and Bill reviewed the original draft of my manuscript. My partner, Meta Zimmeck, has been a tower of strength and a candid critic: she has read the manuscript with great care, suggesting improvements to it and eliminating a number of blemishes, as well as helping me through the dark times when I wondered if I would ever complete the task I had set myself. Finally, I need to add the conventional but necessary caveat: any errors of fact, judgement or taste in what follows are the sole responsibility of the author.

Abbreviations

ACEVO	Association of Chief Executives of Voluntary Organisations
ACU	Active Community Unit
ARNOVA	Association for Research on Nonprofit Organizations and Voluntary Action
AVAS	Association of Voluntary Action Scholars
BASSAC	British Association of Settlements and Social Action Centres
CAF	Charities Aid Foundation
CIC	Community Interest Company
CIU	Club and Institute Union
COS	Charity Organisation Society
CVS	Council of Voluntary Service
DSC	Directory of Social Change
ESRC	Economic and Social Research Council
EVDC	England Volunteering Development Council
IS	Independent Sector
ISTR	International Society for Third Sector Research
LSE	London School of Economics and Political Science
LSVT	Large Scale Voluntary Transfer Housing Association
MDU	Management Development Unit
NAVCA	National Association for Voluntary and Community Action
NatCAN	National Community Activists Network
NACVS	National Association of Councils of Voluntary Service
NCIA	National Coalition for Independent Action
NCSS	National Council for Social Service
NCVO	National Council for Voluntary Organisations
NEF	New Economics Foundation
NGO	Non-Governmental Organisation
OCS	Office for Civil Society
OTS	Office for the Third Sector
PORTVAC	Programme of Research and Training into Voluntary Action

PQASSO	Practical Quality Assurance System for Small Organisations
QSTG	Quality Standards Task Group
RCC	Rural Community Council
SORP	Statement of Recommended Practice
STVS	Strengthening the Voluntary Sector
TAA	Total Activities Analysis
TSRC	Third Sector Research Centre
VCSE	Voluntary, Community and Social Enterprise
VE	Volunteering England
VSSN	Voluntary Sector Studies Network
VSU	Voluntary Services Unit
UNV	United Nations Volunteers
WEA	Workers' Educational Association

1
Introduction: Why the Theory and Practice of Voluntary Action Need Rethinking

This book is rooted in my experience of working in and with volunteers and voluntary organisations over more than 40 years as a practitioner, manager, trustee, researcher and teacher of postgraduate students. It is an attempt to address my growing unease or anxiety about how the ways in which we understand and discuss the nature and purpose of voluntary action and the ways in which we go about it have changed over the past two or three decades. I have increasingly come to believe that these changes threaten the health and vitality of a kind of behaviour that has played a key part in shaping the kind of society we live in and has made an important contribution to the quality of our lives.

During the last 20 years or so, voluntary organisations have come to be seen as ever more significant actors on the stage of public and social policy, while successive governments have looked to volunteering as a means of addressing a variety of social issues. Urged on by 'second tier' or 'infrastructure' bodies such as the National Council for Voluntary Organisations (NCVO), those who manage and lead voluntary organisations have enthusiastically embraced the opportunities created by these developments (and the resources which go with them) with little, if any, reflection on the implications of their decisions. At the same time, the growth of academic interest in voluntary action has not led to a body of theory which could throw light on these changes by providing a persuasive explanation of why voluntary organisations are qualitatively different from their counterparts in the public and private or 'for profit' sectors, or an authoritative account of the distinctive kind of behaviour involved in volunteering. In the past few years concerns about the implications of recent developments for the autonomy of voluntary organisations have led to the establishment of the National Coalition for Independent Action (NCIA) in 2006 and the setting up of a

Panel on the Independence of the Voluntary Sector by the Baring Foundation in 2011. The need to rethink voluntary action, however, is driven not just by concerns about independence but, more fundamentally, by anxiety about the possible loss of the distinctive *identity* of voluntary organisations and volunteering.

This opening chapter will provide an introduction to the book by discussing in turn:

- my own experience of voluntary action and the ways in which it has shaped the perceptions and perspectives that inform the book;
- the need to challenge the narrow double-headed paradigm that sets the terms for much of the contemporary discussion of voluntary action. This provides the conceptual underpinning of much of the book's argument; and
- the way in which the book is structured and why.

At this point, however, it might be helpful if I were to clarify the way in which some key terms will be used throughout the book. The term *voluntary action* is used to embrace both the activities of individuals (volunteering) and collective or organised action (by voluntary organisations). The *voluntary and community sector* is my preferred name for the heterogeneous collection of organisations that are not part of the state (or public sector) or part of the market (or private, for-profit sector). At times I may abbreviate this to *voluntary sector*. The terms used by other writers, including *non-profit sector*, *third sector* and *civil society*, are, broadly speaking, synonymous, although they may carry some ideological nuances. *Voluntary organisation* (or *voluntary sector organisation* or *voluntary and community sector organisation*) is used to mean any of the various organisational forms to be found in the voluntary sector. By contrast, the use of *voluntary agencies* is applied only to those voluntary organisations which employ paid staff. Other terms will be defined as and when they appear in the text.

My own experience and perspectives

I have decided to provide an account of my own 'adventures' in the world of voluntary action at this stage for two reasons. In the first place, it will provide the reader with an insight into the kind of experiences that have shaped my approach to the book; it is a part of the data on which I have based my arguments. In the second place, it is intended to highlight some of the possible limitations on my vision; it is my experience that people who work in the voluntary sector rarely have a clear view of the sector as a whole in all its variety, but tend instead to see it through the distorting lens of the kind of organisations with which they are most familiar. I have tried to transcend this kind of myopia, but have provided the means by which the reader can judge how successful my efforts have been. In a sense I am following a similar path to that taken by Marilyn Taylor, who described her book on *Public Policy and the Community* as 'an odyssey – a journey through experience, discussion and reading' (Taylor, 2011: xi), and, like her, I need to make that experience explicit.

My serious involvement with voluntary action began in 1968 when I joined the Workers' Educational Association (WEA) as a tutor-organiser. The WEA's work of organising adult education classes was carried out by a network of local branches entirely staffed by volunteers, and my responsibilities included nurturing and supporting the work of 15 such local units as well as teaching a number of evening and day-time classes. As a result my initial engagement was with the kind of 'grassroots associations' (as David Horton Smith (2000) has called them) that formed part of what was later to be known as the 'community sector'. After three years in the field I joined the staff of the WEA's national headquarters, where, as well as retaining responsibility for the well-being of the association's local branches, I broadened my experience to include participation in a number of national voluntary organisations – including the forerunner of the NCVO, the National Council for Social Service, and liaison with the education department of the Trades Union Congress and individual trades unions. And I began to appreciate the dynamics of organisational change (although it was only with hindsight that I understood what was going on) as the WEA grappled with a slow but irreversible shift of power from the periphery to the centre and the emergence of its professional staff as an important feature of an organisation which had hitherto depended on the voluntary efforts of its members.

Following this extended introduction to the world of voluntary action, I spent nine years as the Head of Cambridge House and Talbot, the Cambridge University Settlement in Camberwell, South London. Cambridge House was the centre for a variety of forms of voluntary action, some directly managed by the settlement itself and others provided by the voluntary agencies, projects and community groups that shared the building. The spectrum of activities encompassed survivals of nineteenth-century philanthropy such as organising country holidays for children in need; the provision of more contemporary services such as legal advice and assistance, adult literacy tuition, work with children and young people, and activities for people with learning disabilities; community development work with local tenants' associations and other bodies; self-help and mutual aid groups such as Gingerbread for one-parent families; a social club run by its members; and a miscellaneous collection of leisure-time activities including martial arts and spiritual healing. As well as managing Cambridge House's own in-house activities and engaging with the dozens of paid staff and hundreds of volunteers associated with the settlement's wider activities, the Head was expected to involve him or herself in the work of other organisations at both local and national levels. In my case this included participation in the work of the local Council for Voluntary Service as a trustee and with the Volunteer Bureau as chair, and involvement in the settlement's national umbrella organisation – the British Association of Settlements and Social Action Centres (BASSAC) – in a number of capacities. My period at Cambridge House, therefore, gave me not only the experience of directly managing a complex voluntary agency but also a much broader knowledge of different forms of voluntary action and insights into the ways in which voluntary organisations interacted with the local and national state.

In 1987, after almost 20 years as a practitioner, I left the settlement and embarked on a new career as an organisational consultant, researcher and lecturer, first at the London School of Economics' (LSE) Centre for Voluntary Organisation (which became the Centre for Civil Society) and subsequently at Roehampton University, where I established the Centre for the Study of Voluntary and Community Activity. During this second half of my engagement with voluntary action, my portfolio of interests was varied: it included governance, religious and faith-based organisations, volunteering, relationships between government and the voluntary sector, and the work of 'second-tier' organisations. Within this range of interests, however, was a strong bias towards smaller and less formal organisational forms like community sector organisations (Rochester, 1992, 1997, 1998) and very small voluntary agencies (Rochester, 1999a, 1999b; Rochester *et al.*, 1999). I have also been interested in the ways in which the work and aims of voluntary organisations have been shaped by their past and, with Rodney Hedley and Justin Davis Smith, founded the Voluntary Action History Society in 1991.

During the past ten years or so I have felt increasing disquiet or discomfort about the ways in which many voluntary organisations, individually and collectively, were going about their affairs. There was less evidence that they were fulfilling the crucial role of identifying need and developing ways of responding to it rather than providing the kinds of services for the kinds of user prescribed by the agencies of national and local government. Increasingly, moreover, they were adopting the managerial approaches developed in the world of business and introduced to the statutory sector in the guise of New Public Management; those who lead voluntary agencies became known as 'chief executives', their committees of management were increasingly referred to as boards, and, in an attempt to respond to calls for them to be more 'business-like', they increasingly saw themselves as businesses and their beneficiaries and funders as 'customers'. The period also saw the emergence of volunteer management as a new profession, which increasingly saw itself as a branch of human resources management and adopted 'off the shelf' techniques based on managing paid staff rather than the 'home-grown' approaches to supporting volunteers and organising their work which had developed on the ground (Zimmeck, 2000). And, finally, the campaigning and advocacy edge which voluntary organisations had brought to the public and social policy arena was dulled by the engagement of many of them in a range of partnership arrangements based on the government's view that the interests of the voluntary sector (and the corporate world) were more or less identical with their own and that apparently intractable social problems could only be tackled by a joint approach by all three sectors.

Alongside my growing dismay at the ways in which voluntary organisations were losing the ability to pursue new ways of addressing need, the confidence to manage their affairs in a distinctive way and the commitment to providing the people and the communities they served with a voice, I also felt more and more concerned about the direction being taken by the growing voluntary sector research community. David Billis in the UK (1993a, 2010a) and Roger Lohmann (1992) and David Mason in the USA (1995) have developed important theories to explain why and how voluntary organisations are qualitatively different from their counterparts in the for-profit and public sectors, while David Horton Smith (2000) has provided not only an incisive critique of the concentration of much scholarly attention on the minority of voluntary organisations which are led by professional staff but also a comprehensive account of the organisation and behaviour of the 'grassroots associations' which make up the majority of the sector's population. These have, however, had remarkably little influence on the ways in which researchers have gone about their business, and there are few examples of the use of these theoretical frameworks to explore and explain how the distinctive characteristics of voluntary organisations influence and affect what they do and how they do it. And, as a result, the academic literature contains little to challenge or slow down the way in which the role and behaviour of voluntary organisations have been changing.

It was these concerns that led to the idea of a book on 'rethinking voluntary action'. I began to develop this analysis in a lecture entitled *A Decade of Civil Society under New Labour* that was delivered at the British Academy in February 2009 (Rochester, 2009). The exploration of the dominant paradigm in volunteering formed an important strand in a book that I co-authored with Angela Ellis Paine and Steven Howlett (Rochester *et al.*, 2010). And the ideas that underpin this proposal were presented and subjected to critical analysis at a series of seminars on *Rethinking Voluntary Action* that were jointly organised by the Centre for the Study of Voluntary and Community Activity at Roehampton University and NCIA and held at the University of Roehampton during 2010 and 2011. The seminar series provided an invaluable opportunity to present some of my emerging thoughts on the issues to an informed and critical audience and has enabled me to develop the argument that is put forward in this book and the confidence to offer it for publication.

Two paradigms

At the centre of the book's argument is the contention that the theory and practice of voluntary action are constrained by two narrow paradigms which set the boundaries for the ways in which we look at voluntary organisations, on the one hand, and volunteering, on the other. In both cases they involve 'taken-for-granted' and implicit assumptions about the nature of the phenomena that are based on the features of just one part of the full spectrum of voluntary organisations and volunteering, respectively.

- The *voluntary sector paradigm* – which shapes the actions of voluntary organisations and those who promote and support their work – characterises organisational expressions of voluntary action as formally constituted and managed agencies with conventional hierarchical structures that are controlled and led by paid managers. They employ staff to carry out their operational activities, which take the form of the provision of services to one or more kinds of user. It also involves the assumption that voluntary agencies operate in the general arena of social welfare.

- The *dominant paradigm in volunteering* characterises it as a gift of time that is analogous to a gift of money – a philanthropic activity to help someone less fortunate than oneself. It sees volunteers as being active in the field of social welfare (broadly defined); taking up opportunities provided mainly by large, professionally staffed and formally structured organisations; and undertaking activities that have been pre-determined by the volunteer-involving agencies. Volunteering is thus seen essentially as unpaid work that needs to be managed.

Organised voluntary action, however, takes a variety of forms; performs a number of different roles or functions; and plays a part in the full gamut of human activities. The great majority of voluntary organisations are totally dependent on the voluntary efforts of their members and supporters, and only a small minority employ paid staff. They include a variety of organisational forms including membership associations, self-help groups and informal groupings around common concerns and interests. They may address their own needs rather than those of others and, rather than providing services, they may direct their energies to advocacy and campaigning, to mutual support and self-help, or to providing opportunities for creative activities or other forms of expressive behaviour. They are as likely to be found in the fields of sport, recreational and cultural activities and in concerns for the environment (and for the well-being of animals) as in the area of social welfare.

Similarly, the volunteering paradigm does not take account of the many different motivations that prompt people to become involved, the engagement of volunteers in a variety of fields beyond social welfare, the diversity of organisational contexts within which volunteering takes place, and the range of roles undertaken by volunteers. Reasons for involvement may be rooted in self-help and mutual aid rather than altruism, or may be driven by the intrinsic satisfaction of taking part in a cultural or recreational activity. Volunteers are active in a range of public policy areas such as transport, town planning and the environment, and, beyond that, play a key part in the full gamut of educational, cultural and recreational activities. Volunteering takes place in a variety of formal and less formal organisational contexts and involves a variety of roles beyond that of the unpaid helper. Volunteers lead and manage the work of associations and small agencies, and their contributions in the world of sport and the arts include coaching, teaching or tutoring others; acting as directors, conductors or managers; and officiating at matches and judging competitions.

The book will therefore seek to present a new paradigm – a more rounded, more adequate and more deeply rooted account of voluntary action – with which to replace the set of assumptions on which the current theory and practice of the voluntary sector and volunteering are based.

Structure of the book

The main body of the book is organised in four parts, which present in turn: a review of the historical context for our current thinking about voluntary action; an analysis of the pressures and influences that have shaped and continue to shape its theory and practice; alternative perspectives on some of the key elements of the current paradigms of voluntary action; and the main features of a more rounded paradigm of voluntary action and its implications.

Part I consists of three chapters that provide the context for what follows.

Chapter 2, 'Revisiting the Roots of Voluntary Action', offers both a critique of the inadequacy of the current state of the historiography of voluntary action and an attempt to show how its limitations can be addressed. It argues that the roots of voluntary action extend beyond the twin impulses of philanthropy and mutual aid identified by Beveridge in 1948 to include conviviality; non-party politics; and the pursuit of 'serious leisure'. This more inclusive approach provides the basis for a comprehensive review of the history of volunteering and voluntary organisations, and the chapter concludes by considering the implications of this broader view of voluntary action history for the ways in which we view the contemporary scene.

Chapter 3, 'The Invention of the Voluntary Sector and its Consequences', looks in more detail at the past three decades or so, during which the idea of a voluntary *sector* has become such an influential concept. It discusses the circumstances in which the voluntary sector was 'invented' and reviews the growing acceptance and usage of the term both as a means of distinguishing voluntary action from the 'public' or 'governmental' and the 'private' or 'for-profit' sectors and as a badge of identity for voluntary organisations. The chapter looks at the impact of the wide range of sector-specific initiatives and institutional responses which followed, and outlines the ways in which the notion of a sector has had an impact on the relationship between voluntary organisations and the state.

Chapter 4, 'The Invention of Voluntary Work and its Consequences', discusses the ways in which the creation and acceptance of the idea of a sector as a means of categorising and giving meaning to the organisations involved in voluntary action have been accompanied by a similar but less remarked process through which voluntary action by individuals has come to be seen as 'voluntary work'. While the phrase itself has by no means attained the currency of the sector metaphor, it has had a powerful impact on the way in which volunteering has been perceived, discussed and promoted. This chapter explores the roots of this perspective; discusses its implications; and assesses its impact.

Part II, 'Pressures and Influences', consists of four chapters that explore the key factors that have shaped the contemporary understanding of the voluntary sector and volunteering.

Chapter 5, 'A Perilous Partnership? Voluntary Action and the State', acknowledges that much of the history of voluntary action – especially in the broad field of social welfare – cannot easily be disentangled from its relationship with government at national and local level, but argues that the degree of influence – both direct and indirect – exercised by government over the work and conduct of voluntary agencies has become a major threat to their independence of thought and action during the past 15–20 years. The chapter reviews the ways in which the relationship has developed and assesses its impact on volunteering and voluntary organisations in terms of both the kinds of activities they undertake and the ways in which they organise their affairs.

Chapter 6, 'Selling Out? Voluntary Action and the Market', analyses the extent to which voluntary agencies have been influenced by the rules and values of the market. It traces the shift of thinking in voluntary organisations from a concern to be 'business-like' to a commitment to behaving like a business. Voluntary sector managers increasingly talk about 'growing their businesses'; 'meeting the needs of their customers'; and 'looking for success in a competitive market place'. The chapter looks for explanations of this change and assesses the impact of this influence on voluntary agencies and those who benefit from their activities.

Chapter 7, 'The Hegemony of the Bureaucratic Model', discusses the way in which bureaucracy has become the predominant organisational model in our society, to the point where other forms of organisation are ignored and forgotten: it has become the 'taken-for-granted' norm by which we assess organisations and judge their effectiveness. The chapter identifies the key features of the bureaucratic form and highlights its virtues and advantages before introducing an alternative kind of organisation – the association – and discussing the comparative advantages of each of the forms (and a hybrid with elements of both) as a means of meeting different kinds of social needs. It concludes by suggesting that the hegemony of the bureaucratic model has increasingly obscured and undermined the importance and value of the distinctive ways in which voluntary organisations have organised their activities.

The last chapter in this section – Chapter 8, 'The Pressure from Within' – turns from the consideration of external pressures on the world of voluntary action to look at ways in which elements within the sector have contributed to the narrowing of the perspective through which we view voluntary organisations and volunteering, and diminished their contribution to our society. In particular, it discusses the way in which a small number of national 'infrastructure' bodies have asserted their leadership of the sector while becoming clients of the government with the honorary status of 'strategic partners'. The chapter then explains how and why the sector has developed in this way and explores the consequences.

Part III consists of five chapters that aim to provide *alternative perspectives* on some of the key elements of the current paradigms of voluntary action.

Chapter 9, 'Governance, Ownership and Control', goes beyond the usual discussion of governance arrangements to discuss the issues of ownership and control that underlie them. Each organisation will have its 'owners' – a constellation of people who care whether the organisation lives or dies and who can exercise control over the key decisions that affect its destiny. The chapter argues that, in many voluntary organisations, ownership and control have increasingly become located in their staff rather than their boards (and the wider interests they may represent) and have tended to pass from the staff as a whole to their managers, and especially to the chief executive. In the process, the users of their services have been reduced to passive recipients of what is provided rather than active participants in the work and governance of the organisation.

Chapter 10, 'What is Voluntary Action For?', provides a critique of the prevailing view that the only yardstick by which to judge the 'success' of organisations is by assessing their efficiency in producing goods or services. It argues that the primary purpose of many voluntary organisations and groups is to provide opportunities for 'expressive' rather than instrumental behaviours; their activities are ends in themselves rather than the means to some external impact. The chapter argues that the archetypal voluntary organisation combines expressive and instrumental purposes. This combination explains why voluntary organisations have been seen as distinctive bodies that are qualitatively different from their counterparts in the for-profit and public sectors.

Chapter 11, 'The Fallacies of Managerialism', argues that the approaches and techniques commonly used in the management of business (and adopted by statutory agencies) are not only unhelpful but also damaging when applied to the leadership and management of voluntary organisations. It suggests that the particular form of bureaucratic organisation which is found in most businesses and many other organisations – command and control – is unsuitable for organised forms of voluntary action. The chapter goes on to look at some more specific examples of the misguided application of managerialism to voluntary organisations and concludes by suggesting that voluntary bodies should be seen as societies or communities which need 'political' leadership rather than machines or warehouses which require technocratic management.

Chapter 12, 'Towards a "Round Earth" Map of Volunteering', addresses the shortcomings of the 'dominant paradigm' in volunteering by outlining an alternative approach that aims to provide a more comprehensive map of the terrain. It argues that the assumptions that have underlined the development of a 'volunteering industry' are based on restricted definitions of volunteer motivation; the areas of social life in which volunteers are active; the organisational context within which volunteering takes place; and the ways in which volunteering roles are defined. The chapter presents a three-perspective map to capture this diversity based on volunteering as service to others (the dominant or 'non-profit' paradigm); volunteering as activism (a 'civil society' paradigm); and volunteering as serious leisure, and concludes by discussing the implications of this more rounded model of volunteering for theory and practice.

The final chapter in Part III – Chapter 13, 'Dissenting Voices: The Case of the National Coalition for Independent Action' – looks at the ways in which voluntary organisations have responded to the challenges to their independence and their distinctive character posed by the pressures discussed in Part II. It focuses on the formation and activities of the NCIA and on the critical analysis it has developed and also looks at the work of the Panel on Independence set up by the Baring Foundation in 2011. The chapter discusses the ways in which those who have expressed concern about the independence of voluntary action have developed their critique and the extent to which they have been able to mobilise support for their views.

The three chapters which bring the book to its conclusion in Part V bring together the arguments set out in the earlier parts of the book and discuss the implications of the outcome of this exercise in 'rethinking voluntary action'.

Chapter 14, 'The Paradox of Sectorisation', begins by highlighting the benefits that flowed from an assumption of a common identity based on a distinctive set of organisational characteristics. The idea of a 'sector' enhanced the status of voluntary organisations, provided a basis for mutual support and helped to develop a 'critical mass' to support professional development. The chapter goes on to argue, however, that, as the concept of a sector has become stronger both internally and externally and given birth to a range of sector-specific institutions and services, the distinctive characteristics of voluntary organisations have been diminished rather than strengthened. The chapter then suggests explanations for the 'paradox of sectorisation' before discussing the implications of this development for theory and practice.

Chapter 15, 'Towards an Alternative Paradigm', brings together insights from two bodies of research-based literature to outline a more 'rounded' characterisation of voluntary action than the one provided by the two linked 'dominant' paradigms. It argues that the 'dark matter' of voluntary action and its essential characteristic should be understood as unmanaged volunteers operating in the non-bureaucratic organisational spaces provided by associations and informal groupings. It sets out the key features of volunteering of this kind and of the organisations in which it takes place and locates them in a typology which draws upon the ideas of ambiguity and hybridisation developed by David Billis (1993a, 2010a) to provide a more complete 'round earth' map of voluntary action and the voluntary sector.

Finally, Chapter 16, 'The Implications of Rethinking Voluntary Action', discusses the implications of the 'alternative paradigm' set out in the previous chapter and the way in which it redraws the map of voluntary action. It reprises the main arguments set out in the preceding chapters that have led to the alternative paradigm presented in Chapter 15. It goes on to argue for a 'shift of focus' in our view of voluntary action; to present an organisational typology to explain the diversity of voluntary organisations; and to explore the implications for the research agenda and for practice of placing unmanaged volunteers in non-bureaucratic organisational settings at the centre rather than the periphery of voluntary action.

Part I
The Context

2
Revisiting the Roots of Voluntary Action

Introduction

People who work in and with voluntary organisations and those who study them are remarkably insouciant about the history of voluntary action. Individual organisations are careless of their archives and only too ready to consign their records to damp cellars or cart them off to landfill in skips. If they do show some interest in their past, this takes the form of 'cherry-picking' their history to provide selected images, incidents and personalities with which to add sparkle to their promotional and fund-raising materials rather than a serious attempt to understand the concerns and the external forces that shaped both their founding mission and the ways in which it has been adapted to changing circumstances. From a wider perspective, the debates about social and public policy and the growing role to be played in it by voluntary agencies have been curiously deracinated. As a result, the discussion has been largely uninformed by any understanding of the historical experience which has formed today's institutions and relationships, while any lessons from the past have been left unlearned. While we do not have to go as far as Marx, who suggested that 'those who do not understand history are condemned to repeat it, the first time as tragedy, the second time as farce' (Marx, 1852), there seems 'to be little doubt that a lack of understanding of past experience represents a serious gap in the armoury of the policy-maker and the social analyst as well as voluntary sector leaders' (Rochester *et al.*, 2011: 4).

But this lack of interest is not the only issue; there is also a serious problem with the nature of the historical material that is available to us, which at best provides only part of the story. This chapter tries to address this shortcoming by providing a critical review of the

15

historiography of voluntary action. It argues that conventional accounts of the development over time of voluntary organisations and volunteering are incomplete, and suggests ways in which we might develop a more inclusive and comprehensive view of the roots of voluntary action. The chapter begins by discussing the way in which the history of voluntary action has been summarised in two guides or handbooks for the voluntary sector that were published in the mid-1990s. It goes on to spell out the key themes that are covered in the historical literature on which these accounts are based. The chapter then introduces two additional perspectives that are largely ignored in this approach to the historiography of voluntary action – efforts to bring about social change and achieve greater social justice, on the one hand, and activities based on conviviality and expressive behaviours, on the other. And it concludes by attempting to show how these additional perspectives can be used to provide a more complete and rounded account of the history of voluntary action and by spelling out the implications of such a view.

The first of the two summaries of the conventional story of voluntary action's history was a chapter by Justin Davis Smith on 'The voluntary tradition; philanthropy and self-help', included in *An Introduction to the Voluntary Sector*, which he co-edited (Davis Smith, 1995). Acknowledging the impossibility of providing a comprehensive review of 500 years in a single chapter, Davis Smith focuses on the 'now famous division...between the two main impulses of voluntary action: philanthropy and mutual aid' (Davis Smith, 1995: 10) made by William Beveridge in his seminal report on *Voluntary Action* published in 1948 to complement his earlier volume which laid the foundations for the post-Second World War welfare state (Beveridge, 1942, 1948). This starting point enables Davis Smith to try to redress the tendency of earlier writers (such as Owen, 1964) to focus exclusively on the history of philanthropy. He does not, however, manage to give anything like equal attention to his two themes; his account of mutual aid occupies less than a third of the space devoted to philanthropy. This imbalance reflects the general state of the historiography of voluntary action, which is also seen in a focus on social welfare on the one hand (and more especially the relief of poverty) and the prominence given to the changing relationship between voluntary action and the state. Davis Smith does, however, provide a tantalising glimpse of a more inclusive approach by suggesting that the 'rich tradition of voluntary activity concerned with campaigning and political protest' seen during the 'golden age' of the late nineteenth century makes a good case 'for extending Beveridge's simple two-fold distinction...and including campaigning activity as a third element in its own right' (Davis Smith, 1995: 15).

The second of these two summary accounts of voluntary action history is found in the chapter on the 'History of the Voluntary Sector' contributed by Marilyn Taylor and Jeremy Kendall to Kendall and Knapp's UK volume in the Johns Hopkins Nonprofit Sector Series (Kendall and Knapp, 1996). Here again, Taylor and Kendall give the history of philanthropy most attention; the main focus is on the relief of poverty and other areas of social policy; and they treat the developing interaction with the state as a major theme. They also cover mutual aid, but give it much less attention than the philanthropic impulse. Unlike Davis Smith, however, Taylor and Kendall mention other manifestations of voluntary action: they refer to the 'growth of more radical middle- and working class organizations pushing for electoral reform' at the end of the eighteenth century; 'an explosion of recreational activities' in response to growing leisure time in the nineteenth century; the flowering of new campaigning organisations in the 1950s and 1960s; and the attention paid to community development in the 1960s and 1970s. On the other hand, their treatment of these activities is rather cursory and hardly justifies their concluding remarks that voluntary action has 'played a major role in change both by the powerful and powerless'; that 'it has been a channel for dissent, both in religion and in politics'; and that it has been 'a way for groups excluded from political and economic power to gain a stake in society, to develop networks, discuss and formulate strategies and gain an organizational base' (Taylor and Kendall, 1996: 39, 44, 55–7, 60).

Clearly it is unreasonable to expect a comprehensive account of several hundred years of voluntary action history in a single chapter, but the choices made by the authors of these two short accounts about what aspects to highlight and what areas to ignore are revealing. Between them they provide us with both the main features of its mainstream historiography and some important indications of its limitations. The next section of the chapter will review the ways in which the roots of voluntary action and the major developments in its history have been treated by the historians, before exploring at greater length the additional aspects mentioned briefly by Davis Smith and by Taylor and Kendall.

The familiar story

The key themes in the familiar account of voluntary action's history were all highlighted in the Beveridge report on *Voluntary Action*. They are: philanthropy or what its author called 'the impulse from above'; mutual aid or 'the impulse from below'; and the 'moving frontier' between the state and voluntary action. This part of the chapter will present in turn some of the more salient developments in the history of all three.

Philanthropy

Much – too much – of the history of voluntary action has been written as the history of philanthropy. And the philanthropic perspective still plays a prominent part in contemporary discussions of voluntary action. We recognise the importance of the motivation that comes from 'love of one's fellow man, an action or inclination which promotes the well-being of others' (Prochaska, 1988: 7) or, in Beveridge's words, 'social conscience, the feeling that makes men who are materially comfortable, mentally uncomfortable as long as their neighbours are materially uncomfortable' (Beveridge, 1948: 93). Much of our thinking about charitable giving and volunteering is based on this perspective.

There is insufficient space here for anything like a full account of the history of philanthropy. All I can hope to do is to identify some of the key developments that have helped to shape our understanding of today's world of voluntary action. Davis Smith (1995) has noted how long the philanthropic tradition has been part of our society and highlighted the way in which charitable organisations flourished in the twelfth and thirteenth centuries, during which 500 voluntary hospitals were founded in England alone. But he begins the story in the sixteenth century, when the legal and administrative foundations of modern charitable endeavour were first laid down. The need for a new framework was clear: the sixteenth and early seventeenth centuries were characterised by economic and social upheaval that created, alongside greatly increased wealth for a new entrepreneurial class, a large population of the landless poor, including in their number beggars and vagrants, who were seen as a major threat to law and order. And the means of relieving poverty and meeting other social needs had been seriously damaged, first, by the dissolution of the monasteries that had provided care for the sick and other rudimentary elements of a social welfare system, and, second, by the enclosure movement and growth of the towns that had undermined the feudal system in which:

> A lord was bound by personal obligations embedded in customary land law to ensure that at least the basic essentials of life were provided for any of his tenants who suffered exceptional hardship.
>
> (Chesterman, 1979: 11, quoted in Taylor and Kendall, 1996)

To fill the gap left by the undermining of these arrangements, the Tudor era developed an organisational form – the charitable trust – 'which was to play such an important role in the history of the voluntary sector over the next 500 years' and an equally significant legal and administrative system for regulating charity. The charitable trust was essentially based on an endowment – 'a gift or bequest made in perpetuity for charitable purposes' (Davis Smith, 1995: 11). This became the predominant form of giving in the sixteenth and seventeenth centuries and was increasingly used for non-religious purposes such as education and health as well as for the relief of poverty. These arrangements were given legal recognition and status in two Acts of Parliament passed in 1572 and 1601. The first Charitable Uses Act was designed to prevent fraudulent activity in the name of charity and established the first 'roving' charitable commissioners to investigate breaches of trust and ensure that the income from the endowment was devoted to the purposes specified by the donor. The preamble to the 1601 Act of the same name provided the basic definition of charitable purposes, which has been the cornerstone of the legal definition of charity ever since.

The second commonly accepted high water mark of philanthropy was the second half of the nineteenth century. Like the earlier period, the nineteenth century was a time of major economic change and social turmoil. Industrialisation and the rapid growth of towns and cities had led to the creation not only of great wealth but also of extensive and profound urban poverty. The scale of the resources devoted to philanthropy at this time was remarkable, although the often-quoted claim by *The Times* newspaper, in the 1880s, that 'the income of London charities was greater than that of several nation states, including Sweden, Denmark and Portugal, and twice that of the Swiss Confederation' (see Owen, 1964: 169) has been questioned (Morris, 2006). Nonetheless, one estimate put the total annual income of British charities in 1896 at £8 million (Davis Smith, 1995: 14). The explosion of philanthropic activity was the product of the degree of wealth created by the industrial revolution; the need to address the dramatic increases in social need; and the development of an organisational form which was fit for the purpose and which has provided the model for the voluntary agency of the twentieth and twenty-first century.

The associational charity – made up of a number of philanthropists and committed to raising funds – emerged in the eighteenth century and became the key vehicle for nineteenth-century philanthropy, ahead of the older form of the charitable trust endowed by a single philanthropist and concerned with spending the income from an endowment.

The new charitable form also developed a separation between those who provided the funds and directed its activities and those who carried out the work of the organisation. They divided along gender lines: very few women were involved as members of the governing bodies of nineteenth-century charities, but their voluntary workforce was almost entirely female. Many middle-class women who were barred from the labour market devoted their time and developed their abilities by engaging in philanthropy; one contemporary estimate was that half a million of them were involved with charitable organisations on a regular or 'semi-professional' basis (noted in Davis Smith, 1995).

The nineteenth century also saw the emergence of attempts to co-ordinate voluntary activity in the shape of the Charity Organisation Society (COS) as a precursor of what are today called infrastructure organisations. Founded in 1869, the COS was intended to rationalise the activities of charities, which had grown in an uneven and random fashion, so that the availability of assistance was imperfectly matched with social need; there was a considerable overlap of activities; and resources were being wasted. To address these evils the COS aimed to establish its local branches as clearing houses for relief through which all requests for assistance would be channelled. It was, however, ultimately unsuccessful in its attempts to impose order on the activities of other organisations which valued their independence. Its commitment to 'scientific philanthropy' did, however, leave a significant legacy. At the heart of the COS philosophy was the distinction between the 'deserving' and the 'undeserving' poor and the belief that philanthropic support should be targeted to those who deserved it because they could, with the help of short-term aid, regain their economic independence and escape pauperism. In order to ensure that the right people were helped, it was necessary to enquire carefully about the circumstances and the character of those requesting assistance, and this task was mainly entrusted to 'lady visitors' whose investigations into each 'case' paved the way for the development of professional social work.

The history of philanthropy does not, of course, end in 1900, but it does increasingly become entwined with the history of the state's involvement with social welfare, and this story will form part of a later section of this chapter. But it may be appropriate to deal with one or two aspects of it here. The COS was a last ditch defender of the idea that government and charity occupied separate spheres of activity based on the distinction between the 'deserving poor' who were suitable recipients of charitable activity and the 'undeserving poor' who would be dealt with by the state. This distinction dates from the sixteenth century and was fundamental to the 1834 Poor Law and the Goschen Minute on 'The Relief of the Poor in the Metropolis' of 1869 – the year in which the COS was formed. By the end of the nineteenth century the principle had been undermined, and it was laid to rest by the Poor Law Commission of 1905–09 and the welfare legislation of the Liberal governments of 1905–14. The COS was superseded by a new form of co-ordinating body and the principle of 'separate spheres' gave way to the ideas of the 'new philanthropy'. Following the pioneering work of Thomas Hancock Nunn in Hampstead, a new form of local organisation that came to be called the Council of Social Service sprang up across Britain, accompanied by the establishment (in 1919) of a National Council for Social Service or NSCC (these were later to become Councils of Voluntary Service, or CVSs, and the NCVO). The 'new philanthropy' that they embodied and promoted was based on the development of partnership arrangements and 'a new technique of co-operation between statutory and voluntary services' (Macadam, 1934: 11).

Mutual aid

Comparatively recently, writing about the history of voluntary action has challenged the near monopoly of philanthropy as an explanation for the motives of those who have engaged in it by 'rediscovering' mutual aid; the 'impulse from below' has taken its place alongside the 'impulse from above'. Beveridge (1948: 93) located the origin of mutual aid 'in a sense of one's own need for security against misfortune, and realisation that, since one's fellows have the same need, by undertaking to help one another all may help themselves'. The historical roots of mutual aid are at least as deep as those of philanthropy; while the claims of the nineteenth-century friendly societies to pre-Christian origins have been described as 'somewhat romantic' by Gosden (1974: 3), there is more convincing evidence of mutual aid activity in ancient Israel (Loewenberg, 1992). But comparatively little is known about manifestations of the 'impulse from below' until the later Middle Ages and, subsequently, the eighteenth and nineteenth centuries.

Self-help in the Middle Ages took three major forms. In the first place, it was found in the craft guilds and livery companies that emerged in the fourteenth century with the rise of the trades that provided their focus. Their primary functions were the protection and regulation of a specific trade or profession, but they also provided support and help to their members who fell on hard times and might also take responsibility for meeting wider social need by, for example, the provision of almshouses (Taylor and Kendall, 1996). The second medieval form of mutual aid was found in the religious fraternities, whose main function was to offer prayers for the dead but which also provided food and shelter for members in need. Membership was not, like the guilds, restricted to practitioners of specific trades or crafts, and was open to women (Davis Smith, 1995). While the guilds and fraternities have been studied in their own right and have been recognised as precursors of the friendly societies of a later period, the third aspect of mutual aid in the medieval period has received very little attention. This is the practice of organising 'church ales' and 'help-ales', for which beer was specially brewed as means of raising money for repairs to the parish church in the first case and the relief of poverty in the second instance (Clark, 2000).

Very little of the medieval approach to self-help survived the sixteenth century. The fraternities were swept away with the monasteries and the chantries under Henry VIII (Davis Smith, 1995) and the help-ales gave way to the Elizabethan institution of poor relief amid a growing disapproval and distrust of the associated 'carnival' atmosphere (Rochester, 2008). For the most part the craft guilds had also ceased to play a part in the provision of welfare by 1600, but the Livery Companies of the City of London were a notable exception and 'remain major, if sometimes mysterious, philanthropic institutions to the present day' (Taylor and Kendall, 1996: 31). And, it has been suggested, 'the legacy of the guilds, with their emphasis on mutual support and democratic control, lived on and was to re-emerge with the development of the friendly society movement in the late eighteenth century' (Davis Smith, 1995: 29).

At their peak in the late nineteenth century the friendly societies rivalled the importance of the philanthropic associations of the time. By 1872 their combined membership exceeded four million (Gosden, 1974). The first friendly societies were established in the late seventeenth century as a means of providing insurance for their members against loss of earnings during times of ill health and meeting the costs of their funerals. Their numbers grew rapidly alongside the growing industrialisation of the eighteenth century, and by 1801 it was estimated that there were about 7,200 societies with a total membership of more than 700,000 members (Gosden, 1974: 12). They were local, independent and quite small-scale organisations with a typical membership of about a hundred which met once a month, usually at a local public house, to collect members' contributions, which were kept in a box secured by three keys, one held by the landlord of the pub where the box was kept and the other two by stewards who served in rotation.

While the numbers of the independent societies continued to grow in the nineteenth century, the main motor for the burgeoning of the friendly society movement – which witnessed a four-fold increase in membership between 1815 and 1874 – was the development of the national federated bodies known as the affiliated orders, such as the Independent Order of Oddfellows and the Ancient Order of Foresters. Starting life as groupings of local societies, they developed into national structures in which the central body was accountable to the representatives of a number of districts whose committees were elected in turn by the local 'lodges' or 'courts' (Gosden, 1974: 12). The affiliated orders provided a more robust and more 'professional' structure than the independent local societies, among which there was a constant risk that their assets might prove insufficient to meet their obligations: 'There are plenty of examples of local societies founded in the late eighteenth century which survived into the twentieth, but there were also many which collapsed financially and left their members bereft of provision' (ibid.: 15–16). Despite these advantages, the affiliated orders themselves came under increasing pressure as the nineteenth century came to an end. On the one hand, the calls on their resources became greater as their members lived longer, and, on the other, they faced a new level of competition for members from the trades unions and commercial enterprises. In the short run, the friendly societies began to move away from their roots in mutual aid and, in the longer run, were supplanted by the development of government measures to provide social security (Taylor and Kendall, 1996).

The decline and fall of the friendly societies did not, however, bring to an end the role of mutual aid or self-help as a feature of voluntary action. Many of the organisations founded in the wake of the Second World War and the establishment of a welfare state have their roots in the mutual aid tradition, although the focus has shifted from social insurance to single issue concerns (Davis Smith, 1995). The parents of children with learning disabilities came together to form Mencap; single parents set up local Gingerbread groups; relatives of people with dementia established the Alzheimer's Disease Society; and the pre-school playgroups movement promoted opportunities for play among young children that actively involved their mothers in providing them. And, at the same time, there has been a proliferation of unaffiliated local groups of people with shared health and social problems, while 'twelve step' groups such as Alcoholics Anonymous became a feature of the landscape of voluntary action (Wann, 1992; Davis Smith, 1995).

The moving frontier

Recent accounts of the history of the relationship between the state and voluntary action have warned of the seductive charms of a 'whiggish' interpretation that treats the voluntary sector as an interesting (or sometimes less than interesting) prelude to the development of the welfare state, and describes 'the inexorable growth of the state following on from the failure and decline of the voluntary response'. The reality is a great deal more complex; the relationship between the state and voluntary action is more accurately described as a 'moving frontier'. While Geoffrey Finlayson suggests that 'it may be argued, the change over the whole period' of his book (which deals with 1830–1990) 'at least until 1979, is consistent with a broadly Whig interpretation of a developing and expanding Welfare State – which even the Thatcherite attempts after 1979 did not, in practice, disturb'. But, he concludes, this is 'much too linear'. 'It was not a matter of launching a "historical trajectory" from voluntarism to state; it was a question of experimenting with "shifting boundaries" between voluntarism and state.' While there were 'varied solutions at different times... these were never entirely coherent and clear-cut. Rather, they always contained elements of ambiguity and tension' (Davis Smith, 1995: 17–19).

Historical models of the relationship between the state and voluntary action thus need to be treated with caution – as accounts which have been simplified so as to highlight some key features and differences. A further complication is judging the point at which the state makes its first appearance on the welfare scene in a form that bears some resemblance to its manifestation in contemporary society. Earlier historians tended to date this emergence in the years after 1870, but more recent scholars have suggested that the process began in 1830 or earlier – some as early as the beginning of the seventeenth century. With these caveats, it is possible to suggest that from 1830 until 1979 there have been three broad models of relationships between voluntarism and the state:

1. For most, if not all, of the nineteenth century voluntary action played the major role in social welfare; the relief of poverty was addressed by the philanthropy of charitable trusts and the new charitable associations on the one hand and friendly societies on the other, while voluntary action also provided social housing, education and healthcare (Harris, 2010). State provision tended to be seen as residual.

2. At the end of the nineteenth and the early years of the twentieth century, there were important developments in the state's

responsibilities for welfare services and a change of attitude towards them on the part of some elements of the voluntary sphere. The former included growing state responsibility for health and education and the reforms introduced by the Liberal Government of 1906–11. These changes challenged voluntary organisations to reconsider their role in the provision of welfare and led to the development of institutions that not only took on the role of co-ordinating and supporting voluntary action but also promoted mutually supportive links between the statutory and voluntary sectors.

3. The post-Second World War welfare settlement gave the major role and the overall responsibility for social welfare to the state. Webb and his colleagues (1975, quoted in Harris, 2010) suggest that 'a subsidiary but important part of the drive towards statutory social services represented a deliberate move away from voluntary provision... Faith was invested in statutory services as a way of guaranteeing provision that was comprehensive and universal, professional and impartial, and subject to democratic control.' The creation of the welfare state did not, however, lead to the marginalisation of voluntary action expected by many at the time. While the services and expertise of a number of established organisations remained indispensable in the new context, new bodies had been conceived during the war and afterwards in response to heightened expectations which had not been met by the statutory services (Davis Smith, 1995).

The survival and further growth of voluntary action after the formation of the welfare state strongly suggests that the state and voluntarism do not compete for the same space. Instead, they are and have been interrelated in an almost symbiotic relationship. This was true even in the nineteenth century, when voluntary action and public provision were, it has been widely suggested, taking place in 'separate spheres'. In fact, they were interconnected on at least two levels – the personal and the financial. In the first place:

Those who sat as Poor Law Guardians would very often be the same people who sat on the committees which controlled schools, hospitals and dispensaries and the other varied forms of charitable organisations; they would often also be among those who took the lead in sponsoring local voluntary efforts in times of disaster or communal celebration.

(McCord, 1976, quoted in Harris, 2004: 29)

And this kind of cross-sector leadership continued into the twentieth century: Margaret Simey, veteran Liverpool activist, moved seamlessly during her long life between local government, the voluntary sector and academia (Clarke, 2004).

Harris also provides examples of the ways in which 'the two sectors supported each other by cross-funding'. Money raised by endowed charities was used to supplement the poor rates, while local authorities (town councils and boards of guardians) made donations from public funds to charitable organisations and subscribed to local hospitals to secure treatment for sick paupers (Harris, 2004: 29).

It does, nonetheless, seem clear that, as Alison Penn (2011) has argued, the reforms of the 1906–11 Lloyd George administration provided a watershed in voluntary action history. Her argument goes further than the incursion of the state onto what had been the territory of voluntarism. She suggests that, once central government became a major player, voluntary organisations felt the need to establish a national presence in order to influence these new actors at national level. A second key issue for her is the adoption by the state of the 'business' model of organisation. Industrial society had created the large 'firm' – a formally organised, strictly hierarchical and increasingly bureaucratic form. This became the organisational template for the new state agencies that began to take shape in the inter-war period and then became the norm for the voluntary organisations with which the state was increasingly allied.

Penn argues that philanthropic charities were best able to adapt themselves to meet this template, while the mutual aid groups were less susceptible to remaking themselves in the image of the firm. Similarly, those organised as a unitary body or with high degrees of control exercised by the central or national body over its branches were at an advantage over looser federations in which local units had a great deal of autonomy, on the one hand, and the typically small, locally based friendly societies, on the other. Mutual aid organisations were displaced and philanthropic institutions remade by the forces of state-sponsored isomorphism. She refers to these processes as the 'metamorphosis of philanthropy' and the 'displacement of mutual aid' (Penn, 2011: 22, 26).

'The road less travelled'

This section of the chapter looks at several aspects of the history of voluntary action that have not found a place in the conventional accounts of its development.

Voluntary action for social change and social justice

As we have seen, both Davis Smith (1995) and Taylor and Kendall (1996) mentioned some aspects of the historical involvement of voluntary organisations in campaigning and (non-party) political activities. This kind of activity tends to be studied through two kinds of lenses. It is seen either as part of the story of the specific issue which is the subject of the campaign (such as electoral reform or changes in the law) or, more generally, as part of the literature on social movements. In the first place, the focus is on the extent to which the organisation or organisations influence change and succeed in its or their aims rather than on the character of the voluntary effort that was involved. In the second place, there are serious limitations on the usefulness of the social movements literature. Empirical studies have been outweighed by 'theorising' about 'the features which distinguish social movements from other forms of political action' (Byrne, 1997: 12), and writers have shown little interest in history earlier than 30 or 40 years ago when, they suggest, the modern social movement began to take shape.

Social movement theory does, however, offer a useful framework for discussing voluntary action as a means of pursuing social change and social justice and, in the process, adding a new dimension to the definition of voluntary action as a whole. Defining social movements is not simple; 'there are many disagreements among theorists' (Byrne, 1997: 12) and 'the term has been used rather indiscriminately ... applied to anything from localised protests over single issues within a particular country to ideological standpoints which have had a global impact' (ibid.: 10). There is also, however, a fair measure of consensus about some of the key characteristics of social movements. In the first place, they are not themselves formally organised, although they may have groups within them that are. They are more in the nature of 'networks of interaction, which may either include formal organisations or not' (Diani, 1992, quoted in Byrne, 1997: 13). Second, they are held together by shared values and have expressive rather than instrumental functions: 'they have beliefs and moral principles and they seek to persuade everyone – governments, parties, the general public, anyone who will listen – that these values are the right ones, but do not compete for political office' (Byrne, 1997: 13). Third, they are 'outsiders' who challenge the existing situation and do so outside the conventional institutions of political society. And, fourth, they employ a variety of tactics that include direct action and might involve breaking the law. Some, but not all, voluntary organisations that are engaged in campaigning activities may be part of these networks of interaction while others will not, and the degree and kind of involvement of those that are connected will vary greatly and may change over time.

The literature on social movements tends to regard them as a feature of the changing political scene of the last 40 years of the twentieth century (see, for example, Della Porta and Diani, 2006) and suggests that they are typified and defined by four major kinds of activity in advanced industrial societies – 'centred on students, women, environmentalists and peace activists' (Byrne, 1997: 26). Two authors, however, have set the social movements of the contemporary world in historical context (Tilly, 2004) and located them in a longer tradition of 'contentious politics' (Tarrow, 1994). Both locate the origins of social movements in the late eighteenth century 'when the resources for turning collective action into social movements could first be brought together over sustained periods and across territorial space' (Tarrow, 1994: 7) and the 'repertoire' of collective action was expanded from individual acts of resistance, such as food riots and peasant revolts, to include demonstrations, strikes, rallies and public meetings. At the same time, contentious action ceased to be locally based and directed at specific concerns and began to address issues that affected many localities and was transformed from isolated and episodic actions into concerted and sustained activity. This transformation was underpinned by the power of a new medium, as printed materials became more widely accessible, and on the new institutional framework provided by the development of clubs, societies and associations (Tarrow, 1994).

The emergence of the social movement in the late eighteenth century can be associated with such diverse interests as the supporters of the radical politician, John Wilkes, on the one hand and the anti-Catholic Protestant Association led by Lord George Gordon, on the other (Tilly, 2004). The early years of the nineteenth century witnessed significant successes for the anti-slavery movement with the abolition of slavery in 1833 and 'the immense social movement mobilization on behalf of parliamentary reform' that led to the Reform Act of 1832 (Tilly, 2004: 46). The Act did not, of course, mark the end of pressure for electoral reform: discontent with its very limited concessions led to the development of a massive national movement known as Chartism, which not only dominated the scene for a decade (1838–48) but also 'provided a seedbed and a template for the nineteenth century's major popular mobilizations', most notably the long campaign for women's suffrage. And, as the steam ran out of Chartism as a national movement from 1848, some of its activists moved into other causes such as 'temperance, cooperatives, local betterment programmes, or... educational, land or property reform' (Tilly, 2004: 48). These and other issues gave rise to social movements in the later years of the nineteenth and into the twentieth century, although little attention is given to them in the social movement literature. Charles Tilly, for example, in his *Social Movements 1768–2004* moves rapidly from the account of the Chartists in his chapter on the nineteenth century to the events of 1968 and the fall of the Berlin Wall in 1989 at the beginning of his account of the twentieth century.

Alongside the emergence of a new wave of modern social movements in the second half of the twentieth century, we can also note the development of new approaches by the kind of voluntary agency that Crowson *et al.* (2009) refer to as 'NGOs' or non-governmental organisations. While the term is normally applied to voluntary organisations active in international aid and development, these authors claim (without any substantial evidence) that 'the NGO is a breed that is increasingly being identified in the sphere of national politics' (McKay and Hilton, 2009: 3). They use the term to mean: 'those bodies seeking or exerting socio-political influence, while belonging to neither the government nor the business sectors. They exist in the overlap between the voluntary sector and the public sphere' (ibid.: 4).

They exist, according to McKay and Hilton, as a consequence of the welfare settlement which followed the Second World War when, in their view, the voluntary sector underwent a fundamental transformation: 'In place of service provision, the sector became more engaged with... the shaping of the broader socio-political agenda' (McKay and Hilton: 5).

While few would accept their generalisation that voluntary agencies turned their attention away from service provision after 1945, McKay and Hilton's argument that the coming of the welfare state provided the conditions for greater and wider voluntary sector activity on the campaigning front is supported by the case studies presented in the book. These range over the territories of the major social movements – peace, women's issues and concern for the environment – and also include poverty, human rights and drugs on the domestic front and international issues such as aid and development, fair trade and the anti-apartheid movement.

Locally based contentious action has also resurfaced in the twentieth century, either loosely connected with wider movements – such as disability rights and environmental issues – or in completely autonomous forms. It has, however, left little mark on the writing of social and political history. Much of this kind of activity lies within the territory of community development, but the relevant literature tends to focus on the professional practice of community workers and the policy contexts within which they operate rather than the groups with which they work. And, when the spotlight does fall on community groups themselves, they are seen as contemporary phenomena and there is little, if any, interest in how their characteristics and their activities might have developed over the years. We can, however, find some allusions to the history of campaigning at the community level. The authors of a recently published 'short guide' argue that one of the main foundations of community development can be found in the housing and planning field: 'The origins of the tenants' movement ... lie in the early twentieth century with campaigns for social housing and rent strikes and the associations formed by tenants of the new local authority housing estates as the century progressed' (Gilchrist and Taylor, 2011: 28). A review of the first 40 years of the *Community Development Journal* reminds us that the late 1960s and early 1970s witnessed an upsurge of activism at a local level: 'action groups protested at the closure of public services including hospitals and schools ... and the action of squatter groups was becoming an increasing concern for local authorities' (Popple, 2008: 13).

Voluntary action as conviviality and expressive behaviour

Conviviality – the enjoyment of festive company – has very deep roots and is a much broader phenomenon than voluntary action. Medieval England celebrated the great church festivals with the kind of festivity and dancing that has been characterised as 'carnival' (Ehrenreich, 2007). Following the Reformation such unorganised, unruly and anarchic behaviour was suppressed as a threat to good order. Conviviality, however, found new expression in the associations and clubs which were such an important feature of seventeenth and eighteenth-century social life. The aim of a typical society 'along with drinking and socializing, was collective improvement' (Clark, 2000: 1), while, by 1800, many of the distinctive features of socialising – 'including drinking, feasting, singing and gambling' – were incorporated into club life, while 'food and drink were fundamental to most club meetings until the end of the eighteenth century' (ibid.: 225). A much quoted view of the English approach to voluntary action from a French visitor to nineteenth-century Britain (quoted by Davis Smith, 1995: 9) observed that:

> In France, men like to meet for the sake of meeting: The Englishman is perhaps less sociable: he requires an object, a community of tastes, a peculiar tie, which draws him nearer his fellow men.

Conviviality has had a long history as an ally of mutual aid. Until the seventeenth century the cost of maintaining the local church or relieving poverty in the parish was met from the sale of food and specially brewed beer at 'church-ales' and 'help-ales'. And friendly societies provided more than insurance; part of the members' subscriptions was used to meet the cost of drink at their monthly meetings at a local inn and an annual feast (Gosden, 1974). Both the Oddfellows and the Foresters (national 'affiliated orders') 'had developed from purely social clubs of the eighteenth century by adding to their traditional activities various financial benefits. In the process of doing this they had never abandoned their social functions' (Gosden, 1974: 48). Not surprisingly, there were concerns that the members' subscriptions would be spent on drink instead of mutual insurance, and there were many attempts to restrict the convivial activities of the societies after the passage of the Friendly Societies Act in 1829. These, however, were 'the cause of many societies breaking up'. 'The critics failed to understand how vital a role the cheerful club evening played in attracting and holding members' (Gosden, 1974: 24).

At first sight, the philanthropic associational charities owe little or nothing to the convivial impulse. They were earnest undertakings aimed at addressing social ills that included drunkenness and were carried out by dignified Victorians of the respectable and upper classes. On the other hand, one of the key ways in which they went about raising money for their causes (and one that remains in the contemporary fundraiser's repertoire) was to invite potential donors to a fairly lavish dinner. It was also commonplace to recognise the work of lady visitors and caseworkers with an annual social event (Prochaska, 1988). And, for some philanthropic activities, conviviality was seen as complementary to education: the first of the founding objects of the Universities Settlement Association, which was responsible for the establishment of Toynbee Hall, was 'to provide education and the means of recreation and enjoyment for the people in the poorer districts of London and other great cities' (Briggs and Macartney, 1984: 9). Indeed, the formation of clubs for all age groups, the organisation of holiday and summer outings, and the arranging of Christmas parties and other social events was a prominent feature of the work of most settlements (see, for example, Rimmer, 1980; Barrett, 1985).

Working men's clubs, which flourished in the late nineteenth and the whole of the twentieth century but which have been largely overlooked by the historians of voluntary action, attracted a wider membership than the other working-class organisations of the time – the trades unions and co-operative societies (Davis Smith, 1995). By 1927 there

were 2,500 'workmen's self-governed and self-supporting' clubs affiliated to the Club and Institute Union (CIU) with a total membership of
more than 900,000 (CIU, 1927: 1). In their case, conviviality was not an
ally to either mutual aid or philanthropy; it was the primary purpose
of their existence. While the CIU claimed a formal and informal educational function – 'pedantic or scholastic', on the one hand, and 'the
vaster and wider flung education which is part of every day's life in a
club', on the other (CIU, 1927: 47) – the main raison d'etre was social:
'The first aim and ideal of the Union is to secure for the workman a
higher and wider level of happiness in his leisure hours and in his daily
personal and civic life' (CIU, 1927: 68).

The desire for conviviality is, in practice, closely allied to recreational activities and the constructive use of leisure time. For many
people, involvement in voluntary action may be prompted by a desire
to learn a new skill or gain knowledge, often for its own sake rather
than for a given end; the impulse for self-expression; and a perceived
need for recreation. This dimension is captured by Konrad Elsdon,
whose approach was quoted by the Code of Practice for Community
Groups (2003) that formed part of the original Compact between the
Government and the Voluntary Sector. The Code (and Elsdon's study)
encompassed:

> Not just those organisations which provide services to the people
> who need help, advice or care; it embraces all those...which peo-
> ple set up because they like to play football or sing, perform plays,
> garden, watch birds, study the heavens or dig up the past, engage in
> politics, worship or take part in Morris dancing.
>
> (Elsdon, 1995, quoted in the Code of Practice for Community
> Groups, Home Office, 2003: 9)

Leisure-time, recreational and expressive activities have been the focus
of a great deal of voluntary action since the late nineteenth century,
when 'For the employed classes, growing leisure time led to an explosion of recreational activities' (Taylor and Kendall, 1996: 45). This brief
overview cannot do justice to the number and variety of the organisations involved. They included philanthropic ventures designed to
distract the working classes from the 'wrong' use of leisure, but also clubs
and associations run by their working-class members and middle-class
societies that were the successors of the clubs of the eighteenth century. Some were national in scope, others were local and yet others were
national federations of local branches or groups. Many of them were

attached to religious denominations. Between them they catered for a wide range of leisure activities, including:

- *Physical activity* – such as rambling and cycling clubs and organised sports, including boxing, rugby and associational football, cricket, hockey and lawn tennis.
- *Holidays* – including camping, youth hostels and the work of the Co-operative Holidays Association and the Workers' Travel Association.
- *Education and self-improvement* – from the Sunday School movement of the late eighteenth century, to the Mechanics Institutes and the Workers' Educational Association and the hundreds of local literary, historical and archaeological societies.
- *Social activities for children and young people* – such as boys' and girls' clubs and the Boy Scouts and other uniformed movements.
- *Clubs and societies for women* – including the Co-operative Women's Guilds, Women's Institutes and Townswomen's Guilds; and
- *The Arts* – music from, for example, the choral societies of the early nineteenth century and the later brass band movement, drama, and painting and sculpture.

Many of these organisations were established in the later years of the nineteenth century and the early years of the twentieth, and many of them have survived until today, despite competition from commercial enterprises on the one hand and local government on the other. As Jones (1986: 6) has pointed out in his review of the period between the two world wars:

> Leisure goods and services provided by commercial enterprises, the State – at both national and local level – and voluntary organisations all expanded. In addition, earlier associational forms of group-created leisure survived and adapted to the new economic and social context.

Conclusion: The implications of a more complete account of voluntary action history

The roots of voluntary action are more numerous than those that have been identified in conventional narratives of its history. Charitable trusts and associational charities continue to play an important role in shaping the landscape of voluntary action, while voluntary organisations based on the principles of mutual aid are still part of the scene, even if they are by no means as prominent as the friendly societies or the medieval guilds were in their day. But the inheritors of the traditions of philanthropy and mutual aid need to take their place alongside other deep-rooted expressions of voluntary action. First, social movements and other forms of campaigning activity have also played a major part in the history of voluntary action and remain significant players. And, second, by far the most numerous members of the voluntary action population are those based on the impulse to conviviality and the pursuit of opportunities for expressive behaviours and recreation.

The implications for the theory and practice of voluntary action of this fuller picture of its roots go further than the need to take account of a more varied set of functions and motivations; they also involve an acceptance of a more varied collection of organisational forms and ways in which people and groups interact and a more diverse set of relationships with the state. The 'networks of interaction' of a social movement and their more or less organised component parts, the short-term local campaign groups, and the voluntary associations and clubs which are the sites of social and leisure-time activities need to take their place alongside the endowed charitable trusts, the voluntary agencies based on the associational charity form and the organisational expressions of mutual aid. And, while the idea of the 'moving frontier' helps us to understand the ebb and flow of the relationship between the state and voluntary organisations involved in the provision of social welfare, the interactions between social movements and other campaigning bodies and the state are very different in character. Whether they adopt an 'insider' or an 'outsider' approach, these manifestations of voluntary action exist to challenge the state and influence the way it acts. For their part, the very large number of organisations which exist to enable people to meet socially and pursue their creative or recreational interests have another – very different – relationship with the state. To a great extent they operate in a separate sphere, and this means that the idea of a 'frontier' is unhelpful. But, on the other hand, their ability to meet and go about their activities can be enhanced or restricted by government action which determines the availability of spaces for their meetings and the terms under which they function.

Finally, we need to recognise the limitations of the framework used for this analysis. Voluntary organisations can be complex phenomena with their roots in more than one of the four broad 'impulses' sketched out in this chapter. The relationship between the roots of an organisation and the form it takes may be far less obvious than the framework appears to suggest; campaigning organisations and recreational bodies, for example, may adopt the associational charity model, while organisations delivering social welfare services might be constituted as purely voluntary associations or mutual aid groups. Similarly, an organisation's interaction with government might not conform to type; recreational organisations might develop a campaigning role, while some providers of social welfare might exist in isolation from government. As well as trying to develop a wider view of the roots of voluntary action, we need to be aware of the complex nature of the origins and development of each individual voluntary organisation.

3
The Invention of the Voluntary Sector and its Consequences

Introduction

We have become so used to the term 'voluntary sector' that the fact that it was invented as recently as the late 1970s can be easily overlooked. This chapter reviews some of the events of the past three decades to explore the ways in which the idea of a sector has become such an influential concept. The adoption of a new label for what had hitherto been described as 'voluntary organisations' or 'voluntary action' was very much a product of its era, and it is striking that the idea of a non-profit sector surfaced in the USA at much the same time. The chapter begins by looking at the circumstances that gave rise to the new way of denoting voluntary action in both countries in the 1970s and at the identity and motives of those who promoted the concept. It highlights the role of the reports of the Wolfenden Committee (in the UK) and the Filer Commission (in the USA) in giving it currency. It notes that the idea of a sector was more influential in this country than across the Atlantic, and puts forward two explanations for this – the way in which the idea of a voluntary sector was socially constructed, on the one hand, and the importance of the almost symbiotic historical relationship between voluntary organisations and the state in the UK, on the other.

The chapter then explores the impact of the adoption of the sector metaphor on the nature of the relationship between voluntary action and the state; more generally on the development of UK public and social policy; and on the development of voluntary organisations themselves. It also charts the ways in which the boundaries of the sector have been redrawn by government and discusses the significance of the transition from a 'voluntary and community sector' via the 'third sector' under New Labour to the idea of a 'civil society' which is favoured by the current governing Coalition. The chapter concludes by drawing out some of the implications of the concept of a sector for the identity and independence of voluntary organisations.

The invention of the voluntary sector in the UK

The idea that the 'voluntary sector' was a more or less conscious invention of the late 1970s has been persuasively argued by Perri 6 and Diana Leat, whose article draws not only on the 'conventional analysis of documents' but also on the 'quite unconventional' use of their personal recollections of a process in which they were both involved, 6 at the NCVO and Leat at the Volunteer Centre UK (6 and Leat, 1997: 34). They argue that the period of some 20 years between the work of the Committee chaired by Lord Wolfenden which reported in 1978 (Wolfenden, 1978) and the report in 1996 of the Commission on the Future of the Voluntary Sector chaired by Professor Nicholas Deakin (Commission on the Future of the Voluntary Sector, 1996) was distinguished by 'the construction of a sub-elite, an interest, a lobby and a field of public policy' (6 and Leat, 1997: 33). In their view, this invention of a British voluntary sector mattered because 'every time we use the concept of a voluntary sector to debate public policy, analyse and compare organisations, or draft laws, we are implicitly recognising specific political claims and interests. Every use of the expression carries specific political freight' (ibid., 34).

The later years of the 1970s can be seen as the time during which the generally accepted post-Second World War welfare settlement had run out of steam and the state provision of welfare services was receiving increasingly critical attention. There were three principal grounds on which the performance of the welfare state was found wanting. In the first place, the 'welfare bureaucracies' through which the state delivered social welfare services were seen as inflexible, inefficient and insensitive. In the second place, they were failing to meet some basic needs: major concerns about housing and homelessness, the persistence of child poverty and an increasingly complex and inaccessible benefits system had led to the setting up of major campaigning organisations and a series of alternative or complementary services. And, third, there was increasing concern about the parts the welfare state was not reaching; the formation of Mencap by the parents and families of people with learning disabilities was perhaps the best known of a variety of initiatives to promote the well-being of people with disabilities or long-term medical conditions in the absence of appropriate public services. These concerns fuelled the development of a set of ideas that came to be known as 'welfare pluralism', the view that the state monopoly or domination of the delivery of service provision should be replaced by a system in which a variety of providers would deliver diverse responses to social need. The advocates of this approach could point to successful examples of provision based on decentralised authority, greater public accountability and the involvement of users or beneficiaries in the design and implementation of services (Hadley and Hatch, 1982).

Welfare pluralism provided an intellectual context in which the idea of a voluntary sector could gain traction by highlighting the need for a set of organisations that could share with the state the role of providing a more varied set of welfare services. The identity of the state's counterpart in this relationship could be identified as a voluntary sector that could take its place alongside the statutory or public sector. The invention of the sector was not, however, simply a matter of embracing an intellectual concept. It was also, as 6 and Leat argue, the product of a 'fragile alliance between the diverging interests of the pressure group world with those of an ageing charity establishment, each fearful of new threats from the new politics' (1997: 43). And the process of invention – from the influential introduction of the sector concept in the Wolfenden Report in 1978 to its consolidation in the report of the Deakin Commission in 1996 – was the work of 'policy entrepreneurs' such as Nicholas Hinton, the Director of the NCSS when it transformed itself into the NCVO, and his successors, and Michael Brophy, Director of the Charities Aid Foundation (CAF). These key actors were aided and abetted by academics like Stephen Hatch, the researcher for the Wolfenden Committee, and Nicholas Deakin, who legitimated the process:

> in order to persuade people of the credibility of imagined threats, to give respectability to unevidenced claims of organisational virtue, to corral the intellectual high ground with the policy communities, and to weave numbers around the concept of 'sector' created for political purposes, one needs intellectuals.
>
> (6 and Leat, 1997: 39)

The process of inventing the sector was more or less complete by the time the Deakin Commission published its report. The idea that the world could be divided up 'by sectors defined by their organisational form' had supplanted an earlier focus 'much more on styles and principles of social action, and upon industries' (6 and Leat, 1997: 33) or specific areas of policy and practice. And the change can be seen as having three important impacts. In the first place, it brought about the creation of what 6 and Leat refer to as 'a policy sub-elite', when the key individuals in a small number of national intermediary bodies, as Wolfenden termed them, asserted their claims to be recognised as leaders of a sector. The extent to which they succeeded in this aim is demonstrated by the award in 2010 and 2011 of knighthoods to the chief executives of the NCVO and the Association of Chief Executives of Voluntary Organisations (ACEVO) and of a CBE to their counterpart at Volunteering England (VE). In the second place, the invention of a voluntary sector changed quite radically the basis for the relationship between the state and voluntary organisations. And, in the third place, the concept of a sector had a major impact on the way in which voluntary organisations saw themselves and how they conducted their affairs.

The Wolfenden Committee

While the report of the Wolfenden Committee was of crucial importance to the development of the concept of a sector, it was less than enthusiastic in its own use of the term. It begins by referring to the 'voluntary field' and the 'voluntary movement' (Wolfenden, 1978: 9, 10) while the idea of the 'sector' only appears in Chapter 2. And the pivotal passage in which the role of the sector is defined as one of four ways of meeting social need uses the term 'system'; the 'voluntary system' takes its place alongside the informal system of social helping based on the help given by family, friends and neighbours; the commercial or market-based system; and the system of statutory provision through national and local government agencies (ibid.: 22–6). This analysis of the ways in which social needs are met provided the underpinning for the idea of a voluntary sector and remains influential today.

The Committee also provided a second important building block for the development of the voluntary sector in theory and practice by suggesting that what it called 'intermediary bodies' played an important role in promoting voluntary action at both national and local levels. Nationally, after a fairly rapid review of statutory bodies as disparate as the Housing Corporation and the Charity Commission, on the one hand, and specialist intermediaries like Age Concern and the Royal National Institutes for the Blind and for the Deaf, on the other, Wolfenden focuses on the 'generalist independent national intermediary bodies', by which it means the National Council of Social Service and its counterparts in Scotland, Wales and Northern Ireland. It argues that they had a major part to play in representing the interests and views of the sector:

> The role of representation is essential in our view. As legislation becomes more difficult and complicated, so it becomes more necessary to have a body able to speak about it on behalf of the voluntary sector, though we realise that there will not normally be a common view on all major points. If there were no such bodies as the councils of national service we believe the government would wish to encourage the creation of organisations on these lines.
>
> (Wolfenden, 178: 140)

But the Committee's view of their role was not limited to representation. There was also 'a clear need for all the national councils to provide, as they now do, an information and support service for voluntary organisations generally' while the development role was also important:

> We believe that the NCSS may well wish to place a greater weight upon this function in future, both in studying the question of whether to set up new organisations to meet new needs, or bodies to attack common boundaries which cross the boundaries of existing organisations, and perhaps in pressing even more strongly the avoidance of wasteful duplication.
>
> (Wolfenden, 1978: 141–2)

The Committee was also firmly of the opinion that these arrangements for the co-ordination, support and development of the sector should be reproduced at local level through the CVSs in the urban areas and the rural community councils (RCCs) in the countryside. In its discussion of the role of local intermediary bodies, there is a tantalising glimpse of what might have been a very different report. This is a reference to a study of CVS that had identified two contrasting ideologies, unitary and pluralistic. The first of these:

> would take as its basic presupposition that all social services agencies are working to the same common ends, and that, given a degree of public spiritedness and rationality on the part of those involved, most problems are administrative in nature and can be solved by joint discussion of what needs to be done and how it may be achieved

in the most effective way. This requires of the CVS that it acts as a coordinator and possibly also as a broker or umpire, to bring this joint and voluntary consensus about.

> (Lansley, 1976: 75, quoted in Wolfenden, 1978: 106)

In the pluralistic model, by contrast:

> the presupposition that all sides are working together to common ends is challenged. So equally fundamentally is the emphasis on voluntary organisations as welfare providers. Instead it is assumed that different groups of providers and receivers within the area of social provision have different and often competing interests, that social planning will at best only be an arbitration between these interests.
>
> (Lansley, 1976: 76, quoted in Wolfenden, 1978: 106)

Lansley goes on to suggest that the pluralistic CVS may facilitate joint action by voluntary groups, but as a temporary alliance related to a particular situation rather than to 'a belief in the desirability of coordination for its own sake'; its 'relation to the local authority will be one of a critic' and it would not 'claim that it was the sole voice of the voluntary movement to which the local authority should listen' (Lansley, 1976: 76–7).

Noting briskly that 'the great majority of CVSs would see themselves as "unitary" rather than "pluralistic"' (Wolfenden, 1978: 107), the report bases its recommendations on the first approach. It argues that local generalist intermediary bodies have four key functions:

- *Development* – 'a process of reviewing existing provision, identifying unmet needs and initiating action to meet them which might include helping to bring new organisation into existence, seeking grants for new work... and initiating research and evaluation projects';
- *Services to other organisations* – including typing and duplicating services, information, advice and training;
- *Liaison* – promoting the exchange of information and opinion between organisations;
- *Representation* – articulating views, protecting interests, pressing for changes through negotiation, and publicity on behalf of the organisations represented. Much of it is concerned with representing the voluntary to the statutory sector.

> (Wolfenden, 1978: 110–11)

The importance attached by the Wolfenden Committee to the work of these local intermediary bodies and these key functions is made clear by the inclusion in their report of a whole chapter devoted to the discussion of ways in which they could be more adequately funded from the national exchequer. This discussion concludes by suggesting that the cost 'would not exceed £2.5 million per annum' and that 'The consequent strengthening of the voluntary sector's contribution would be worth that sum many times over' (Wolfenden, 1978: 179).

The importance of the contribution made by the Wolfenden Report to the process of inventing the voluntary sector is thus two-fold. In the first place, it provided an analysis of the various ways in which social need was met that placed the sector in a framework that distinguished between actors on the basis of their organisational form rather than the field of action or 'industry' in which they were involved or the kind of function they performed. In the second, it argued the need for sector-specific agencies that would provide voluntary organisations with leadership, representation, co-ordination and support, and identified bodies at national and local level that should be recognised as having the potential to perform that role.

The invention of the non-profit sector in the USA

At much the same time as the Wolfenden Committee was helping to kick-start the process of inventing the voluntary sector in the UK, a similar chain of events was unfolding across the Atlantic. The composition of the American counterpart to Wolfenden – the Filer Commission on Private Philanthropy and Public Needs – was different. It was heavily weighted towards the world of business, and John Filer, the chairman, was both a corporate lawyer and the chief executive officer of a major insurance company. Aided by 'a distinguished panel of experts including economists, sociologists, tax attorneys and specialists in non-governmental organizations' (Hall, 1992: 77), the Commission produced, in 1977, 'six weighty volumes' that provided 'a comprehensive multidisciplinary survey of every aspect of charitable tax-exempt organizations' and which 'analyzed the role of nonprofits as employers, as sources of essential health, educational, welfare and cultural services, and as forces in political life. The work also carefully considered the regulatory and tax issues affecting these organizations' well-being' (ibid.: 78) – hardly a surprise, given that one of the key considerations leading to the Commission had been a perceived threat to the tax exempt status of non-profits.

According to Peter Dobkin Hall, however, the Commission's most significant impact was that it:

> gave substance to what, up to then, had only been an idea: that charitable tax-exempt organizations composed a coherent and cohesive 'sector' of American political, economic and social life. This unified conception of nonprofits as part of a 'third,' 'independent,' or 'nonprofit' – or, as the commission preferred to call it, 'voluntary' – sector lay the groundwork for establishing organizations that could give its common interests unified expression.
>
> (Hall, 1992: 78)

For once, an American enquiry looked to the UK for a model, but the Commission's suggestion that the USA needed a Federal Government Agency along the lines of the British Charity Commission that 'would have effectively removed public policy toward philanthropy from the political process' (Hall, 1992: 78–9) fell on deaf ears. Filer's attempt to find an alternative – non-governmental – means of 'bringing the diverse and discordant elements of the tax-exempt universe – the third sector – into harmony' eventually bore some fruit in the creation of a new and not particularly strong body. As 6 and Leat observed (1997: 37), 'while in the UK existing organisations such as NCVO and CAF had to be manoeuvred into new coalitions... in the USA a new advocacy coalition at national level had to be created in the form of the networks that formed Independent Sector in Washington'. It took almost four years to create the new body, and what emerged was the product of a low level of consensus: the new organisation – Independent Sector (IS) – was formed on the basis that it would pursue its mission 'only by working through the vast network of organizations already extant' while its founders were conscious of 'the danger of slipping into a spokesperson role. To do so would not only do a disservice to the sector and society but will bring the wrath of the sector down on the organisation.' And IS committed itself to 'decentralization rather than centralization of planning and decision making' (Hall, 1992: 79).

The UK and the USA

The long struggle to develop a representative body for the sector in the USA and the comparative weakness of the organisation that was eventually established can be seen as one aspect of the differences between the American and the British experience of the impact of inventing a voluntary or non-profit sector. The impact on the UK was much more marked than in the USA, and we can identify a number of explanations for why this was so. In the first place, the composition of the two sectors was significantly different. The organisations that formed the American non-profit sector were essentially defined simply by their tax status, and they included a large number of very large bodies whose counterparts in the UK were not – for various reasons – seen as part of the voluntary sector. The social construction of the British sector was made clear by Kendall and Knapp (1996) in their contribution to the Johns Hopkins cross-national study of the non-profit sector. Their attempt to measure and map the size and extent of the voluntary sector in the UK had to be conducted on two tracks. On the one hand, they measured a 'broad voluntary sector' which corresponded to the definition used by the American proprietors of the study and which could be used for international comparisons. On the other, they identified a 'narrow voluntary sector' that matched British usage of the term by excluding schools and universities; trades unions and professional associations; and recreation and sports clubs. While the voluntary sector in Britain was indeed 'invented', the notion fell on fairly fertile ground in that many people working in voluntary organisations felt that they had a great deal in common that was less tangible and much harder to define than their tax status.

Differences in the composition of the sector contributed to the comparative degree of commitment to the sector ideal in the two countries. There were two important aspects to this. Because it included major non-profit businesses – like hospitals and universities, which in the UK were seen as part of the governmental or public sector – the centre of gravity of the American non-profit sector was much nearer the large and bureaucratic end of the organisational spectrum than in the UK, where a larger number of organisations were much smaller and more likely to seek to augment their resources and expertise by making common cause with other similar bodies. And, second, the contribution and the power of grant-making trusts and foundations were much less in the UK than in the USA. While some foundations played influential roles in the development of the sector – after all, the Wolfenden Committee was set up by grant-making trusts and the Deakin Commission funded by them – they exercised little of the political power of the major foundations in the USA.

Asymmetry was also a feature of the sector's relationship with the state, where the boot was on the other foot. As we saw in the previous chapter, there has been a long and increasingly symbiotic relationship between the state and the voluntary sector in Britain that has remained very different from the 'relationship of the US "nonprofit sector" to the states and the federal government' (6 and Leat, 1997: 36). The British government had, for example, established a small unit to co-ordinate voluntary social services as early as 1964. As a result 'in the UK, Parliament was much less hostile to the charitable world as a whole... than at least some senators and representatives were to the politics of powerful north-eastern foundations, which have no real equivalent in Britain' (ibid.: 37). And, finally, the unitary nature of the British state provided a political context that was very different from the American federal system; it made it feasible both to develop a single focus within government for its relationship with the sector and to promote a unified response to this from the sector itself.

To a great extent, the comparative indifference or hostility of the state and the weakness of sector-wide organisation in the USA have been counterbalanced there by the development of a strong and comparatively well-resourced non-profit academic community and lobby, which has also made a contribution to the vigour of the voluntary sector concept in Britain. Pioneered by the Program on Nonprofit Organizations at Yale and driven on by the massive cross-national study based at Johns Hopkins University, the study of non-profit organisations has become a significant field in the USA, with a major output of PhDs as well as large-scale provision of postgraduate education for the managers and leaders of non-profit organisations. The American academic establishment and its international followers have provided the critical mass that underpinned the successful launch of no fewer than three international academic journals and sustains two scholarly societies – the Association for Research on Nonprofit Organizations and Voluntary Action (ARNOVA) and the International Society for Third Sector Research (ISTR). American scholars have also had a significant impact on the emergence of a similar field of voluntary sector studies in the UK; researchers such as Lester Salamon, who led the Johns Hopkins Study, 'in a series of visits to Britain, have made tireless efforts since the mid-1980s to integrate research and policy perspectives between the US non-profit sector and the British voluntary sector' (6 and Leat, 1997: 36) and there has been a good deal of travel by British scholars and sector leaders in the opposite direction. The impact on studies of the sector in the UK has been substantial and not entirely benign. In a letter to the *Nonprofit and Voluntary Sector Quarterly*, Salamon (1998: 89) summarised the novelty of his approach in the 1980s when:

the prevailing sense was that the world of nonprofit action was inhabited largely by rather small voluntary groups with little economic weight. The idea that this sector also accounted for significant numbers of paid employees and made major contributions to the economy was not on anyone's screen.

The changing relationship between the state and voluntary action

The invention of the voluntary sector in Britain paved the way for two major changes to the relationship between the state and voluntary organisations. In the first place, it facilitated the casting of voluntary sector organisations in a more central role on the stage of social policy. In the second place, it underpinned an increasing emphasis on what Jeremy Kendal (2003) has called 'horizontal' policies – which are intended to impact on the whole of government and the complete range of voluntary organisations – at the expense of their 'vertical' counterparts – which are hosted by a single government department or cover a single service area or group of users. Neither of these shifts was completed before the consolidation of the sector project in the report of the Deakin Commission and the acceptance of its analysis by the incoming New Labour Government in 1997, although important steps towards the new relationshipwere taken under the Conservative administrations led by Margaret Thatcher and John Major.

> The concept of a voluntary sector provided one of the intellectual segues into the radical social welfare reforms seen in the UK in the 1980s and 1990s. Once welfare services were conceptualised as occurring in different 'sectors'... the way was open to propose a 'mixed economy of welfare'. Viable alternatives to the provision of welfare by governmental agencies could be envisaged in both policy and practice. 'Welfare pluralism' could replace 'welfare statism' as a central plank of social policy.
>
> (Harris *et al.*, 2001: 2–3)

The consequences of these changes for voluntary organisations were profound. On the one hand, their importance and their status were significantly advanced as they came to play a more central role in the delivery of social welfare. 'Instead of meeting social needs in ways which complemented, supplemented or provided an alternative to the state, voluntary organisations increasingly took responsibility for delivering "mainstream" services which were previously delivered by statutory bodies' (ibid.: 3). There were, however, limitations on the degree to which voluntary organisations enjoyed an enhanced status; as contractors and providers competing with one another to sell their services to government, they became at best junior partners and at worst powerless supplicants in the new mixed economy of welfare.

The ability of the state to deal with the sector as a whole was also enhanced by the growing influence of the government's specialist Voluntary Services Unit (VSU: located in the Home Office for most of the period but supervised by a cross-departmental Ministerial Group for the Voluntary Sector) and its programme of grants for the headquarters of a number of national voluntary organisations. During the 1980s the VSU launched a number of initiatives aimed at promoting the development of voluntary action at local level (see, for example Griffiths, 1981; Hatch, 1986) and used the allocation of funding to the national bodies with an interest in action at the local level to try to 'rationalise' their activities by promoting mergers between them. The most important evidence that government was able to take a 'horizontal' view of the sector came, however, not from the VSU but from a scrutiny team made up of representatives from six different government departments which 'provided substantial sums to the voluntary sector' who, in 1990, published an *Efficiency Scrutiny of Government Funding of the Voluntary Sector* (Home Office, 1990).

This substantial report covered 'all Government funding whether by direct payment of grants to voluntary organisations or through intermediaries such as local authorities or non-departmental public bodies'. The report's main thrust – captured in its sub-title *Profiting from Partnership* – is frankly instrumental. While it contains a number of recommendations designed to improve the ways in which government agencies administer their funding programmes that were very welcome to voluntary organisations, the main messages are about how to harness the work of voluntary organisations and volunteers and the contribution of their intermediary bodies to the priorities of the government's policy agenda. Government departments were exhorted to 'look actively at how voluntary bodies can contribute to the advancement of their policy objectives. This will include looking at the scope for contracting out services to voluntary bodies' and 'to consider whether they can offer grants for work which encourages volunteering'. And the VSU 'in funding bodies that contribute to the efficiency and effectiveness of the voluntary sector . . . should . . . set priorities for the needs to be met – for example training in management skills' (Home Office, 1990: 27, 30, 37).

The Deakin Commission's Report has been seen as marking the completion of the period of invention of the sector (6 and Leat, 1997: it treats the sector idea as a commonly understood and commonplace way of looking at the world and uses it as the basis for its major recommendations about creating a more just and equal relationship between the voluntary sector and the state. At the centre of these was the idea of a 'concordat' between the two parties that was accepted by the incoming Blair government and became the *Compact on Relations between Government and the Voluntary and Community Sector in England* (Home Office, 1998. Similar national compacts were also agreed in Scotland, Wales and Northern Ireland). At the time of writing it now seems clear that the Compact's long life is drawing to a close in England (although not in Wales and Northern Ireland), but, in its day, it can be seen as the culmination of the process set in train by those who created the idea of a sector in the late 1970s.

The Compacts were a highly ambitious attempt to create a new kind of partnership between the state and the voluntary sector that would be 'based on shared values and mutual respect'. They were intended to be comprehensive; on the government side they were to apply to the whole range of statutory agencies at national, regional and local level, and encompassed the complete spectrum of voluntary action, from the largest national charity to the smallest local community group. And, while they were stronger on aspirations than on enforceable actions, they covered a range of issues, including the terms on which government should provide funding to voluntary sector organisations; good practice in conducting consultation processes; and respect for the rights of voluntary organisations to criticise government and take part in campaigning activities. At national level in England, this involved the beefing up of the role of the VSU (which evolved into the Active Community Unit (ACU), the Office for the Third Sector and eventually the Office for Civil Society) under the leadership of a minister for the voluntary sector; and, on the other side of the relationship, the setting up of a Working Group on Government Relations (which became the Compact Working Party and then Compact Voice) based in NCVO to champion the views of the sector. But the impact of the compacts was not felt only – or mainly – at national level. They were 'rolled out' across the country as well as across the various organs of central government, and, by 2005, practically every local authority in England had agreed – or was negotiating – a local compact with the voluntary sector in its area; in the jargon of the time, 94% of the 388 authorities were 'compact-active' (Craig *et al.*, 2005). This development enhanced the visibility of local CVSs as representatives or leaders of the sector locally. Thus, the Compact was made possible by the idea of a voluntary sector and, in turn, helped to ensure that the term was used systematically at both national and local level (for a full examination of the development of the Compact family and its impact, see Zimmeck *et al.*, 2011; Rochester and Zimmeck, 2013; Zimmeck, 2013).

While the Compact provided an overarching vision of partnership between successive New Labour governments, it was not the only policy development that was based – at least in part – on the idea of a sector. At national level this involved the recognition of a growing number of national voluntary organisations as the government's 'strategic partners'. While the practice of providing funding to the national headquarters of voluntary organisations was far from new, the rationale that such funding was justified as part of a strategic vision for the development of the voluntary sector gave it a novel and very different flavour. At local level the sector was used as one of the building blocks for policy initiatives aimed at improving the performance of local government in addressing some of the deep-seated problems of social cohesion and social disadvantage. One important initiative was launched in 2001. This required local authorities to convene Local Strategic Partnerships that brought together representatives of the public, for-profit and voluntary sectors together with members of the local community to devise Local Strategic Plans aimed at tackling key social needs and then guide their implementation. Here, again, local CVSs were expected to play an influential part in facilitating the participation of voluntary sector representatives. By 2008 the health of the voluntary sector had itself become a measure of the performance of local authorities and local authority partnerships; among the 199 national indicators set out in the framework for the new comprehensive area assessment was one that rated the extent to which authorities could claim to have an 'environment for a thriving third sector' (Department for Communities and Local Government, 2008).

Impact on the development of voluntary organisations in the UK

The second major impact of the invention of the sector was on the way in which voluntary organisations were led and managed. From the start, the inventors of the sector were interested in the management of voluntary organisations. As early in the process as 1981, the report of a working party on 'Improving Effectiveness in Voluntary Organisation', set up by NCVO and chaired by the management 'guru' Charles Handy, pointed to the need for the sector to embrace some of the management practices of business and led to the establishment by NCVO of a Management Development Unit (National Council for Voluntary Organisations, 1981). The front-page headline in the first issue of their *Bulletin* raised a number of issues by pointedly asking 'Can the salt of the earth be managed?' before rapidly concluding that they could (NCVO, 1983). This was the beginning of the growth of a small-scale industry in which free-lance consultants and trainers, units based in universities and commercial companies competed for a share of the growing market for their wares, while national headquarters organisations and CVS and other local intermediaries increasingly saw the provision of organisational development and management training as a key function (for the impact on CVSs see Rochester, 2012).

The first university-based programme of research, training and postgraduate education was established by David Billis at Brunel University in 1978 and relaunched at the LSE in 1987. The Open University set up its voluntary sector programme in 1988, and a number of small units and one-man bands began to specialise in the study of the sector in a growing number of universities. By 1993 the number of academics interested in the field had become sufficient to support a series of seminars on 'Challenges for Voluntary Agencies in a Changing Social Policy Landscape', organised by Margaret Harris and Colin Rochester at the LSE and funded by the Economic and Social Research Council. Those taking part in the seminars established the Voluntary Sector Studies Network to provide a forum for continuing discussions, and this has gone from strength to strength until, in 2010, it was able to launch its own journal, *The Voluntary Sector Review*.

New Labour's enthusiasm for its partners in the voluntary sector led it to invest both in the education and training of the managers and leaders of voluntary organisations and in academic research on the field. The vehicle for the first of these was the £80 million Change Up programme launched in 2004 and the establishment of a quango called Capacity Builders four years later. The programme had two main thrusts – the establishment of national hubs of expertise (which later became rebranded as national support services) and the reconfiguration of the support provided by CVSs and other local 'infrastructure' bodies. The hubs were designed to improve the quality of the support available to voluntary organisations in six 'key areas of expertise': finance; governance; ICT; performance; volunteering; and workforce. An evaluation of this part of the programme (Durning, 2006: 19) reported 'quite widespread dissatisfaction' with its quality and recommended that it should be refocused 'in order to do less better'. Instead, however, the six hubs became nine 'work streams' and three 'priority programmes' that continued until terminated by the Coalition government in 2011. The attempt to restructure the regional and local infrastructure was also ineffective. A great deal of effort was put into devising strategic plans for the future development of more effective and uniform support services, but of the 109 plans generated by the process fewer than half were of reasonable quality, and, in any case, the resources needed to implement them were generally lacking (Siederer, 2006).

The government's investment in academic research was to co-fund with the Economic and Social Research Council (ESRC) and the Barrow Cadbury Foundation the establishment in 2008 of a Third Sector Research Centre (TSRC) led by the Universities of Birmingham and Southampton. This is intended to create a 'critical mass' of researchers in one centre in place of the many small-scale units that existed before. TSRC has concentrated on producing data – creating an evidence base about the sector – and has paid comparatively little attention to developing critical theory about voluntary organisations and their place in the wider social and political environment. The effect of its work has been to consolidate a conceptual framework and a policy field based on the idea of a sector.

While some of the early scholarly attention paid to the sector focused on the distinctive characteristics of voluntary agencies and emphasised the significant differences between them and private sector businesses or statutory agencies (see, for example: Harris, 1990; Billis, 1993a), critical commentary on the utility of adopting management theory derived from the world of business by the national intermediary bodies has been muted. The casting of voluntary agencies in the roles of government's partners in delivering welfare services has been accompanied by an assumption that they will need to behave not just in a business-like manner but as if they were businesses, and that the techniques and approaches used by the managers of private enterprise are those that are needed to run a voluntary organisation.

It is also worth noting at this point that the boundaries of the sector and the way it has been defined have changed over time. The idea of the voluntary sector was expanded by Deakin to become the voluntary and community sector and include small grassroots and less formal organisations alongside agencies led and managed by paid staff. It was this expanded version of Kendall and Knapp's 'loose and baggy monster' with which the Compact was agreed. As New Labour's policy towards the sector became more and more instrumental and 'partners' became 'providers' and 'contractors', it decided that the term 'third sector' would better reflect the identity of the charities, voluntary agencies and social enterprises that were equipped to fulfil these roles. The Coalition originally opted to use the term 'civil society'; exactly what it intends that to mean will only become clear in time. It has tended to be inconsistent in its use of terminology, and a recent announcement by the Cabinet – of the appointment of a 'Crown representative for the voluntary sector' – refers to the 'voluntary, community and social enterprise (VCSE) sector' (Last, 2012b).

Some conclusions

The invention of the voluntary sector has indeed created a policy field as well as developing a policy sub-elite made up of those who lead the intermediary bodies and those who act for government at central and local level, together with some 'useful' fellow-travelling intellectuals. Their achievement has been to gain widespread acceptance of one narrative about the role and function of voluntary organisations in public and social policy and one view of organisational effectiveness and efficiency. In the process they have co-operated with government on the redefinition of voluntary and community organisations as a single 'governable terrain' or sector which enables them to 'impose an institutional and normative order as a whole onto to an otherwise privately organised and variably regulated group of organisations' (Carmel and Harlock, 2008: 156). In the process they have also brought into question the heterogeneity of voluntary organisations, their ability to act independently and the way in which they construct their own identity. These three consequences of the invention of the sector will be explored in the later chapters of this book.

4

The Invention of Voluntary Work and its Consequences

Introduction

The creation and acceptance of the idea of a sector as a means of categorising and giving meaning to the organisations involved in voluntary action has been accompanied by a similar but less remarked process through which voluntary action by individuals has come to be seen as 'voluntary work'. While the phrase itself has by no means attained the currency of the sector metaphor, it has had a powerful impact on the way in which volunteering has been perceived, discussed and promoted. This chapter explores the roots of this perspective, discusses its implications and assesses its impact. It traces the modern usage of 'voluntary work' back to the influential Aves Committee's report on *The Voluntary Worker in the Social Services*, published in 1969, and explores the way it has permeated the ideas and practices of volunteer-involving organisations, volunteering infrastructure organisations and the academic study of volunteering as well as shaping a series of policy initiatives by successive governments aimed at promoting volunteering.

The history of volunteering in the UK does not, of course, begin with the work of the Aves Committee. The stereotype of the Victorian volunteer as 'Lady Bountiful' had ceased to be a reality (if it ever was accurate) by the 1880s, when the social background of those involved in voluntary action and the level of training or preparation for their roles were broadly similar to those of today's volunteers. There is evidence that the number of volunteers increased significantly in the years between the two world wars, while the belief that the scale and scope of volunteering were substantially reduced by the post-Second World War welfare settlement led by state provision has been challenged: 'Undoubtedly the post-war period saw the employment of greater numbers of professional social workers by both statutory [agencies] and voluntary associations, but ... this did not necessarily lead to an immediate decline in the number of volunteers, but rather reflected that the overall volume of work increased' (Brewis, 2011: 10). We should also be wary of accepting the common view that a slump in volunteering activity in the late 1940s and the 1950s was followed by a boom in involvement in the 1960s (see, for example, Sheard, 1992). On the other hand, the Aves Committee met at a time when attitudes to volunteering were changing, and it made a major contribution to the creation of the modern volunteering 'industry'.

Sheard's claim that there was a volunteer boom in the 1960s is based on two foundations. On the one hand, he argues that there was a new interest in the contribution volunteers could make to the quantity and quality of social welfare provision; 'after the welfare state had been in operation for a decade or so' it had become apparent that 'the professionals were not able to meet all the needs – and that sometimes their methods could be rather too remote and bureaucratic' (Sheard, 1992: 12). As a result, there were renewed efforts to involve volunteers in the National Health Service. From 1962 onwards the Ministry of Health issued guidelines for the recruitment, deployment and support of volunteers and promoted the employment of paid voluntary service co-ordinators in hospitals. The first two appointments of this new kind of professional staff were made in 1963, and there were no fewer than 200 of them in post by 1973 (Davis Smith, 1996). The enthusiasm for volunteers, moreover, was not limited to the NHS but also encompassed the criminal justice system and social services delivered by local government. A review of the Probation Service by the Reading Committee in 1967 called for the involvement of volunteers in the Probation Service (Reading Committee, 1967) while the Seebohm Report of 1968 that led to the creation of the modern local authority Social Services Department argued that it would 'be necessary for local authorities to enlist the services of large numbers of volunteers, and the social service department must become a focal point to which volunteers can offer their services' (Seebohm, 1968: 157).

On the other hand, Sheard argues that there was a new interest in volunteering in the 1960s because of a growing concern about antisocial behaviour by young people. From the late 1950s onwards, the older generation felt that the social order was under threat from a series of phenomena such as Teddy Boys, Mods and Rockers, Hell's Angels and the student revolutionaries of 1968. 'It was against this background', writes Sheard (1992: 13), 'that volunteering began to be perceived in a new role; as a safe, constructive outlet for the otherwise unpredictable and destructive energies of disaffected young people'. Organisations like Community Service Volunteers (founded 1962), Task Force (1964) and the Young Volunteer Force Foundation (1968) as well as smaller locally based agencies were created to address this need. This concern with the anti-social tendencies of young people has helped to shape the policies adopted by successive governments to promote volunteering in more recent years, but proved less influential at the end of the 1960s and the beginning of the 1970s. Rather than contributing to the development of mainstream voluntary work, Task Force and the Young Volunteer Force Foundation were relaunched as community development agencies and became part of the 'community work boom' of 1968–75 as volunteering changed direction under the influence of the Aves Committee, which decided not 'to isolate young volunteers for separate treatment.... Young volunteers are essentially part of the whole picture and in many respects, we find them to be distinguishable from their elders only by age' (Aves, 1969: 26).

The Aves Report

The Aves Committee was a joint venture between the NCSS (which subsequently became the NCVO) and the National Institute for Social Work Training. It was set up in June 1966 'to enquire into the role of voluntary workers in the social services and in particular to consider their need for preparation and training and their relationship with professional social workers' (Aves, 1969: 15). Its chair, Miss (later Dame) Geraldine Aves, had been Chief Welfare Officer of the Ministry of Health, and her colleagues were a mix of academics, local government officers and voluntary sector representatives. The Committee's report 'represented something of a watershed in the development of volunteering'. In the first place it provided the modern volunteering 'movement' with a clear orientation; volunteering was 'a way in which people of all ages and backgrounds could be enabled to make a contribution to community services and activities' and 'an integral part of social services provision with volunteers complementing the services of professional staff' (Sheard, 1992: 15). Second, it laid the foundations for the 'infrastructure' of a volunteering industry by calling for a national focus and local centres for promoting and supporting volunteering. And, third, it led – eventually – to the emergence of a new profession of volunteer manager. In the process, the Aves Committee has made a major contribution to shaping how we discuss the theory and practice of volunteering through the creation of a 'dominant paradigm'.

A view of volunteering

The title of the Aves Committee's Report refers to 'the voluntary worker', and this is indicative of its approach to volunteering. It used the terms 'volunteers' and 'voluntary workers' as synonymous and looked upon them essentially as resources that could be deployed to help meet a range of social needs:

> Social services had become more comprehensive and complex than ever before.... The aims of the services were becoming more explicit; their limitations as well as their potentialities were more clearly recognised; shortages of suitably equipped staff were constantly deplored, and there were doubts about the wisdom – even if it had been practicable – of trying to meet all these needs by the use of paid staff. In short, it had become apparent that only by the intelligent mobilization of every resource could society hope to realize its aspirations to meet a very wide range of human needs. Among these resources the services available from volunteers clearly needed careful evaluation.
>
> (Aves, 1969: 16)

From this starting point the Committee went on to explore the current involvement of volunteers and the potential for enhancing it; to consider the value of volunteer work and the most appropriate uses to which it could be put; and to make recommendations about how to get the most out of the contribution that volunteers could make.

As well as collecting evidence from voluntary workers themselves and from the 'clients', as they called those who benefitted from their activities, the Committee sought the views of central government departments, local authorities and social workers – but not, interestingly, from voluntary organisations. They found that 'The attitude of the central government departments with major responsibility for the personal social services, the Ministry of Health [as it then was] and the Home Office, is one of encouragement and appreciation of the present and future place of voluntary work in these services', while other departments 'tended to welcome the contribution which voluntary workers can make' while remaining 'uncertain about what this means in terms of precise function' (57). It found that local authority chief officers were less positive about voluntary workers and had given 'comparatively little thought . . . to extending the use made of volunteers or increasing its scope'. Social workers also had concerns about the use of volunteers. They were concerned about the impact on their professional standing of sharing the work with lay people and anxious about the harm that 'unskilful workers' might do: 'For the most part, however, their anxieties relate to the difficulty of finding the time and manpower required to make effective use of volunteers' (Aves, 1969; 53, 57, 67).

The Committee also emphasised the variety of functions carried out by voluntary workers and the scope for further involvement: 'We are left with a conviction that the social services as we know them, and as they are developing, give almost unlimited scope for voluntary effort. The range of tasks available for volunteers is such that gifts and interests of every kind can be utilised.' In an attempt to capture the variety of tasks and type of work performed by volunteers, the Committee classified them 'according to the type of commitment and the various degrees and kinds of knowledge, skill and understanding required'. The result was a three-fold division between practical tasks; work requiring a special skill or knowledge; and work involving personal relationships. Practical work included flower arranging, answering the telephone and checking linen in hospitals; driving for community transport schemes; and cleaning and decoration of houses and community centres. Work that involved the use of specific skills or knowledge included activities in which volunteers made use of abilities they already possessed – using language skills to help others become proficient in English or providing legal advice – or where they had developed the skill or knowledge needed, such as first aid for the Red Cross and giving advice for the Citizens Advice Bureaux service. And work which involved personal relationships might be focused on individuals and families; residential settings; group work; those alienated from societies; and in the emergency services (Aves, 1969: 92, 69).

On the other hand, this very wide range of contributions by voluntary workers did have some boundaries. The Committee felt it important to discuss 'what we believe to be another reason for unevenness in the use of voluntary workers, namely the lack of any clear policy or agreement as to what their proper function is and in what ways the services they offer can most appropriately be used' (86). And, while the Committee felt that the boundary of what was and was not appropriate work for volunteers was not set in stone, there were some key principles that should not change. In the first place, volunteers should not be used as substitutes for professional workers: 'the use of volunteers can lead to

a better service; but this cannot be achieved by employing fewer qualified staff'. And, second, it rejected the view that voluntary workers could
be used by public services to undertake manual or domestic tasks that
would otherwise be performed by paid staff – except in an emergency.
Instead, it argued that the key factor in developing a strategy or policy
for the involvement of volunteers in any organisation was the need to
ensure that the best use was made of what it called 'the special contribution of voluntary workers'. This was based on the view that volunteers
were able to provide a different kind of service to the beneficiaries of
their activities; they could establish a more relaxed and less formal relationship with them and devote more time to a single individual than
those who were constrained by their professional terms and conditions.
As generally part-time workers, they were, on the one hand, less likely
to experience stress and, on the other, could offer a more independent
view and some constructive criticism of the ways in which a service was
being delivered (Aves, 1969: 86, 87, 91).

The organisation of voluntary work

To make effective use of volunteers and to address the concerns
expressed by government agencies and social workers, the Aves Committee called for a strategic approach to the involvement of volunteers
in various contexts: 'The place of voluntary workers in each service or
area of need should be re-examined, in order that their roles may be clarified and greater purpose and direction given to their work.' And it also
provided – in three central chapters – more detailed guidance about the
organisation of voluntary work; the recruitment and selection of volunteers; and the need to provide them with suitable training and support.
The Aves Committee was uncompromising about the need to organise
the work of volunteers: '(I)t is very necessary in any service using volunteers that there should be some form of organization of their work', by
which 'we mean the provision of a system within and through which
volunteers are enabled to carry out their work, as far as may be possible,
effectively, smoothly and with satisfaction to their clients, themselves
and the services which need their help'. This involved addressing seven
main functions:

- Identification of the needs for voluntary work and allocation of
  appropriate individuals to carry out the relevant tasks;
- Ensuring that volunteers are not exploited or neglected;
- Providing volunteers with appropriate preparation or training;

- Making sure that volunteers receive the help and support they need;
- Ensuring that the service provided by the volunteers is of a satisfactory quality;
- Enabling volunteers to meet one another for mutual encouragement; and
- Making sure that the volunteers are aware of the extent and nature of their involvement; the lines of accountability for their work; and the practical details such as payment of expenses and insurance cover.

And, to ensure that these functions were carried out, each service or agency needed to employ a dedicated voluntary service organiser: 'There should be a full-time or part-time organizer of the work of volunteers in every service in which they are employed: the post may be held by a paid or voluntary worker without professional qualifications; or in certain circumstances by a social worker.' While recognising that there were wide differences between organisations – and between the kinds of services they provide – the Committee argued that there were, nonetheless, some common elements in the work of the organizers, 'and one of the most important is the concern for each volunteer which will enable him to give of his best'. It also suggested that people taking on the organiser role would benefit from a short training course that would cover 'the selection of volunteers, and some teaching about management, staff relations, group behaviour and ethical principles' (Aves, 1969: 53, 93, 195, 113, 114).

Recruitment and selection

The Aves Committee found that the recruitment of voluntary workers was heavily dependent on 'word-of-mouth' methods; half of the organisations surveyed reported that 75 per cent of their volunteers came from this source. Other methods included giving talks to groups or societies; appeals via churches or schools; posters and leaflets in libraries and elsewhere; and, for a few organisations, paid advertising. Organisations appeared to be satisfied with this situation, and some of them expressed doubts about the quality or suitability of people recruited in this way rather than approached as the result of a recommendation from an existing volunteer. The Committee, however, felt strongly that more varied and active recruiting methods were needed in order not only to increase the numbers of volunteers coming forward but also to broaden the fields from which they were drawn. Where the Seebohm Committee had emphasised the need to broaden the composition of the volunteering workforce, Aves was particularly interested in the recruitment of older people and those who had recently retired. The challenge of ensuring that volunteers are recruited from all sections of society rather than limited to a narrow social segment has continued to exercise commentators since Aves. In 1992 Hedley and Davis Smith included 'widening the base of volunteering' as a key element in a response to the 'dual crisis in volunteering, the crisis of supply and the crisis of identity' (Hedley and Davis Smith, 1992: 5). And, the best part of 20 years later another survey of 'volunteering and society' (Rochester *et al.*, 2010) included a chapter on 'making volunteering inclusive' among four 'enduring challenges for volunteering'.

Recruitment by word of mouth also meant that procedures for selecting volunteers from among those coming forward were comparatively undeveloped at the time when the Aves Committee was sitting. It distinguished between two kinds of selection: the systems needed to ensure that candidates would be able to meet the demands of exacting roles – such as counselling or providing advice services – and the processes by which organisations that involved volunteers in a number of different roles determined which volunteers were best suited for the various tasks involved. It also heard from large organisations that did not have any selection procedures, either because the range of functions carried out by volunteers was so wide that they could be confident of finding work for all those who offered their services or because their need for volunteers was always greater than the supply, which meant that they could not afford to turn anyone away. Others felt that they should not, as a matter of principle, tell people that they were not suitable for voluntary work and 'Sometimes a great deal of trouble is taken to find a suitable niche for a volunteer who seems unlikely to fit into any of the more usual kinds of work' (Aves, 1969: 124).

The recommendations of the Aves Committee pay little heed to the idea that organisations might have a responsibility to find a role for everybody who offered their help. Instead, it focused on the need for a targeted approach – the need for agencies to 'formulate their requirements more precisely and specify more clearly what kinds of people are wanted for particular services or specific jobs' and 'develop selection procedures applicable to their work, and apply them' (Aves, 1969: 196–7).

Preparation and training

Given that an approach that treats volunteers as unpaid workers and emphasises the need for clarity about the tasks they will perform will also regard preparation and training as a key requirement, it is not surprising, then – especially in the report of a committee set up in part by the National Institute for Social Work Training – to find that the Committee devoted 12 of the 32 recommendations to this area. Some of these are about the wider dissemination of ideas about volunteering (through, for example, use of the mass media) and about opportunities for early involvement at school. But at the heart of this section is a very unambiguous approach to the issue. While 'methods... should be informal and flexible', training is a requirement rather than an option and part of a way of 'managing volunteers' that is made clear in four key recommendations:

17. *Preparation.* All volunteers need preparation for their work...

21. *Organization of training.* In each agency there should be a person who is responsible for the promotion of training for its voluntary workers, and for ensuring that they are able to obtain it...

24. *Supervision.* Supervision, consultation and advice should always be available to volunteers, and are particularly important for those whose work involves close personal relationships with clients ...

28. *Financing training.* Statutory and voluntary agencies should regard the cost of training for volunteers as an essential item of expenditure and make provision for it.

(Aves, 1969: 197)

The volunteering infrastructure

In order to promote and support its approach to volunteering, the Aves Committee recommended the establishment of a national 'focus for all aspects of the work of volunteers' and the development of 'a comprehensive network of volunteer bureaux, as centres of advice and information for volunteers and to assist statutory and voluntary bodies which need their help'. It also called for the formation of local joint committees involving statutory agencies and voluntary organisations which involved volunteers in their work to assist the co-ordination of training provision and provide a local forum for the discussion of training issues.

The role of the proposed national focus – the Volunteering Foundation, as it was called – initially featured in the report as a co-ordinating body for the work of the local committees. Its role was to contribute to the development of training by evaluating methods, advising on syllabuses and arranging conferences and short courses. By the end of the report, however, the Foundation's remit had been clarified and extended to encompass a wider and more strategic role; it would 'serve as a focus for all aspects of the work of volunteers in the social services'. The Committee argued that it would be of the greatest importance for the future of volunteering: 'Without such a body we think it unlikely that the necessary impetus and guidance will be available to achieve what we regard as urgently needed developments' (Aves, 1969: 192).

The Committee recommended that the Foundation should be established as a freestanding and independent body – to the chagrin of the National Council of Social Service, which would have been happy to take on its functions (6 and Leat, 1997). It would be supported financially by government, especially in its early days, and could be expected to attract the interest of 'organisations which are associated with volunteers in any way' that would be encouraged to become paid-up members. It:

> would require a small staff, able through their qualifications or experience, to communicate easily with volunteers, social workers and administrators, to assemble information, promote studies and pilot projects, advise on training schemes and methods; and generally encourage a positive attitude to the whole field of voluntary work.
>
> (Aves, 1969: 192)

The Committee had also been impressed by the work of the local volunteer bureaux that had been established in some parts of the country. By the time it was gathering evidence, 23 councils of social service had set up bureaux that collected information about opportunities for volunteering in their local areas, provided advice and information to potential volunteers and referred them to the local organisations in need of their help. These arrangements did not take the place of 'the organization of voluntary work which is required within any particular service', but it was 'easy to see the advantages of having in any area a central source from which all would-be volunteers can obtain advice and comprehensive information'. It therefore recommended that 'There should be a comprehensive network of volunteer bureaux.' As well as offering services to potential volunteers, they would also be expected to 'assist statutory and voluntary bodies which need their help. Their functions would include recruitment and preliminary selection and the keeping of records of volunteers.' And their major source of income should be local authority grant aid (Aves, 1969: 105, 196).

The impact of the Aves Report

The Aves Committee's report has had a considerable influence on the development of volunteering in the past 50 years. This has been made up of some direct impacts and some less than direct, but nonetheless significant, contributions to shaping the ways in which volunteering is organised and the ways in which it is perceived and discussed. Its direct impacts include the development of a national and local volunteering infrastructure and the acceleration of the process of employing paid staff as volunteer co-ordinators in volunteer-involving organisations across all three sectors. Less directly, it has provided a stimulus for government action to promote and support volunteering, paved the way for the emergence of volunteer management as a new profession and shaped a powerful dominant paradigm in the theory and practice of volunteering.

In the first place, the Committee's report led directly to the establishment in 1973 of the Volunteer Centre UK as an independent, publicly funded national focus for volunteering. While both the name and remit of this body have changed over the years, it has remained a constant presence until 2012, when it was absorbed by NCVO. As a consequence of the devolution of powers to the national administrations of Scotland and Wales in 1998, its remit was limited to England and it became the National Centre for Volunteering until 2004, when it merged with the national body for local volunteer centres – Volunteer Development England – and a body which administered funding of the Department of Health's Opportunities for Volunteering Fund to form Volunteering England (VE). The merged organisation's mission was defined as 'supporting, enabling and celebrating volunteering in all its diversity' and its work aspired to link 'policy, research, innovation, good practice and programme management in the involvement of volunteers' (www.volunteering.org.uk). This was very much in keeping with the original vision developed by Aves, as was its 'diverse membership drawn from the public, private and voluntary and community sectors'. On the other hand, until recently, its staff could not be described as the small team envisaged by the Committee.

The establishment at national level of what became VE was paralleled at local level by the development of volunteer bureaux or, as they are now known, volunteer centres, although the local joint committees proposed by Aves to co-ordinate the training of volunteers failed to materialise. While the number of volunteer centres and their coverage have grown significantly since 1969, the network remains well short of comprehensive and the strength and levels of activity of individual centres have been very uneven. The network reached its peak in 2005–06 when the number of volunteer development agencies belonging to the national network accredited by Volunteering England stood at 320 (Brostomer, 2006). At this point VE had developed a ten-year plan to 'modernise' the network. It argued that, with the help of central government funding, the network could be restructured to match the boundaries of county councils and unitary local authorities, and the smaller number of volunteer centres that this would create could be funded to ensure that they were all able to perform their core functions (as defined by VE) to a satisfactory level. These six functions add up to a more ambitious role than the remit proposed by the Aves Committee and are:

- brokerage;
- marketing;
- developing good practice;
- developing volunteering opportunities;
- providing a 'voice' for volunteering; and
- facilitating its strategic development.

In the event, central government declined to pursue this approach just as its predecessors had rejected the Wolfenden Committee's earlier recommendation of a national funding programme for local intermediary bodies (of which volunteer centres are a species). This left volunteer centres dependent on the attitude of their local authorities and increasingly vulnerable after the cuts on local government expenditure imposed by the Coalition government after 2010. By 2011 the number of affiliated centres had fallen to 276 (Ramsay, 2012) and, in the following year, the Chief Executive of Volunteering England warned that, faced with an average cut of 12% from local government funding, the network was under threat of fragmentation (Young, 2012).

None of the recommendations of the Aves Report was addressed to government (except for the suggestion that the new national focus should be 'financed initially from public funds'), but the Committee is often seen as a starting point for the active engagement of successive governments in a series of initiatives aimed at promoting volunteering (see, for example, Sheard, 1992). While these schemes and programmes varied considerably as to aim and focus, two themes that ran through many of them and surfaced at regular intervals were key concerns of the Aves Committee – on the one hand, the recognition of the contribution that unpaid workers could make to 'improving the reach, quality and cost of public services' and, on the other, the need to broaden the social composition of the volunteering workforce (Zimmeck and Rochester, 2013a). It would be easy to exaggerate the influence of the Aves Report: the instrumental view of volunteering as 'a very cost effective way of providing desirable services', as it was described in the Efficiency Scrutiny of 1990, did not exclude the acknowledgement of its inherent value 'as a desirable activity in its own right' in the same document (Home Office, 1990: 18). But, as we shall see, the view of the volunteer as valuable unpaid labour continues to make a major impact on the thought and action of government, and of other parties too.

Its impact on volunteer-involving bodies and the organisations that supported their work was to encourage the development of a managerial approach to volunteers and the creation of a cadre of paid staff to exercise this function. As we have seen, the Aves Committee highlighted methods of recruitment and selection; the need for training and support; and the recruitment of paid organisers to address these tasks as the central issues for volunteer-involving organisations. These messages were generally well received and were reinforced by the national and local organs of the new volunteering infrastructure and, in turn, by government itself. The numbers of paid co-ordinators and organisers continued to grow rapidly and increasing attention was given to the ways in which they carried out their functions. The adoption of an explicitly managerial approach loosely based on the techniques of human resource management applied to paid employees – known as the workplace model – can be seen with hindsight as the eventual (but not necessarily inevitable) consequence of this process. In 1996 there was opposition to the adoption of formalised forms of management of this kind (Davis Smith, 1996) and, five years later, Zimmeck (2000) identified an alternative model – the 'home-grown' product – which involves a less hierarchical approach with a minimum of rules and procedures. But the writing was on the wall; as part of its ambition to build the capacity of the voluntary sector, New Labour turned its attention to the management of volunteers and adopted the 'workplace model' as the way forward. One result was the establishment of a Volunteer Management Programme as part of the CapacityBuilders initiative and another was the establishment of a set of National Occupational Standards that define the skills and knowledge required to manage volunteers. And, alongside this 'top-down' pressure, there has come a bottom-up approach to developing a professional identity through the formation of the Association of Volunteer Managers (Howlett, 2010).

The dominant paradigm

If we can trace the development of what is sometimes called the volunteering industry, with its infrastructure and an increasingly professional approach to the organisation of volunteering, back to the Aves Report's emphasis on the value of the voluntary worker as a resource for those delivering social services, we can also find in it the seed of what has grown into the 'dominant paradigm' of volunteering. This is the 'default setting' for any discussion of volunteering: it involves the unspoken assumption that volunteering is essentially about unpaid work undertaken for the benefit of people less fortunate than oneself and which involves carrying out pre-determined tasks for a formal, bureaucratic organisation which employs staff to manage its volunteer labour. This view excludes other kinds of motivation; different fields of activity; a variety of organisational contexts; and other kinds of intra-organisational relationships to focus on just one form of volunteering.

It has dominated the academic study of voluntary action: the attempt by my co-authors and myself to do justice to the diversity and reach of volunteering in our recent book on *Volunteering and Society in the 20th Century* (Rochester *et al.*, 2010) was stymied by the lack of research that looked beyond the field delineated by the dominant paradigm. And its wider influence can be seen in the report of the Commission on the Future of Volunteering (2008), which began with an inclusive definition of volunteering which embraces 'not only formal volunteering, through clubs and organisations, but also informal volunteering, often carried out on a more individual basis' and includes 'mutual aid or self-help; philanthropy or service to others; participation; and advocacy or campaigning' (Commission on the Future of Volunteering, 2008: 5) but ends with a series of recommendations which make sense largely in the context of a much narrower conception of voluntary action by individuals. We shall return to this dominant paradigm and discuss a more rounded view of volunteering in Chapter 12.

Part II
Pressures and Influences

5
A Perilous Partnership? Voluntary Action and the State

Introduction and prologue

This, the first of four chapters that review the key forces and influences that have shaped the dominant view of voluntary action in the early years of the twenty-first century, discusses the growing impact of the state on voluntary organisations and volunteering. It acknowledges that, as discussed in Chapter 2, much of the history of voluntary action – especially in the broad field of social welfare – cannot easily be disentangled from its relationship with government at national and local levels and that the 'moving frontier' between them has been an enduring theme. The chapter argues, nonetheless, that the degree of influence – both direct and indirect – exercised by government over the work and conduct of voluntary agencies has become a major threat to their independence of thought and action during the past 20 years or so. It reviews the ways in which successive governments have sought to engage voluntary organisations in the achievement of social and public policy objectives and the delivery of public services and attempted to use volunteering as a panacea for a number of social ills. The chapter also charts the growing dependence of voluntary organisations on government funding and the changing and increasingly disadvantageous terms on which this support is provided. It concludes by assessing the impact of governmental influences on volunteering and voluntary organisations, in terms of both the kinds of activities they undertake and the ways in which they organise their affairs.

While the relationship with the state has been a more or less continuous part of the history of voluntary action, we can perhaps date the beginning of a new era from the innovations in social policy implemented by the Liberal administration led by Lloyd George in 1906–11. These laid the foundations for the emergence of an enlarged role for the state in the provision of social welfare that, in turn, had a significant impact on the ways in which voluntary agencies were structured and managed. As central government came to play an ever-increasing part in securing the welfare of its citizens, voluntary organisations adapted their structures to enable them to influence the ways in which statutory bodies went about their business and make themselves more attractive as partners with which government could collaborate. On the one hand, they developed national headquarters that could form relationships with government departments and, on the other, they followed the example of statutory bodies by adopting the organisational template provided by the private sector 'firm' with its centralised bureaucracy. As Alison Penn (2011) has argued, some forms of voluntary action were better equipped for this new organisational model: philanthropic charities thrived while mutual aid societies were relegated to the sidelines, and unitary bodies with power concentrated at their centres were better able to make their way than looser federations with branches that enjoyed considerable local autonomy.

First act: The 'mixed economy' of welfare

The period between the Lloyd George reforms and the 1980s was not without twists and turns in the relationship between the state and the voluntary sector. But they had little impact on voluntary organisations and volunteering compared with the radical attempts to remake government and social policy during the years following the election in 1979 of a Conservative government led by Margaret Thatcher. The new administration's ambition of 'shrinking the state' was rooted in a perceived 'crisis' in social welfare provision that was experienced in many developed societies during the 1970s. Widespread criticism of the welfare settlement reached at the end of the Second World War was based both on economic considerations – the growing proportion of national income devoted to social welfare was seen as unaffordable – and what were seen as operational failures – the welfare state had failed to meet the expectations of its architects and the needs of its service users. While these concerns were expressed by representatives of all shades of political opinion, it was the academics, think-tanks and politicians of the right who developed the most radical diagnosis of the problem and offered a clear alternative and a way forward. In their view 'the public sector, in welfare and elsewhere' was 'essentially beyond redemption, since it is by definition chronically inefficient' (Deakin, 1996: 23). They argued that government agencies were bound by inflexible rules and procedures and thus unable to respond to the needs of their users. In the absence of the benign discipline of the market they were prone to 'capture' by the self-interested producers of services in the form of self-serving senior managers, on the one hand, and greedy trades unions, on the other. The remedy for this state of affairs was to replace the system of state-run monopoly provision with a market-based approach in which providers would be required to meet the demands of their users or customers under the pressure of competition from their rivals.

The first step in the process of implementing these far-reaching changes in welfare provision was to bring the public sector to heel. At central government level this involved a frontal attack on the Whitehall monolith by the creation of a new breed of semi-independent agencies charged with the implementation of policy and the delivery of services and organisationally distinct from the departments of state, whose responsibilities were now concentrated on policy development. The new arms-length agencies became the major employers of rank-and-file civil servants and were required to model the ways in which they operated on private sector business practices. Local authorities were brought to heel by the imposition of new forms of regulation and limits on their ability to raise and spend money and then required to reorganise themselves to become 'enablers' and 'purchasers' of services rather than directly providing them.

Central government's efforts to 'shrink the state' were founded in part on the assumption that voluntary agencies could and should play a larger part in the provision of social welfare. The Government's Efficiency Scrutiny of voluntary sector funding identified the virtues it saw in voluntary action:

The voluntary sector is an important force, which complements public services, and has the potential to do more. It is:

  i.   able to get close to the customer
 ii.   innovative and able to respond to new needs
iii.   able to work in a wide range of fields
 iv.   able to operate at less cost than government.

(Home Office, 1990: 6)

And:

> The Government has an interest in encouraging volunteering, both
> because it is a desirable activity in its own right, and because it is a
> very cost effective way of providing desirable services.
>
> (ibid.: 18)

What is clear, however, is that the recommendations of the Efficiency
Scrutiny report are nakedly instrumental. Voluntary action may be desirable in its own right, but government should only fund those aspects of
voluntary sector activities that help to advance its own policies. It rec-
ommends that the government should make it clear that 'In future, it
will expect a closer match between its own objectives and the bodies it
core funds' and suggests that:

i.   Departments will look actively at how voluntary bodies can
     contribute to the development of their policy objectives. This
     will include looking at the scope for contracting out services to
     voluntary bodies;
ii. Departments will examine existing grants and schemes against
     their policy objectives, and will phase out any which no longer
     contribute to their objectives.

> (ibid.: 27)

While the Efficiency Scrutiny provides evidence of the government's
view of the sector, it was at local rather than national level that the
impact of the new approach to the role of the state was to have the
greatest impact on voluntary organisations.

The NHS and Community Care Act 1990 was designed to usher in a
new set of arrangements for social welfare that came to be known as
'the mixed economy of care'. The Act called for three kinds of change.
In the first place, it authorised a shift from the provision of residential care to providing support to people in their own homes. Second, it
transferred responsibility for social care from the NHS to local authorities. And, third, it introduced a major change in the identity of care
providers by specifying that 70% of provision should be made by the
'independent sector' – voluntary agencies and private companies. And,
to enable the third of these changes to take place, local authority social
services departments were to be restructured; there was to be a clear division between those responsible for purchasing services from external
providers and those that would continue to organise the department's

own provision, while a third part of the organisation would provide a beefed-up inspection service.

The impact on voluntary organisations that became contractors under the new arrangements was not felt overnight. It took time for local authorities to adopt the culture and practice of purchase-of-service contracts and, in the early days of the contract culture, many local voluntary organisations did not face competition from other providers. But, over time, the effects of contracting began to emerge. In the first place, the nature of the work they carried out began to change. Organisations increasingly concentrated their efforts on providing services rather than supporting self-help, engaging in community development and undertaking campaigning activities. Their services moved from the less formal to the more formal or intensive – instead of luncheon clubs they provided day centres or sheltered accommodation. This was accompanied by a change in the profile of their users; those working with older people increasingly focused on the needs of the most frail and dependent, while groups providing play facilities gave higher priority to children believed to be 'at risk'. And, at the same time, paid staff replaced volunteers in many agencies, generalist workers gave way to people with specific kinds of expertise, and organisations increasingly appointed staff to manage or direct their operations (Billis and Harris, 1992).

Second act: New Labour and the politics of partnership

The arrival in 1997 of the New Labour Government led by Tony Blair did not halt this move towards a more professional engagement of voluntary organisations in the delivery of more formal services to dependent users. It did, however, set the largely instrumental involvement of the sector in service provision within an overarching vision of a different kind of relationship between voluntary organisations and the state. Its vision, set out in the Compact, was of a partnership based on 'shared values and mutual respect' (Home Office, 1998: Foreword) which was underpinned by a formal statement of the principles that should inform the relationship between government and the voluntary and community sector. It was an ambitious enterprise that was intended to guide the behaviour of all of the departments, agencies and non-departmental public bodies that made up the apparatus of government in their dealings with the full range of organisations that constituted the voluntary and community sector. The English Compact had counterparts in the other countries of the UK and in practically every local authority. Together, this family of compacts appeared to offer the prospect of achieving the aim of the Commission on the Future of the Voluntary Sector (1996) of changing 'the culture of government in its dealings with the voluntary sector' by turning it into 'a listening, responding and engaging body' (Jochum and Rochester, 2012: 8).

In the event, the high hopes invested by many in the national and local compacts were disappointed – although they did make a valuable impact in Wales, and on some parts of central government and on some local authorities in England and Scotland. The comparative failure of what was, after all, a very high-profile policy initiative can be explained by a lack of consistent commitment and leadership at ministerial level; insufficient resources for the key part of the machinery of government; the inadequacies of the lead body for the sector; and weaknesses in the machinery for liaison and accountability (Zimmeck *et al.*, 2011). But this is only part of the story: the Compact and the model of an equal partnership based on mutual respect that it embodied were overtaken by changes in the government's policy orientation.

> New Labour was 'hyper-active' in its generation of policies, programmes and initiatives (Kendall, 2003), and over its thirteen years in power it changed its priorities in ways that also changed the environment in which the Compact operated.
>
> (Zimmeck and Rochester, 2013b: 9)

The first of these shifts was a move away from general support for the full range of voluntary organisations, no matter what activities they were involved in, and towards particular support targeted on those organisations that contributed to the delivery of public services. Voluntary action was no longer seen as valuable in its own right but as useful to government as a means to achieving its own ends. The second major set of changes involved an increasingly prescriptive approach to local authorities: this involved establishing cross-sector bodies like local strategic partnerships; tightening controls over spending; introducing stringent performance targets; and imposing detailed monitoring requirements. A third shift of policy was signalled by the redefinition of the sector to make room for the social enterprises which were seen as the latest 'magic bullets' in the campaign to deliver public services at lower cost. The concept of the 'third sector' redrew the boundary of the voluntary and community sector in two ways: on the one hand, it was stretched to include social enterprises and, on the other, it was redrawn to exclude smaller community-based bodies and others whose activities were not solely or mainly devoted to delivering services. In these changed circumstances the Compact ceased to be the principal defining feature of the government–voluntary sector relationships and became, instead, just one of the ways in which the relationship was managed.

New Labour's rhetoric of partnership was also brought into play in its relationships with a collection of national organisations described by the Wolfenden Report as 'intermediary bodies' that provide support 'individually and collectively' for the voluntary organisations which comprise their membership (Wolfenden, 1978: 100). These – now known more commonly as 'infrastructure' organisations – flourished under New Labour administrations that gave them both a higher profile and an enhanced income. Some of them – like NCVO and VE – had been funded by central government for a number of years, while others joined the payroll during the period of New Labour rule. Grants of this kind – which supported the running costs of organisations and, thus, their very existence – had originally been seen as 'core funding'. The idea of supporting an organisation's 'core costs' rather than rewarding it for providing services that contributed to the achievement of government's own policy objectives, however, was not seen by the administration led by John Major as a legitimate form of statutory funding. Faced with the desirability of continuing to support some key intermediary bodies, however, the government relented, but covered its retreat by renaming its grants 'strategic funding'. With a further adroit use of language New Labour changed the label once more and committed itself to funding a series of 'strategic partners' who secured often quite generous financial backing by committing themselves to government-led strategies for involving voluntary organisations in delivering public services. The number of such 'strategic partners' had ballooned to 42 (receiving a total of £12.2 million per year) by 2010, when the Coalition began to cut their numbers before phasing out central government funding to the last remaining survivors.

Grants to a growing number of 'strategic partners' did not, of course, represent the only form of investment by New Labour in the voluntary sector. The Deakin Commission had not only aimed its recommendations at government but had also argued that the voluntary sector had a responsibility for putting its own house in order by developing its organisational capacity and thus making itself a fit partner for government (Commission on the Future of the Voluntary Sector, 1996). This had prompted a number of initiatives, of which the most significant was the work of the Quality Standards Task Force set up by NCVO under the leadership of Rodney Buse (Jochum and Rochester, 2012). In the wake of the Cross-Cutting Review of the sector carried out by the Treasury in

2002, New Labour embarked on an ambitious programme to build on these beginnings and bring about a transformation of the voluntary sector's capacity to contribute to the delivery of public services. This had two key aims:

- to enhance the skills and especially the managerial techniques of those who managed and led voluntary organisations; and
- to 'modernise' or reconfigure the sector and its institutions through mergers and the development of consortia and other methods of collaborative working.

Implementation had three principal components. The first of these was the establishment of national programmes aimed at improving 'key areas of VCS expertise', originally defined as raising and managing finances; governance; ICT; performance improvement; volunteering; and human resource management. Following a review of the first three years of the programme (2003–06) the streams were reconfigured into a larger number of national support services which included, alongside many of the original areas, collaboration and partnership; responding to social change; marketing and communications; and campaigning and advocacy. These delivered a mixture of training programmes; bespoke advice and support; opportunities for sharing information and experience; and web-based and other resources. The second element was a major investment in 'modernising the sector's infrastructure at regional, sub-regional and local level' to address the 'lack of capacity and patchy public investment in sector infrastructure' that were 'barriers to increasing the involvement of the VCS in service delivery' (Active Community Unit, 2003: 3). And the third component – FutureBuilders – was a vehicle for providing loans to third sector organisations to enable them to bid for, win and undertake contracts for the delivery of public services.

The impacts on voluntary sector organisations of the policies of New Labour governments over their 13 years in power have been profound. In the first place, the rhetoric of partnership embodied in the Compact and in the idea of strategic partnerships with key national bodies created an environment in which the 'taken-for-granted' assumption is that the interests of governments and voluntary sector organisations are broadly identical and that the dialogue or interaction between them is focused on how they can work together to achieve shared purposes. The resulting 'mood music', as Andy Benson of the NCIA has called it, makes it increasingly difficult for voluntary organisations to remember that the interests of their beneficiaries may be very different from those of the government and to voice disagreement or dissent.

Second, the concentration on service delivery as the main or sole purpose of voluntary action has undesirable effects. It relegates other historical functions of voluntary organisations, such as self-help and mutual aid, community development and campaigning or advocacy roles, to the margins. At the same time, it shifts the focus of interest from the needs of those the organisation exists to serve to the demands of those providing the means of addressing them. And organisations and those who manage them are increasingly behaving as 'producers' whose interests are not necessarily those of the users of their services.

Third, attempts at 'modernising' the sector have helped to create or entrench the power of the kind of 'sub-elite' identified by 6 and Leat (1997) as the inventors of the concept of a sector. Directly (through the funding of strategic partners) and indirectly (through contracting with the same few intermediary bodies to provide capacity-building support services), government has identified sector 'leaders' and co-opted them onto its 'modernisation' project.

And, finally, voluntary organisations have been nudged, bribed and sometimes coerced into becoming more and more similar in their structure and behaviour to the bureaucratic agencies of the state and the market. The ChangeUp programme of national hubs and support services was entirely based on two key principles that have not received the level of critical scrutiny they require. In the first place, it was based on a deficit model of capacity: rather than attempting to identify existing strengths and build on them, it started from the assumption that voluntary sector organisations were lacking in key skills or knowledge that prevented them from playing a larger role in society. And the approach to making good the deficit was based on a bottomless faith in private sector models. Being 'business-like' was the desirable characteristic, and that was interpreted to mean imitating the approaches and techniques used in the private sector without questioning how appropriate and/or helpful they might be in organisations that were based on very different values and principles.

Third act: From contracting to commissioning

A final twist in the ways in which New Labour's policy shifted over time – and one whose impact was not felt until after New Labour had lost power and been replaced by the current Coalition – was a segue from contracting to commissioning as the preferred method of outsourcing the work of statutory agencies. The shift from grant aid to contracting after the 1990 NHS and Community Care Act was an important change in the relationship between statutory bodies and voluntary organisations. Historically, grants had enabled voluntary sector organisations to negotiate funding to enable them to address the needs and wishes of their users in ways they felt were the most appropriate. Contracting shifted the initiative towards government and enabled statutory agencies to specify more clearly and in more detail the scope and scale of what they were prepared to fund – although in many cases there remained a degree of negotiation about how needs should be addressed as well as the terms of the financial arrangements.

Commissioning leaves no space of that kind: government decides exactly what kinds of services it wants, how much it is prepared to pay, what outcomes it expects and how the services are to be delivered. The only decision left to a voluntary organisation is whether it wants to join the competition to try to secure what is on offer. Commissioning is not adapted to meeting social need: one senior civil servant has been quoted as saying that 'we will procure social care in exactly the same way as we commission submarines or paper clips'. And it makes no concessions to any special qualities voluntary organisations may bring to the table; they are required to compete on an equal footing with private sector bidders and no account is taken of 'local experience, local focus or degree of "embeddedness" within local communities' (Adur Voluntary Action and NCIA, 2010: para. 3.35) or a track record of successfully running the service in the past. And the emerging trends in commissioning do not bode well for the sector. Some local authorities have indicated that they will not be inviting more than a small minority of voluntary organisations in their areas to submit tenders, while the tendency of commissioners is to bundle services into fewer and larger contracts that favour very large organisations and give an advantage to private sector contractors. For many voluntary agencies the future may be restricted to acting as sub-contractors to these major players.

The financial reckoning

For most of the period under review, voluntary organisations have attracted a steadily increasing volume of funding from statutory sources, both in absolute terms and, less dramatically, as a proportion of the total income received by the sector. Figures from the 2010 NCVO Almanac (Clark *et al.*, 2010) estimate that the total income from public funds received by voluntary organisations rose from £8 billion in 2000–01 to nearly £13 billion in 2007–08. And the figures also reflect the shift from grants to contracts and commissioning. In 2000–01 slightly more funding came in the form of grants than was received as the result of contracts, but by 2007–08 grant income had fallen slightly (from £4.1 to £3.7 billion) while receipts from contracts had more than doubled (from £4.0 to £9.1 billion). As a share of the total income received by the sector, receipts from statutory sources rose over the same period from just under 32 per cent to a fraction over 36 per cent.

The state has also tried to stimulate private giving. The Conservative administrations that developed an instrumental approach to public funding for voluntary organisations by insisting that it was conditional on the ability of the organisations so funded to help government achieve its policy objectives also professed an interest in the broader role of the voluntary sector. They paid tribute to this wider range of useful activities, but saw them as something to be supported by private donations rather than statutory funding. The role of government was, thus, to encourage altruism and make giving easier and more rewarding. This led to the introduction of new forms of 'tax-efficient' giving in the shape of payroll giving – when donations could be deducted at source before tax was paid – which was introduced at the end of the 1980s, and Gift Aid, which enabled charities to reclaim the tax paid by donors in respect of their donations, which was introduced in 1990 and extended to all levels of gifts in 2000 (NCVO and CAF, 2005). These measures contributed to an increase in payments from individuals from £9.4 billion in 2000–01 to £13.1 billion in 2007–08, but the proportion of income from this source remained at 37% of the total, which is very slightly ahead of the percentage for income from statutory sources, while the gap between these two sources has narrowed quite considerably.

The politics of volunteering

Since the 1960s successive governments have sought to promote volunteering through a plethora of policies, programmes and initiatives. These have often been driven by attempts by individual government departments to use volunteering as a means of taking forward their policies. Some stemmed from the personal interests of leading politicians; the mentoring and befriending programmes sponsored by both Tony Blair and Gordon Brown are prime examples. And a comparatively small number of them were based on a general conviction that volunteering was, in itself, a desirable activity that deserved support in all of its manifestations; these included New Labour's backing for promotional campaigns such as the Year of the Volunteer in 2005 and, perhaps most significantly, the Major government's Make A Difference Campaign of 1994. Few, if any, of these activities, made any significant impact on volunteering. While the headline figures for the numbers involved in formal and informal volunteering produced by the surveys conducted at intervals since 1981 (Field and Hedges, 1984; Lynn and Davis Smith, 1991; Davis Smith, 1998; Attwood *et al.*, 2003; Home Office, 2004a; Kitchen *et al.*, 2006; Low *et al.*, 2007; Kitchen, 2009; Drever, 2010; DCLG, 2011; Cabinet Office, 2013) are not strictly comparable (due to differences in sample sizes and some variations in response rates), they have not provided any evidence of an upward trend.

There are a number of explanations for this apparent lack of impact, and these are summarised in an evaluation of the Make A Difference scheme. While this programme can be seen as one of the better-designed interventions of recent decades, it fell short of achieving its ambitious aims: 'Its failures were due to a combination of insufficient resourcing, lack of strategic thinking and inability to translate high strategy into workable solutions on the ground' (Davis Smith, 2001: 197). Subsequent programmes reproduced these shortcomings as governments failed to learn from past mistakes and continued to launch ill-considered and under-resourced short-term projects rather than investing in the kind of long-term and unglamorous support that volunteering needs (Zimmeck and Rochester, 2013a).

That government's ventures into promoting volunteering are generally regarded as ill-conceived and poorly executed is widely accepted, but few of those who work in volunteer-involving organisations or the volunteering infrastructure would regard its engagement as anything but benign. Indeed, the Independent Commission on the Future of Volunteering, chaired by Julia Neuberger, called for more – not less – commitment by the state, albeit with a different orientation:

> Government can contribute in many ways – not by setting up new initiatives or projects, but by setting the strategic direction, acting as a facilitator and enabler and by removing barriers to volunteering.
> (Commission on the Future of Volunteering, 2008: 32)

There are, however, serious causes for concern about the way the actions of government might encroach on the autonomy and the integrity of volunteering. The first of these is that government can distort the volunteering agenda by promoting or supporting certain kinds of activity while neglecting other forms of involvement. Evidence from volunteer infrastructure bodies and volunteer-involving organisations submitted to the Neuberger Commission revealed a great deal of unease that priorities were being imposed by government bodies that were out of touch with what was happening at ground level. One submission summed up this feeling: 'Government should stop inventing new volunteering schemes and support existing organisations and infrastructure. The sector already knows what it is doing and should be trusted to get on with it' (Gaskin *et al.*, 2008: 119). The second cause for concern is the damage done to the image of volunteering by government-sponsored schemes of what Kearney (2001) has called 'mandated volunteering'. This phenomenon is by no means as commonplace in the UK as it is in the USA and Canada, but it is becoming a growing feature of the current government's approach to social security, where the receipt of benefits has, in some cases at least, been made conditional on claimants undertaking unpaid work.

A third issue – so far of potential rather than current concern in the UK – is the possibility of 'government volunteerism'. One contribution to discussions that preceded the UN International Year of Volunteers 2001 argued that volunteering ought to 'be recognised as a strategic resource which can be positively influenced by public policy' (quoted in Rehnborg, 2005: 94). The outstanding example of this approach is the USA Freedom Corps, the latest and broadest of a series of volunteering programmes developed by the Federal Government, which was set up following the terrorist attacks of September 2001 to 'inspire and enable all Americans to find ways to serve their community, their country or the world' (ibid.: 109). The fourth and final threat to volunteering from the state lies in the power of governments to create an environment in which volunteering can or cannot flourish. Evidence submitted to the Commission on the Future of Volunteering pointed, for example, to inappropriate and onerous forms of regulation that curtail the activities of small, local groups and the growing difficulties of accessing space for their activities when local authorities are required to charge market rents for the use of rooms in schools and other public buildings and playing fields and other community facilities are sold off to the private sector (Gaskin *et al.*, 2008).

These specific concerns about the impact of the state on volunteering underline the need for a broader debate about what governments should – and should not – do. Much of what could be called the volunteering 'establishment' has supported the idea of a strategic role for the state (Commission on the Future of Volunteering, 2008: 32), the need for 'a strategic policy framework' for volunteering and a 'healthy partnership between volunteering and the state' (Davis Smith, 2000). On the other hand, the former executive director of the UN Volunteers suggested that 'in many cases the most important thing that governments can do is to get out of the way' (quoted by Kearney, 2001: 32), while Ralf Darhendorf (2001) argued that a vigorous volunteering sector that was independent of the state (and thus did not include volunteers in statutory agencies and in voluntary organisations funded by government) was an essential condition for a healthy democracy. And the Conservative Party, in opposition, felt that government policy should be 'to encourage, invest and, where necessary, simply get out of the way' (Conservative Party, 2008: 8). The lack of such a debate shows up the absence of a body capable of challenging government and acting as an advocate for volunteering. At national and local levels, VE and volunteer centres have generally accepted the role of 'infrastructure' organisations as providers of support and services to volunteer-involving organisations rather than representing their interests and the interests of volunteers. An organisation – the England Volunteering Development Council or EVDC – was set up in 2004 for the express purpose of providing 'a high level representative and advocacy mechanism for volunteering' but, apart from setting up the Neuberger Commission, appears to have done little and has remained largely invisible.

Epilogue: The Conservative–Liberal democratic coalition

The coming to power of a very different government in 2010 with an overriding commitment to 'austerity' and balancing the nation's books and a Thatcher-like mission to reduce the scope and range of the government's role has not only changed the environment in which voluntary organisations operate but also exposed the weakness of their position as clients of the state. Cuts in public spending hit voluntary organisations hard; the network of strategic national partners was dismantled; and the Compact turned out to be the 'umbrella for a sunny day' it had been characterised as by some of its critics. The scale of the impact of the reductions in public expenditure on the income of voluntary organisations has been significant. A survey by ACEVO found that charities in the UK were experiencing cuts of at least 7.6 per cent in 2011–12 (Last, 2012a) but that, in their worst case scenario, the figure could be much greater. NCVO's estimate was that the sector would lose at least £2.8 million in real terms over the period 2010–11 to 2015–16, which would represent a cumulative decrease of 6.2 per cent in funding from central government and of 8.9% of its income from local government (Kane and Allen, 2011). Studies also showed that the cuts were not being applied proportionately. NCVO reported that more than half of local authorities were reducing their funding of voluntary organisations to a greater degree than was consistent with the government's head-line target (ibid.). In London, information from 19 of the 33 authorities showed that the sector was losing an average of 11.5% of its income against a reduction in central government support to the local bodies of 5.2% (van der Feen, 2011). The number of national strategic part-ners receiving funding was rapidly reduced from 42 to 15, and those that survived this initial cull had their grants reduced and phased out over a three-year period. The national Compact was hastily rewritten to reflect the Coalition's narrowly instrumental view of the sector (after a flawed consultation process which was not itself Compact-compliant) and the resources available for its implementation drastically reduced by the inclusion of the Commission for the Compact in the government's 'cull of the quangos' (Zimmeck *et al.*, 2011). At local level a good deal of anecdotal evidence suggests that compacts not only failed to protect voluntary organisations from the disproportionate cuts but also had no effect on the way in which authorities made decisions about the future of services without taking account of the views of the local voluntary sector.

Conclusion: Assessing the impact of the state

At this stage a note of caution needs to be sounded. The impact of gov-ernment policies on the majority of voluntary sector organisations is largely indirect. The NCVO's Civil Society Almanac calculates that only 38,000 voluntary organisations (or 22% of their total number) receive any kind of funding from central or local government (Clark *et al.*, 2010). Nearly four-fifths of the total were not subject to direct pressure from the state. But many of them were affected by the actions of gov-ernment; they were subject to onerous forms of regulation – including checks for volunteers working with children and vulnerable people and the often heavy-handed implementation of health and safety require-ments – while their work might be hindered by the cost of accessing spaces to meet in public buildings. For the minority, the impact was both more direct and more significant. In the first place, the narrowing of the scope for statutory funding and the tightening of the terms on which it was made available led, first, to a much greater emphasis on service delivery rather than mutual aid, campaigning or advocacy and community development and to a progressively more detailed prescription of what was to be provided, to whom and in what ways. Voluntary organisations have increasingly acted as agents of government rather than as independent providers with their own agendas and approaches. In the second place, they were subject to isomorphic pressures, both directly, though the kinds of contract they committed themselves to, and indirectly, through the 'capacity-building' programmes in which they were expected to participate. As a result, they became more like other providers and lost the distinctive characteristics that had been the principal reason why their contribution had been valued in the first place. And, third, many of the intermediary bodies that existed to provide a voice for voluntary organisations at local and national level accepted the rather more restricted role that was signalled by their re-designation as 'infrastructure' bodies whose function was increasingly to equip their members to contribute to the provision of services that were designed and defined by government. Finally, and perhaps most significantly, these three major changes to the activities of the minority of voluntary organisations and the ways in which they conducted their work took place – at least until 2010 – in the context of an increasingly powerful narrative of 'partnership' based on the assumption that the interests and concerns of the state and those of voluntary sector organisations were essentially the same.

6
Selling Out? Voluntary Action and the Market

Introduction

The previous chapter reviewed the ways in which the policies, programmes and initiative of successive governments presented increasing challenges to the autonomy, identity and integrity of voluntary organisations and volunteering over the past 20 years. This chapter focuses attention on another powerful influence that has shaped the way in which the theory and practice of governing and managing voluntary sector organisations has developed over a similar period. It looks at the impact on the sector of the process through which, it seems, the culture and values of the market have pervaded every facet of contemporary society. In a way that would have been unthinkable 30 years ago and unusual ten years after that, the leaders and managers of voluntary organisations refer to them as 'businesses' and have developed 'business plans' which are based on securing greater 'market share' as they successfully pursue 'customers', who tend to be those who pay for the costs of the services or 'products' provided by the organisations rather than those who directly benefit from their activities. They have gone well beyond the commonsense aspiration to be 'business-like' as they go about their work and have become increasingly difficult to distinguish from the commercial enterprises whose forms and practices they have adopted.

This chapter will explain how the values of the market and the model of business organisation have come to dominate our society and social institutions over the past 30 years and identify the ways in which they have impacted on voluntary sector organisations and volunteering. It will then conclude with some thoughts about the wider and deeper consequences of the hegemony of the market for voluntary action and for society more generally.

The extent and depth of this change in the culture and practices of voluntary organisations have been made clear by a recent debate that has taken place in the on-line discussion forum of the Voluntary Studies Sector Network (vol-sector-studies-network@jiscmail.ac.uk). Sparked off by a request for information about organisations that had been forced to change their 'business model' by changes in the availability of funding, the discussion has been one of the liveliest and longest in the history of the forum. It has revealed a clear divide in the approaches of the researchers, consultants and practitioners who have contributed to the debate.

One set of contributors took the view that the adoption of business models, values and practices by a sector that was hybridising and changing was unproblematic. For them the business approach offered a means of clarifying aims and objectives; improving organisations' understanding and focus on where they 'added value'; making the most efficient use of resources; adapting to changes in the environment; and developing a culture of improvement. They thought the future lay in the adoption of the business approach by a new generation of young social entrepreneurs who 'wanted to achieve social outcomes more than personal gain, but who did not think in terms of sectors'. One contributor felt that the voluntary sector was 'clinging to outdated modes of operation' and 'failing to connect with the new generation who were blending approaches from different sectors'.

Those taking the opposite view argued that 'the push to become more business-like' focused on 'the instrumental role of voluntary organisations in delivering services' at the expense of their more fundamental contribution of providing a means of 'questioning, challenging, critiquing and promoting the voices of those usually unheard by those making decisions'. Rather than 'speaking truth to power', one contributor suggested, the tactic of the new generation of social entrepreneurs was 'to try to speak to power and get a bit of the cake'. Another contributor referred to a wider 'confusion in strategy between citizenship (and how to engage with it) and consumption/consumerism (and how to engage with it)'. In their view, voluntary sector organisations are qualitatively different from businesses or statutory agencies, and the adoption of the business approach is at best inappropriate and at worst threatens to undermine the rationale and identity of any voluntary agency that embraces it.

The rise of neo-liberalism

The permeation of voluntary organisations and volunteering by the values and norms of the market is part of a profound and far-reaching change in the political culture not only of the UK but also of much of the world. In the 1970s and 1980s the ideas of Milton Friedman and the Chicago School of economics came to dominate the thinking of the International Monetary Fund and the practice of many national governments, among which Reagan's USA and Thatcher's Britain were notable examples. While one major element of the teaching of Friedman and his followers – monetarism – has been largely discredited, their more general views on the primacy of the market remain influential. The principle of monetarism was that the key to managing the economy and controlling national output, rates of inflation and levels of unemployment was the management of the money supply. Both 'the United States and the United Kingdom tried to put monetarism into practice at the end of the 1970s' and 'both experienced dismal results' (Krugman, 2007). Despite the failure of his main economic prescription in action, Friedman's wider vision of how economies did – and should – work remains influential.

Paul Krugman has described the history of economic thought in the twentieth century as analogous to the upheavals in Christian beliefs in the sixteenth and seventeenth centuries brought about by the Protestant Reformation and the Catholic Counter-reformation. Until Keynes appeared in the role of Martin Luther, the free market orthodoxy of classical economics held sway. But its central belief that 'the answer to almost all problems was to let the forces of supply and demand do their job' offered neither explanation of nor solution to the crash of 1929 and the subsequent depression. Arguing that 'free markets could not be counted on to provide full employment', Keynes and his followers created 'a new rationale for large-scale government intervention in the economy' that shaped government thinking and practice in the UK and underpinned a post-war political consensus that survived until the end of the 1970s. Krugman casts Friedman as St Ignatius of Loyola, founder of the Jesuits. 'Like the Jesuits, Friedman's followers have acted as a sort of disciplined army of the faithful, spearheading a broad, but incomplete, rollback of Keynesian heresy. By the century's end, classical economics had regained much though by no means all of its former dominion, and Friedman deserves much of the credit' (Krugman, 2007).

As well as reinstating classical market economics to a leading posi-tion among teachers and students of the subject, Friedman's 'laissez-faire absolutism' had a powerful and far-reaching impact on decision-makers and opinion-formers. His belief that markets always work and that government intervention was never justified was widely shared and 'contributed to an intellectual climate in which faith in markets and dis-dain for government often trumps the evidence' (Krugman, 2007). This provided the conditions in which the neo-liberal agenda of minimal reg-ulation of the market; the shrinking of the state; and the privatisation of national assets and service delivery held sway. And blind faith in the beneficence of the market still has a hold on the hearts and minds of those in charge of the world's financial and political institutions, despite the evidence that it has led to the most serious economic crisis since 1929 and a degree of inequality between the richest and the poorest in many societies that can be seen as 'intolerable' (Stiglitz, 2012).

In Britain we can date the implementation of the neo-liberal agenda from the election in 1979 of the Conservative government led by Margaret Thatcher. This brought to an end more than 30 years of bipar-tisan consensus about the foundations of economic and social policy forged as a social settlement in the aftermath of World War Two. While the two main political parties disagreed about details and boundaries, there was broad agreement between them that the country should have a mixed economy based on public as well as private ownership and that the state had a duty to meet its citizens' needs for health, education, housing, employment and a range of social services 'from the cradle to the grave'. The demolition of these pillars of the post-war settlement was not only the main feature of the Conservative administrations led by Thatcher and John Major between 1979 and 1997, but also formed a continuing agenda for the New Labour administrations of Tony Blair and Gordon Brown which succeeded them. The power of the neo-liberal laissez-faire approach was such that, as well as providing the driving force for Thatcher's radical reforms, it also led to a new multi-party consensus about the parameters and driving forces of public and social policy. For this reason, 1979 is increasingly seen by historians and com-mentators as a milestone which should take its place alongside 1945 as a marker of a new phase of political and social history.

Privatisation

The twin set of radical changes made by Thatcher and her successors involved, on the one hand, the privatisation of public assets and services and, on the other, the reform of what remained of the public sector. The selling off of public assets to the private sector was perhaps the most radical and certainly the least easily reversed of the changes. The key public utilities – electricity, gas and water supplies – were followed into private ownership by the telephone service and the railway system, and continuing attempts have been made to transfer the postal service into private hands. As well as 'selling off the family silver', as former Prime Minister Harold Macmillan described it, the government also reduced the state's stock of social housing by selling off individual homes to their tenants at substantial discounts and encouraging the transfer of what was left from the ownership of the local authorities that had built them to newly created organisations called large-scale voluntary transfer housing associations (LSVTs).

The second means of reducing the scope and scale of the public sector adopted by the Thatcher administration and used by its successors was the out-sourcing of functions and services to private companies and – to a much lesser extent – voluntary sector organisations. On one level this involved the use of outside experts to address complex or special-ist issues that government agencies were ill-equipped to tackle, such as major developments in information technology for the National Health Service and Her Majesty's Revenue and Customs. Increasingly, however, services that had been performed by public servants were out-sourced to private companies in the belief that they would be able to deliver a better service at lower cost. And the discipline of the market meant that contractors who failed to meet expectations could be replaced by more efficient rivals (although this has happened less often in practice than envisaged in theory). Under successive governments it came to seem that there was very little that could not be delegated to the private sector. Increasingly, delivery of the criminal justice system, including the administration of courts, the movement of prisoners and the man-agement of some prisons, was out-sourced, while the Welfare to Work programme and its successor, the Work Programme, were entirely dele-gated to the private and voluntary sectors, and responsibility for many hospitals and other medical services will be transferred to for-profit companies under the latest changes to the National Health Service intro-duced by the Conservative/Liberal Democratic Coalition that came to power in 2010.

The privatisation of public services was not restricted to the agencies of central government but was also a factor in a general trend towards a weakening of the powers of local authorities. We have already noted the transfer of much of the housing stock in England and Wales from municipal control to the new LVSTs, and another major step in the same direction was introduced by the NHS and Community Care Act of 1990. There were three key elements to this important piece of legislation. In the first place, it changed the focus on care for people with disabilities and long-term medical conditions from institutional to home-based provision. In the second place, it transferred responsibility for community care from the NHS to local authorities. And in the third place, it changed the primary role of local authorities in this area from providers of services to enablers that would purchase the great majority of the services needed from voluntary sector and for-profit providers who were lumped together in central government's guidance as the 'independent sector'.

More generally, local authorities controlled by all political parties have out-sourced basic functions such as refuse collection, administration of their council tax payments and rents, and management of their leisure facilities, while some leaders of Conservative-controlled authorities developed ambitious plans for transforming them into 'virtual councils' whose sole function was to manage the contracts of the private companies which would deliver all their services. This approach, originally articulated by Nicholas Ridley, Thatcher's local government minister, in the 1980s, has enjoyed a renaissance under the Coalition, but in 2012 all the signs are that the tide is beginning to turn, as a number of the most fervent supporters of large-scale privatisation at the local level have lost power (Butler, 2012).

Public sector reform

What was left of the public sector after the privatisation of public assets and the out-sourcing of governmental functions was subjected to a process of 'reform' aimed at turning it into as close a facsimile of the private sector as possible: if the statutory agencies which remained could not be transferred to the for-profit sector, they should be made to behave as if they were private companies. There were two mechanisms for achieving this: the introduction of markets (or 'quasi-markets') to areas of public life and the restructuring of statutory agencies in the image of the private company. As we have noted, the NHS and Community Care Act 1990 was intended to create a market for community care in which voluntary organisations and for-profit companies (and some parts of local statutory agencies) competed to provide services under contract to local authority purchasers. A similar split between 'purchasers' and 'providers' and 'a state-financed internal market, in order to drive service efficiency' was introduced into the NHS following the 1989 White Paper, *Working for patients (NHS reforms)*. More recently the Coalition has taken the application of market principles to the NHS to its logical conclusion by opening up the competition to provide health services to 'any willing provider' – which essentially refers to those from the for-profit sector.

Alongside the introduction of market rules and principles to the public sector, a number of major changes have been made to the ways in which statutory agencies are structured and administered. This collection of measures has been labelled 'New Public Management'. As Deakin has pointed out, this term 'lumps together under a single heading a variety of different approaches, which have been introduced at different times in different services and different locations' but, as he also argues, 'all the currents of reform have three features in common; they are focused on management issues; they require the recipients to services to be seen as customers; and they have been implemented "top-down" from the centre'. Deakin stresses the importance of the first of these features:

> The managerial emphasis is crucial: whatever the structural changes, the motivation of those with executive responsibility for service delivery has been seen as central to the project. It is best achieved through changing the culture of the organisation and the inculcation of alternative key values expressed in slogans, acronyms and mission statements.
>
> (Deakin, 2001: 25)

On the other hand, the importance of operational and structural changes should not be underestimated. By the early 1990s the Civil Service had been transformed by the introduction of the 'Next Steps' programme. This involved the division of the major government departments between slimmed-down central units responsible for the development of policy and semi-independent 'agencies' to which were devolved the implementation of policy and the delivery of services. The new 'agencies' were modelled on private sector companies, and there was a good match between their structures and the new managerial ethos and culture. And, in many cases, there was a good 'fit' between the public-facing activities of agencies dealing with services such as pensions and benefits and the reshaping of public sector bodies as businesses whose primary concern was their customers. Nor did the slimmed-down rumps of the central departments escape reorganisation in the mould of the private company. They are subject to the corporate governance of departmental boards that help them to be 'business-like through drawing on the expertise of senior business leaders who sit on the boards as non-executive board members' (HM Treasury and Cabinet Office, 2011). And they are required to draw up and work to annual business plans setting out their vision and detailed proposals for implementing the policies and priorities of the government (see, for example, Cabinet Office, 2010).

The dominance of the ethos and practices of the market in Whitehall is also reflected in the choice of people to head major reviews of the working of government and policy in a whole range of areas. The die was cast when the review of Community Care that preceded the 1991 Act was entrusted to Sir Roy Griffiths, a director of the Sainsbury supermarket chain, and a series of other leading figures in the corporate world followed him down the corridors of Whitehall. They included Philip Hampton, also from Sainsbury (regulation); Sir Peter Gershon, Chairman of Tate and Lyle (efficiency in the public sector); Derek Wanless, former chairman of NatWest Bank (resourcing the NHS); and Lord Hodgson of Astley Abbots, a former merchant banker (charity law). And, on another level, the pervasiveness of corporate management norms contributed to – and was in turn reinforced by – new opportunities for senior managers to pursue their career through a sequence of posts across the public, private and – to a lesser extent – voluntary sectors. This was made possible by the acceptance of the idea that they brought with them generic management skills that were transferable to a variety of organisational settings. This idea also informed a new approach to the deployment of civil servants, who were no longer expected to master the brief of a specific department but to develop their generic skills in a series of relatively short-term assignments to different parts of the service.

The impact on the world of voluntary action

The programme of privatisation and public sector reform that has been carried forward by successive governments since 1979 and the development of a wider climate in which the values and practices of the market dominate British society have had a marked impact on the organisation and behaviour of voluntary agencies, on attitudes to volunteers and the way in which their activities are shaped, and on the development of the voluntary and community sector as a whole.

The first – and most immediate – change to the environment in which voluntary agencies operate was a significant recasting of their relationships with the state. In the first place, the basis on which voluntary organisations received funding from central and local government shifted from grant-aid to purchase-of-service contracts. Much of the discussion of this change has emphasised the comparative disadvantages of the new regime: grants are seen as giving organisations a greater measure of autonomy and imposing looser and less demanding requirements for accountability. On the other hand, contracting offered a greater degree of security and certainty of funding, as well as a clearer mutual understanding of the basis on which payment was made and more explicit agreement on how organisations could demonstrate that they had applied the funding to the purposes for which it was given. Above all, contracting changed the nature of the underlying relationship between the two parties from one based essentially on patronage – with the voluntary organisation in the role of supplicant – to one based on a mutually advantageous deal negotiated between bodies which were more equal in their status (if not in their power).

The post-1979 world, however, brought another and perhaps more significant change in the relationship. Embedded in the bipartisan settlement of 1945 was the assumption that the state had accepted broad responsibility for the welfare of its citizens. As a result, the activities of many voluntary organisations were directed towards ensuring that government accepted that its responsibilities included providing specific services or meeting the needs of different groups (MENCAP, for example, came into being to fight for the inclusion of people with learning disabilities in the educational system) or towards improving the quality of the provision that was already being made (see, for example, the work of Shelter in campaigning for better housing). The roles of many other organisations were seen essentially as complementary or supplementary to the 'mainstream' services provided by the state. In the new market-dominated social policy environment, voluntary sector organisations had to find new ways of influencing government, on the one hand, and adjust to the new expectation that they would be providing services previously provided by the state rather than working alongside them, on the other.

Second, changes in social policy and the wider environment of market hegemony also had a number of impacts on the way voluntary agencies were organised, including changes in their governance, their managerial values and practices, and the composition of the human resources they deployed. Membership of the governing bodies of many organisations changed in response to the perceived needs to secure the skills and expertise that would help them thrive in the new commercial environment in which their survival depended on the ability to secure contracts to provide services. Those with experience of financial management in the commercial world and people who could interpret the legal requirements of contracts became more attractive as board members than those with specialist understanding of the field in which the agency operated. Similarly, people who were seen as 'good decision-makers' with experience of assessing risks and opportunities were valued more than those who had first-hand knowledge of the communities served by the organisations or those who used their services. At the same time, boards became increasingly business-like rather than 'hands-on' (their role memorably described as 'not rowing but steering') and frequently reduced to a kind of critical audience for the senior managers who alone had the knowledge of day-to-day operations and the details of contracts to lead the organisation.

Changes in the governance system were matched by developments in the agencies' organisation and management. Their organisational structures increasingly came to resemble the model of the 'for-profit' company organised as a hierarchy that faced upwards towards a chief executive and his or her senior management team. And they adopted key managerial techniques such as strategic planning; quality or performance measurement systems; and approaches to marketing from the business world. This meant that the assessment of managerial competence was based on the deployment of generic skills and owed little to any in-depth understanding of the organisation's user group or field of activity. Whereas many leaders of voluntary agencies had built their careers on commitment to a specific cause, the new generation of managers tended to have proved their ability and honed their skills in a sequence of posts in a variety of organisations.

A third important change affected the identity of those who carried out the main work of the organisations. In order to meet the demands of the new contracts for reliability in meeting the targets set in them, agencies tended to reduce the part played by volunteers or replace them with paid staff and to employ trained specialist staff rather than well-meaning or highly committed generalists. Where organisations continued to involve volunteers in their work, the terms of engagement were very different: Scott and Russell (2001: 59) reported that some of the agencies they studied 'tended to formalise the role of volunteers. This included tighter specification of tasks, increased supervision and performance review' as well as a more selective approach to the recruitment of volunteers. Instead of welcoming more or less anyone who wanted to help and finding a means of enabling them to make a contribution to the work of the organisation, agencies took on only those volunteers who it judged could perform specific – pre-determined – functions to a certain standard. At the same time, the demands of the market-led 'contract culture' accelerated changes that were taking place in the roles played by volunteers and their relationship to the organisations in which their volunteering took place. 'In many ... organisations volunteers have been moved out of decision-making and strategic roles into "less risky" and ancillary front-line service roles' and 'are being positioned as resources to be used rather than owners, members or even co-producers' (Ellis Paine *et al.*, 2010: 98).

To a similar but lesser extent the relationship between voluntary agencies and their paid staff has also changed; the new managerial approach associated with contracting also tends to treat employees as 'resources to be used' rather than as integral parts of the organisation who are committed to its values and aspirations and contribute to its decision-making. It is increasingly difficult to argue that working in the voluntary sector is different from employment in statutory agencies or private sector companies. Other relationships have also been remade in the image of the business sector. The users of an organisation's services are viewed as customers – passive recipients of what is provided for them rather than active participants in the design and development of services and their delivery. In other words, they have been defined as a consumer rather than as a citizen (Lewis and Glennerster, 1996), and the implementation of 'user involvement' – one of the key slogans of the 1990s – has been largely restricted to 'limited decisions about services in areas defined by the organisation' rather than 'participation in structures of governance and decisions on strategy' (Locke *et al.*, 2001: 205). Market pressures have also led to a changed relationship between organisations working in the same field; rather than seeking to work together for the greater benefit of those whose interests they promote and protect, agencies increasingly view their counterparts as business rivals with whom they are in competition for a greater share of their 'market'.

As well as having a significant impact on individual organisations, the widespread adoption of the principles and the practices of the market have also changed the character of the voluntary sector as a whole. One characteristic aspect of this change can be seen in the work of what are now called 'infrastructure' – or, less commonly, 'second tier' – organisations, and especially NCVO at national level and the network of CVSs locally. During the last decade there has been a shift of emphasis in the activities of many of these organisations towards providing services to front-line organisations – many of them in the service of 'capacity-building' – at the expense of their historical functions of identifying social need, developing and supporting networks and ensuring that the views of their members were heard. This has led to a change in the relationship between some CVSs and their constituents in which the CVS is seen as a separate body offering services to other organisations rather than as the combined efforts of its members (Rochester, 2012). And, as the provision of services increasingly resembles a commercial enterprise, successive governments have suggested that these activities could be entirely or largely funded by charging CVSs' members for the services they receive (Rochester, 2012).

A second symptom of the changes to the voluntary sector brought about by the influence of the market has been the rise to prominence of the Association of Chief Executives of Voluntary Organisations (ACEVO). Under the aggressive leadership of Stephen Bubb, this trade union for voluntary sector managers has acquired what seems to many to be a disproportionate degree of influence with government as well as within the sector. This can be seen as a reflection of the way in which, under the influence of the market model, authority within voluntary agencies has become increasingly concentrated in the hands of their most senior members of staff at the expense of their governing bodies.

There is also a bigger picture in which the wider significance of the impact on the sector as a whole has been highlighted by Margaret Harris (2001: 219). The changes that have taken place, she argues, may well be advantageous for the individual organisations, which have become more business-like; attracted greater resources; and gained increased reach and status. But there may be a case that:

> the cumulative impact of the pursuit of individual voluntary *agency* advantage is to the detriment of the survival of a distinctive voluntary *sector* in welfare. If the third sector has no distinctive organisational features, no separate voice or voices, no alternative responses to social need, no different ways of doing its work, what will be the rationale for its inclusion within a mixed economy of welfare in future?

The 'market society' and its limitations

The extent to which our political and social institutions have been permeated by the business model has been captured by the suggestion that Britain is not just a society with a market economy but a 'market society'. The difference has been explained by Michael J. Sandel (2012: 10–11):

> A market economy is a tool – a valuable and effective tool – for orga-
> nizing productive activity. A market society is a way of life in which
> market values seep into every aspect of human endeavor. It's a place
> where social relations are made over in the image of the market.

Sandel argues that market values have crowded out non-market norms in a whole series of arenas where public goods – 'the good things' in life – are corrupted or debased by being turned into commodities. 'So to decide where the market belongs, and where it should be kept at a distance, we have to decide how to value the goods in question – health, education, family life, nature, art, civic duties and so on. These are moral and political questions, not merely economic ones' (Sandel, 2012: 10–11). But there are 'daunting obstacles' in the way of rethinking 'the role and reach of markets', which include 'the persisting power and prestige of market thinking, even in the aftermath of the worst market failure in eight years'. Sandel's analysis is based on his native USA, but the relevance to the market society that has developed in Britain is clear.

Voluntary organisations used to exist in a very different moral uni-verse, and their leaders continue to point to their values base as a defining characteristic (see, for example, Blake et al., 2006). But how far have these been compromised by the permeation of our society by the norms of the market? The answer varies according to differences in the kinds of organisation within the sector. Clearly, those agencies that have enrolled under the banner of social enterprise have iden-tified themselves with the market, while there is some evidence that religious and faith-based organisations retain a different set of values (Rochester and Torry, 2012). In between these two poles, the balance between the traditional values of voluntary action and the norms of the market varies from one organisation to another, but the tide is running in the direction of the latter.

Conclusions

Voluntary organisations and the sector as a whole have not been free from the development of a market society in Britain. They have been influenced directly by the adoption of the market model by successive governments and the expectation that the orthodoxy of the 'New Public Management' should apply across all the sectors. And they have been influenced indirectly by the more general acceptance of the power of the market and the permeation of its values into many areas of our public and social life. In the process, the distinctiveness of the ways in which voluntary organisations have responded to need has been called into question, while the extent to which the values that underpinned their activities have been eroded is – or ought to be – a major cause for concern.

7
The Hegemony of the Bureaucratic Model

Introduction

This chapter discusses the way in which bureaucracy has become the predominant organisational model in our society to the point where other forms of organisation are ignored and forgotten: it has become the 'taken-for-granted' norm by which we assess organisations and judge their effectiveness. The chapter begins by highlighting the key features of the bureaucratic form as well as highlighting its virtues and advantages. It goes on to argue that bureaucracy is not the only organisational form through which voluntary action can be undertaken, and introduces an alternative form – the association – that has been described by Billis (2010c) as the ideal type of voluntary sector organisation. It identifies the distinctive features of this kind of organisation along with the uses to which it can be put. It then uses the ideas of David Billis, that voluntary agencies are fundamentally ambiguous organisations that have been subject to a powerful trend towards hybridisation, to suggest that the intellectual hegemony of the bureaucratic model is an obstacle to the better understanding of the organisational expressions of voluntary action.

The world of bureaucracy

We owe the concept of bureaucracy to the German sociologist Max Weber (1864–1920), whose principal contribution to the study of organisations was a theory of authority structures. Weber distinguished between *power* – the ability to make people do what you order them to do – and *authority* – where orders are voluntarily obeyed by those receiving them because they perceive them to be legitimate. Weber identified three 'ideal-types' of authority structure: the charismatic, the traditional and the rational–legal. In the first or charismatic type, legitimacy is based on the exceptional personal character of a 'charismatic' individual whose orders are accepted because they are perceived to possess supernatural, superhuman or heroic qualities. In the second or traditional type, legitimacy is based on custom and precedent; positions of status and power are inherited. In the third or rational–legal type, legitimacy derives from meeting specific goals (rational) and following a set of rules and procedures, and is attached to those who occupy certain offices rather than to individuals (legal). The rational–legal type underpins the bureaucratic model that Weber compared to a machine and described as the most efficient kind of organisational arrangement.

The characteristic features of Weberian bureaucracy are that:

- The organisation is structured as a *hierarchy* of offices and positions in which 'each lower office is under the control and supervision of a higher one'.
- *'A specified sphere of competence'* is attached to each office. This involves both 'a sphere of obligations to perform functions' and 'the provision of the incumbent with the necessary authority to carry out these functions'.
- *Salaried employees* are appointed to all offices. They are selected through a process of open recruitment on the basis of technical qualifications. Employment in the organisation should be seen as a career for officials. An official is a full-time employee, and anticipates a lifelong career. After an introduction period, the employee is given tenure, which protects the employee from arbitrary dismissal.
- The organisation is run according to a set of clear and explicit *formal rules* that govern official decisions and actions.
- And it maintains *written records* of all 'administrative acts, decisions and rules' including 'preliminary discussions and proposals' and 'final decisions'.

(Weber, 1947, in Pugh, 1990: 3–15)

The bureaucratic model has been generally accepted as offering clear advantages over the earlier forms of organisation based on traditional or charismatic forms of authority. It eliminated nepotism and favouritism, provided clear and consistent lines of accountability, and defined the boundaries to the functions and autonomy of individual officers as well as offering them security and opportunities for promotion. Such are these advantages that bureaucracy has become the standard approach to organisational design, to the extent that it is assumed that any organisation should and would take a bureaucratic form. It is the 'default setting' and 'taken-for-granted' norm against which we measure organisational effectiveness.

Over time the way in which we have defined and discussed bureaucracy has moved some distance from Weber's 'ideal-type'. The idea of bureaucracy in current usage is a narrower or simplified version of the original idea and now tends to mean no more than 'a hierarchically stratified employment system in which people are employed to work for a wage or salary' (Jacques, 1976: 49, quoted in Billis, 1993a: 9). It rests on a view of organisations that Billis has called the 'ABC division' (see Figure 7.1).

The 'traditional model' involves a clear-cut division between three separate elements. The first of these – A – represents an *association* that may consist of the shareholders of a private sector company; the elected members of a public body; or the members or trustees of a voluntary organisation. The association is responsible for the appointment of the second constituent part of the organisation, a bureaucracy – B – made up of the paid staff who deliver services or produce goods for the third part of the model, the clients or customers – C. Each of these elements is seen as quite separate, and the focus of much of the literature on organisational behaviour and theory is restricted to just one of them – understanding 'the core management task of making the system of roles of paid staff – the bureaucracy – B – work' (Billis, 1993a). This not only

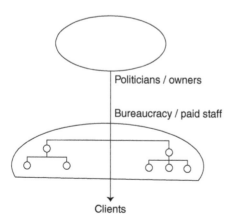

Politicians / owners

Bureaucracy / paid staff

Clients

Figure 7.1 The traditional ABC model

defines the content of academic study but also provides the foundation on which the writings of management 'gurus' are based and the focus of the plethora of manuals and textbooks produced for managers.

But, as Billis concluded at the very beginning of his pioneering search for a theory of the voluntary sector, 'The ABC division just could not manage the complexity of voluntary organisation' (Billis, 1993a: 14). Users or beneficiaries could also be members of the governing body of an agency or might play their part in its operational activities. Paid staff might have been recruited from those who use the organisation's services and they, or former employees, might also be members of the board. And other members of the governing body might also make a direct voluntary contribution to the work of the organisation as well as playing a more hands-off governance role. As well as the blurring of roles and functions, voluntary agencies also experienced tensions between the expectations that the commitment of staff to the cause was open-ended and the need for job descriptions and conditions of employment, and between collaborative and collegiate ways of working and organisation into a bureaucratic hierarchy.

In the second place the current view of bureaucracy is that it is essentially 'top-down' in its approach – authority is initially located at the apex of the organisation and 'delegated' piecemeal to lower levels. Clearly there are considerable advantages to this approach to accountability and control: authority is unambiguous and the entire resources of the organisation can be deployed strategically to maximise its effectiveness and efficiency. But it may be more appropriate in some circumstances than others: it is likely to be more successful in the case of large-scale production involving the repetition of standardised tasks than as a means of managing the work of comparatively small numbers of employees addressing the complex demands of customers needing 'bespoke' responses to needs which managers cannot predict in detail. And much depends on the management style or the 'business culture' that determines how the top-down approach is implemented on the ground. All too easily it can become what Simon Caulkin (2007, 2008), a former business editor of the *Observer*, has called a command-and-control model. He found that:

> By far the most commonly experienced management styles...were bureaucratic, reactive and authoritarian and they were becoming more 'overbearing' and 'controlling'. An uncritical adoption of the business culture of the US has led to a situation where 99% of employees, whether in the public or private sector, work

in command-and-control organisations; in effect centrally planned dictatorships that are set up to take orders from the CEO rather than the customer.

(Caulkin, 2007: 2)

While Caulkin's 'centrally planned dictatorships' take the top-down tendency of bureaucracy to its limit, the formulation does help to highlight the difference between a traditional style of organised voluntary action and the idea of a rational machine which is at the heart of the contemporary orthodoxy about how organisations should work. Historically, voluntary organisations prided themselves on their ability to address the full range of needs presented to them. This meant leaving a great deal of discretion to the staff and volunteers on the front line to decide how to respond to the requests they received and how far they were prepared to go to help each user. In a command-and-control agency that discretion is tightly circumscribed and 'appropriate' levels and kinds of service are prescribed.

In the third place, the current view of bureaucracy is that it involves a machine-like approach to achieving specific objectives. This is a purely *instrumental* view of the nature and purpose of an organisation. It exists solely to produce goods or services, and the test of its effectiveness is its ability to deliver them reliably and at the lowest possible cost. There is, of course, an instrumental aspect to most – if not all – voluntary organisations: they exist because people have decided that something needs to be done and they remain active as long as they can attract support to achieve that goal. But they also have an *expressive* dimension. This has two aspects. On the one hand, it is the expression of a set of values, and organisations are judged not only on what they do but also on the way in which they go about their activities. The focus on vocation that distinguishes the Christian social welfare organisations studied by Jeavons (1994: 212), for example, underpins a dual-faceted organisational mission which combines witness and service; 'to maintain such a mission requires that boards and executives – and all the other participants in these organizations – be consistently attentive to questions about *what statements are made and what messages are sent*, as well as what practical needs are met by the work these organizations do'. On the other hand, voluntary organisations provide the means of satisfying personal needs to take part in activities that are intrinsically rewarding and of providing opportunities for socialising and making friends: 'People participate in and support [organizations] some of the time because there is something they want to do (an expressive need) and some of the time because there they want something done (an instrumental need). Voluntary organizations can accommodate either purpose' (Mason, 1996: 3).

The bureaucratic form of organisation explained in the theory inherited from Weber's rational-legal type is widely accepted as the paradigm through which we can understand how organisations work and how they can be made to function more effectively. The application of this theory to voluntary organisations is, however, of limited value for two main reasons. In the first place, the traditional ABC model with its three largely self-contained constituent parts simply cannot cope with the complexity of roles and functions within a voluntary agency. And, in the second place, it explains only the instrumental element of the voluntary organisation and ignores or excludes from consideration its equally important expressive dimension. Furthermore, the way in which the bureaucratic form has developed in the great majority of statutory agencies and private sector companies in practice – the command-and-control model – is incompatible with the historical emphasis on flexibility and responsiveness to user needs that has been one of the distinguishing features of voluntary action.

Another organisational form – the association

Bureaucracy is not, however, the only organisational game in town. The great majority of voluntary organisations in the UK today are constituted as *associations*, an organisational form that, according to David Horton Smith, pre-dates Weber and bureaucracy by some thousands of years: being 'ancient in origin, going back at least 10,000 years to the Neolithic revolution of primitive humans as they changed from roving nomadic bands to more settled villages of larger size' (Smith, 2000: 243). The great majority of registered general charities in England and Wales have an annual income of less than £10,000 and this suggests, as we shall see, that they are organised as associations. It we add to their number the greater number of unregistered bodies, the total population of all kinds of voluntary organisation in the UK has been estimated (by Elsdon, 1995: 3) at 'far more than a million'. Some of these 'under the radar' groups, as they have been described by researchers at the TSRC (Soteri-Proctor and Alcock, 2013), are informal groupings of the kind reviewed later in this chapter, but many of them are formally organised as associations.

Voluntary associations have been defined by Billis (1993a: 160) as 'groups of people who draw a boundary between themselves and others in order to meet some problem, to do something'. The key feature of the association is membership; this defines the 'boundary' between those who are part of the organisation and those who remain outside. Other defining characteristics include:

- adoption of a name in order both to differentiate the association from the external environment and to enable it to negotiate with the outside world;
- selection by means of elections of individuals from among the membership to act as officers (chair, secretary and treasurer) and/or to form a committee to take responsibility for its day-to-day activities;
- depending for its resources largely on money (in the form of subscriptions) and volunteer effort provided by its members; and
- agreement of some basic rules about how its affairs are conducted.

In a later book Billis has argued that 'the ideal type of the third sector is best typified by the association' and provided a summary of the ways in which it goes about its activities:

> The defining characteristics of associations are the linkage and logical flow between its ownership by members, principles of governance, reliance on volunteer resources for its operational work and principles of membership accountability which together enable it to function as a robust and effective organization. Critically, although there may be clear differentiation in the roles of governing body, committees and volunteer workers, all will usually be part of the active and membership/ownership groups.... In addition, those receiving services may be past or present members, or have close links through family, neighbourhood, friendship and other groups. Active members will be dedicated to the cause which may be expressed tangibly both through financial contributions and through a preparedness to take on unpopular and sometimes unpleasant work, readiness to recruit others into the organization and, if necessary, advocacy – the determination to persuade those outside the group of the rightness of the mission.
>
> (Billis, 2010c: 53–4)

The differences between the associational and the bureaucratic forms of organisation are clear. In the first place, the traditional ABC division simply does not apply; it is impossible to disentangle the operational activities and those who perform them from the rest of the organisation. Second, the organisation is not arranged as a hierarchy; decisions are made collectively and in a collegiate manner and there is very little of the kind of arrangement in which a 'superior' gives instructions to an 'inferior'. 'Authority' relationships, where they exist, tend to be narrowly technical: the treasurer may insist that conditions are met before they write a cheque and the chair has the necessary powers to call and manage meetings, but the great majority of actions are based on choice and consent rather than command and control. Similarly, associations do not conform to the 'horizontal' dimension of the bureaucracy through which strict limits are imposed on the range of responsibilities and activities to be undertaken by each person. The contribution of the active members who provide the labour in an association is bounded, on the one hand, by the amount of time and energy they are able to provide and shaped by their interests and the extent to which they feel comfortable in specific roles and, on the other, by the willingness of their fellow members to give them the opportunity to play them.

Underpinning these differences is a basic distinction between 'two principles of human association: freely given shared commitment and legal principle/coercion' (Fuller, 1969, quoted by Smith, 2000: 11). While bureaucracies largely consist of 'fully remunerated staff associating on the basis of legal principle (explicit or implicit work contracts)', associations are characterised by 'shared commitment to some goal(s) based on voluntary altruism' (Smith, 2000: 11). Finally, the health and vitality of an association tends to depend on the way in which it balances meeting the needs of its members with the pursuit of public benefit – 'about whether to focus activities primarily on the needs of the immediate members, or whether to take a more outward-looking approach towards the needs of the community' (Harris, 1998: 32). This balancing act can be seen as trying to reconcile the ability of the association to meet expressive as well as instrumental aims.

Ambiguity and hybridisation

For Billis (1993a: 159), bureaucracy and association together with the 'personal world' provide three unambiguous 'worlds' in which social needs are met and 'that have reasonably clear terms of reference, or what may be called "rules of the game" '. While the first two of these 'scenes of human existence' have been defined above, the nature of the third needs some clarification. 'In the personal world social problems are resolved by relatives, friends, neighbours on a private basis' and there are three important features of these arrangements: in the first place the relationships are informal: 'It is not usually found necessary or appropriate to establish contractual arrangements between the parties.' Second, roles are not made explicit: 'Problems are responded to without recourse to categorising either those who have the problem or those who respond.' And, finally, the demands of the personal world are boundless: unlike the bureaucratic or associational worlds, they have no 'beginning or end' (Billis, 1993a: 159–60).

Billis envisaged the three worlds as overlapping circles, as depicted in Figure 7.2.

The key to understanding the distinctive nature of voluntary sector organisations is found in the areas of overlap that are populated by two kinds of 'ambiguous' bodies. Where the bureaucratic and the associational worlds meet is located the ambiguous voluntary agency, and in the intersection between the personal and the associational world we find what Billis calls 'unorganised groups'. The latter, which 'represent the first step from the personal to the associational world' (Billis, 1993a: 162) but lack some of the key features of a formal organisation, such as a constitution or legal identity, will be discussed later in this chapter. The main thrust of Billis' original work, however, was to explain the tensions inherent in ambiguous voluntary agencies and the complexities of managing them. The key feature which means that an organisation has crossed the boundary from the associational world into ambiguous territory is the employment of paid staff to carry out operational tasks. An association may employ staff – such as part-time secretaries or caretakers – to support the active members to perform the work for which it has been formed, but the delegation of some or all of those operational functions to paid staff means that it has begun to engage with the bureaucratic world and is no longer an unambiguous association but an ambiguous voluntary agency.

Ambiguous voluntary agencies bring together the organisational logic and 'rules of the game' found in two very different forms of

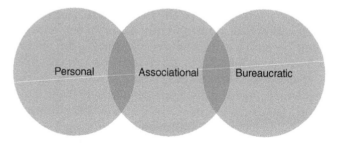

Figure 7.2   The Billis 'worlds' theory

organisation. On the one hand, they retain the comparatively informal working practices of the association, whose members play an active role in the work of the organisation and where authority is vested in officers elected by their fellow members. On the other, they have taken on board the more formal, instrumental approach of the bureaucracy with its hierarchy of paid staff and managers. The process involves 'increased differentiation of roles' such as ' "committee member", "volunteer", "staff", and "director" ' but also a great deal of ambiguity about these statuses (Billis, 1993a: 164), which is the result of tensions between the formal characteristics of the bureaucratic world based on rules and the less formal approach of the association based on freely shared commitment.

While the ambiguity of the voluntary agency appears to be a recipe for conflict and organisational incoherence, it is this characteristic which explains much of the attraction of the voluntary organisation to those responsible for social policy and provides it with a 'comparative advantage' in certain kinds of welfare provision. Billis and Glennerster argue that the direct relief of poverty through financial aid is most efficiently delivered by the state through the social security systems that have replaced charitable subventions. But states of personal and societal disadvantage (affecting people with disabilities and long-term medical conditions and those who are blamed or stigmatised) may best be addressed by voluntary agencies which have 'a comparative advantage over other sector agencies in areas where their distinctive ambiguous and hybrid structures enable them to overcome problems of principal-agent gap, median voter reluctance, weak messages from politicians to staff and lack of market interest' (Billis and Glennerster, 1998: 95).

In a later book, Billis (2010a) has moved on from discussing ambiguity as a means of understanding voluntary sector organisations to an analysis of the related idea of 'hybridisation', which he defines as a process through which organisations with their roots in one sector (public, private and voluntary or 'third') take on characteristics of their counterparts in another. While this can happen in any one of the sectors, Billis is concerned with the impact of hybridisation on 'third' – or voluntary – sector organisations. In his view this can take one of two forms – 'shallow' or 'entrenched' hybridity. The former 'is not a new phenomenon. For many years, some organizations have moved into hybridity in a rather gentle fashion, causing minor disturbances, but not necessarily calling into question their basic third sector identity' (Billis, 2010c: 58–9). This movement might involve changes in the composition of the governing body to include people with business or public sector backgrounds; new forms of funding requiring more bureaucratic forms of accountability; or, most significantly, the recruitment of paid staff to undertake some or all of the organisation's operational work that meets the needs of its users. The new ways of doing things, however, are more or less successfully grafted on to the rootstock of the associational model to form an emergent ambiguous voluntary agency.

The 'entrenched' form of hybridity represents a more profound change:

> At the operational level, entrenchment arises when paid staff become dominant in the delivery of the operational work of the organization and a management structure with several hierarchical levels is established. Then the organization can be considered to have embedded in its structure core features of the [private sector] firm and the [public sector] bureau. The rules of the game begin to change and associational principles have to co-exist with alien principles drawn from the public and private sectors. ... This is because maintaining a structure of staff leads to increased pressure towards considerations of individual and organizational survival.
>
> (Billis, 2010c: 60)

The 'entrenched' hybrid can, therefore, be seen as a fully fledged ambiguous voluntary agency with the 'comparative advantage' to deal with certain kinds of social need and the challenges for those who lead it of having to manage the tensions and deal with the complexity it embodies.

Unorganised groups

The second ambiguous organisational form identified by Billis' 'worlds' theory is found where the personal world of family and friends overlaps with the associational world. These 'unorganised groups' which inhabit what Billis has called 'the primordial organisational soup' have also been termed 'informal associations' (Smith, 2000) and 'transorganizations' (Milofsky, 2008). These groups 'represent the first step from the personal to the associational world. They may be differentiated from the latter by the fact that they do not have a constitution or legal identity. People just come together on an informal basis to resolve their own or others' social problems' (Billis, 1993a: 162). While less is known about the workings of associations than bureaucracies, these unorganised groups have been the subject of very little study, and we know very little about their organisational grammar and working. But we can distinguish them from more formal expressions of voluntary action:

> Their boundaries are permeable. They often are more about the process than the products of their work or the tasks people seek to accomplish. They may disappear when their signature problem is not present as a community concern only to reappear when a new crisis arises. They may change character when new members join. Their expressive value is often equal to or even greater than their instrumental value. They may not own resources but rather depend on relationships and history and the willingness of people to contribute what is needed when the time comes for work to be done. Their leaders may not be self-conscious entrepreneurs but rather may be citizens who are raised up by acclamation or by the needs of the moment. They are settings or venues where community happens and as such are inseparable from the larger system that is this amorphous thing we call community.... Organizational theory struggles with these entities because it is not clear that they are organizations as understood by contemporary students of nonprofit organizations or management.
>
> (Cnaan and Milofsky, 2008: 2)

Conclusions

The study of organisational theory and behaviour and the wider general climate of our society both tend to assume that there is a single form of organisation – the bureaucracy – and that there is, therefore, a single set of rules of the organisational game. This chapter has argued that the bureaucratic model does not provide us with an adequate understanding of how many voluntary sector organisations are structured and function or a guide to how they should be designed and managed. It has argued that, instead of a single organisational model, we need a range of types through which to explore and understand the diversity and complexity of the organisational expressions of voluntary action. Drawing on Billis' 'worlds' theory and his later work on hybridisation, we have identified four kinds of organisational arrangements. These consist of two unambiguous forms – bureaucracy itself and the association (which is by far the most common set of arrangements for voluntary action) – and two ambiguous types. The first of these – the ambiguous voluntary agency – is located where the world of bureaucracy overlaps with the associational world and can be sub-divided into 'shallow' and 'entrenched' forms of hybridity. The second ambiguous form – the unorganised group – is located where the associational world overlaps with the private world of family and friends. Much of the academic and practitioner writing which seeks to explain how voluntary organisations work and to help their leaders and managers ensure they are effective is limited by the use of a single – bureaucratic – lens rather than an approach which recognises the complexity of the sector's organisational landscape.

8
The Pressure from Within

Introduction

Writing about the introduction of New Public Management in the 1990s, Nicholas Deakin (2001: 26) noted the important role of the 'product champions' who adopted and promoted the changes from a mixture of motives, including the opportunity for personal advancement. This chapter focuses on the analogous role of the sector 'insiders' who welcomed the embrace offered by government in the form of 'partnership'; happily adopted the values and habits of the market; and assumed that the bureaucratic paradigm provided all they needed to know about organisational theory and behaviour. It will identify the kinds of people who championed the new consensus about the role of voluntary organisations and the ways in which they should go about their business before offering an account of some of their main activities and an assessment of their contribution to the three sets of changes discussed in Chapters 5–7.

Who were the 'champions'?

Four sets of people and organisations have made a significant contribution to the development of the current world of volunteering and voluntary organisations. They are:

- Those who controlled the national and local 'infrastructure' or 'second-tier' organisations which had been established to support the work of front-line agencies and provide them with a voice;
- The senior members of staff in many voluntary agencies – who adopted or acquired the title of 'chief executive' – and the body that represented their interests;

- A rather more heterogeneous collection of consultants, trainers and researchers who found a new market for their wares; and
- A small but significant number of people employed by national and local government bodies to promote their interests in voluntary action and manage their relationships with voluntary organisations.

Intermediary or second-tier organisations

The first set of champions of the new world of voluntary action consisted of the intermediary, second-tier or infrastructure organisations. In 1978 the Wolfenden Committee highlighted the importance of what it called 'intermediary bodies', and they had gone on to play a central role in the development of the idea of a voluntary *sector* (which is discussed in Chapter 3). At national level, Wolfenden had reviewed the roles of a number of national organisations before identifying NCSS (later NCVO) and its siblings in Northern Ireland, Scotland and Wales as key players in the future development of the sector: 'To sum up we are convinced that there is a strong case for the generalist independent intermediary bodies in each of the four main parts of the United Kingdom and that their role in future is likely to be more important than ever' (Wolfenden, 1978: 145). The Committee saw that role as three-fold – encompassing liaison between voluntary organisations; representation of their interests; and the development of new forms of voluntary action. But, while 'the role of representation' was 'essential', the Committee recognised some of the limitations on the ability of NCSS to perform it: the organisation's own evidence stated that 'The NCSS plays a large part in the voluntary sector as a whole but has made it clear to us that it does not claim to speak for all voluntary organisations, nor for all registered charities. It would repudiate any idea that there is such a thing as the "voluntary sector" in any finite sense with the NCSS as "headquarters" ' (ibid.: 130).

And it was not the only potential voice for the sector. There were a great many specialist intermediaries focused on specific areas of activity or distinct types of organisations that acted 'as a collective voice for their constituent organisations in negotiations with statutory bodies affecting their objectives and in influencing and informing public opinion' (Wolfenden, 1978: 127). They formed a large and heterogeneous group in 1978, and their numbers have, until recently, grown. It was from their number that most of the 65 organisations were drawn that made up the reference group to which the Working Group on Government Relations reported as it negotiated the Compact in 1997–98 (Zimmeck *et al.*, 2011), and many of them received funding from the New Labour governments as 'strategic partners'. At the time of Wolfenden, furthermore, there was another important national generalist body in the shape of the Volunteer Centre, which 'covers both statutory and voluntary services, with the remit to encourage voluntary service generally' (ibid.: 124). This was the original form of what became VE, the key institution in the volunteering infrastructure until its takeover by NCVO at the beginning of 2013 following its loss of central government funding.

Two further generalist bodies have emerged at national level since 1978. The first of these is the National Association for Voluntary and Community Action (NAVCA), whose roots are in the Standing Conference of Councils of Social Service administered and supported by NCSS. This became an independent organisation called the National Association of Councils of Voluntary Service (NACVS) in 1991 and subsequently changed its name (in 2005) to accommodate a wider membership of 'local support and development organisations'. In 2012–13 it was involved in ultimately unsuccessful negotiations for a merger with another ex-NCVO body, Community Matters (formerly the National Association of Community Associations), whose members run local community centres. NAVCA has sought to position itself as a voice for local voluntary action and has worked closely with successive governments. The second is ACEVO, which is essentially a kind of trade union for the sector's chief executives. Through an aggressive policy of self-assertion, and led by an energetic chief executive, it has succeeded in positioning itself as an alternative to NCVO as a 'voice for the sector'.

The core membership of NAVCA consists of the local generalist intermediaries known as CVSs, whose historic functions, according to Wolfenden (1978: 100), consisted of developing new forms of voluntary action to meet social need; services to other organisations; liaison between local organisations and statutory agencies; and representation. They can thus be seen as the counterparts of NCVO at local level and have played a significant part in the acceptance of the idea of partnership with the state and the dissemination of managerial techniques and culture across the country.

Promoting partnership

All four national generalist bodies in England have accepted and promoted the idea that the relationship between the state and the sector is essentially collaborative and based on shared aims and values and, within that, involves a larger role for voluntary agencies in the delivery of public services. The early running was made by NCVO. While the Deakin Commission on the Future of the Voluntary Sector (which published its report in 1996) enjoyed genuine independence in the way in which it went about its work (Jochum and Rochester, 2012), it had been conceived and brought into being by NCVO, and it was NCVO which took forward its key recommendations. These included the idea of a compact between the government and the sector that did not only embody a general statement of principles underpinning the aspiration to create 'a new approach to partnership ... based on shared values and mutual respect' and a more positive relationship (Home Office, 1998) but also went on to set out new 'rules of the game' aimed at improving the terms on which voluntary sector organisations were funded (Home Office, 2000). The voluntary sector's interests in the negotiation and agreement of the Compact were represented by a Working Group on Government Relations convened by NCVO, and its successor bodies (Compact Working Group and Compact Voice) have continued to depend on servicing by NCVO. Indeed, the constitution adopted by Compact Voice in 2009 makes it clear that it 'operates under the aegis of NCVO'; that 'NCVO provides management and organisational support to the Compact Voice team'; and that 'The trustees of NCVO have legal governance responsibilities for Compact Voice' (Zimmeck *et al.*, 2011: 44).

NCVO's commitment to the idea that the relationship between government and the sector was essentially collaborative and based on shared aims and values was also expressed in its involvement in a range of government initiatives and its recognition as one of central government's 'strategic partners', a status also conferred on ACEVO, NAVCA and VE, among a much larger number of more specialist bodies. The closeness of the relationship between NCVO and government at the height of the New Labour years is illustrated by the career of NCVO's Director of Public Policy, Campbell Robb. He was seconded on a part-time basis to the Treasury to advise on sector issues before he went on to become the director general of the Office of the Third Sector in 2006, and thus responsible for the 'most wide-ranging ever consultation with the third sector and the subsequent creation of ten year government strategy for the sector' until he became the chief executive of the housing charity, Shelter, at the beginning of 2010 (Shelter, 2013).

NCVO was joined in the work of promoting the partnership agenda by the other key second-tier bodies – ACEVO, NAVCA and VE – and, to a lesser degree, by the wider body of 'strategic partners'. As part of the conditions of receiving funding as a strategic partner, each of them was required to support the Compact, but they were already on board. VE had been intimately involved in developing the Volunteering Code, one of the codes of conduct that extended and added detail to the Compact and, like ACEVO and NAVCA, took its place on the board of Compact Voice. While its attempt to emulate the Deakin Commission – the Independent Commission on the Future of Volunteering chaired by Julia Neuberger (who became the volunteering 'czar' in Gordon Brown's 'government of all the talents') – made little impact, its conclusions were firmly rooted in the partnership approach: it recommended, *inter alia*, that 'government ensures that a cabinet minister takes responsibility for volunteering, with a cross-cutting brief across all departments, as well as ensuring that one permanent secretary holds responsibility both for volunteering by government employees, and the topic of volunteering as a whole' (Commission on the Future of Volunteering, 2008: 32). And it was the core membership of NAVCA – the CVSs – that took on the responsibility of developing, negotiating and implementing the 'roll-out' of the Compact at local level. They also provided the main mechanism for securing the participation of the voluntary sector in the Local Strategic Partnerships, set up by the government from 2000 onwards to co-ordinate the delivery of public services, and other formal arrangements for collaboration across sector borders. The degree of importance attached to these roles was reflected by the adoption by NACVS (which became NAVCA) in 2004 of an additional strategic function for their members: 'working in partnership at strategic level is now a central part of the work of a CVS' (NACVS, 2004: 12).

Service delivery

Alongside the crucial support NCVO has provided for the government's partnership agenda, it has also been a consistent advocate of a greater role for voluntary agencies as providers of public services. This advocacy became a little less uncritical over time but remained a key part of NCVO's stance. Addressing concerns that increasing commitment to providing services funded by government might inhibit the ability of voluntary agencies to campaign for changes in government policy for the benefit of their users, Stuart (now Sir Stuart) Etherington riposted that 'voluntary organisations can and do bite the hand that feeds us on a regular basis' and argued that 'with good governance, with good management and good contracts' they could combine providing services with campaigning (Etherington, 2004, quoted in Billis, 2010b: 11). His counterpart at ACEVO, Stephen (now Sir Stephen)

Bubb, has been even more energetic in promoting the involvement of voluntary organisations in delivering an ever-wider range of public services on increasingly 'business-like' terms. One contributor to a debate that took place in 2009 in the on-line publication *Civil Society* about whether managing prison services could be seen as charitable activity commented: 'my suspicion has always been that ACEVO and Steven (sic) Bubb would be in favour of privatising or "voluntarising" anything that isn't bolted down'. Two years later, he again made headline news in the voluntary sector press by arguing in his evidence to the Public Administration Select Committee that grant funding could 'be a much more problematic form of funding than contracts'. He also stoutly defended the role of charities in public service delivery after the chair of the Select Committee accused some charities of being too dependent on public funds (Public Administration Committee, 2011).

More recently, the extent to which the leaders of what are now conventionally termed the sector's 'infrastructure' bodies are prepared to go in seeking access to government contracts for their constituencies has been revealed in an open letter to the economic secretary to the Treasury, signed by 14 of them.[1] Ignoring the contested nature of the government's policies of making sweeping cuts in public services and welfare benefits and accelerating the programme of out-sourcing services to the private sector, they have declared that the voluntary sector is willing 'to make a greater contribution to the Government's Open Services Agenda'. Their letter discusses 'how our sector, and volunteering, can make a greater contribution to the next stages of public service reform' and then goes on to say:

> As the government's welfare reforms take effect we know that some of the most vulnerable people in the country will be affected – including children. Our sector will be at the frontline – helping individuals and families prepare for and manage change. Naturally, the Government wants to support people off benefits and back into jobs wherever possible. But we know that it can end up costing Government more if vulnerable people are not supported through these processes appropriately: the costs associated with contested work capability assessments are an example of this.

> We therefore ask Ministers to give special consideration to the important work that our sector...can play in relation to welfare reforms and preparing for their impact.
>
> (NAVCA, 2012: 2)

This explicit commitment to assist the government to implement its radical changes to social and public policy might have passed unnoticed but for the NCIA, which has challenged the right of these 'self-elected leaders' to speak for the sector as a whole and has pointed to the opposition of many voluntary organisations and groups to the government's 'reforms', which it believes are better seen as 'cuts'. It believes that the proper role of voluntary action is to oppose measures that will adversely affect many of those people whom voluntary organisations exist to serve rather than to contribute to the implementation of policies of this kind (NCIA, 2012c). The NCIA's response – a letter headed 'not in our name' – had been signed by just over a hundred people at the time of writing (January 2013) but had made no impact on the views of the signatories of the original letter. Bubb, for example, found it 'amusing to see the "national coalition for independent action", whatever this is, denouncing NCVO, NAVCA and ACEVO (amongst others) for having apparently signed up the voluntary sector to privatisation and the dismantling of the welfare state' (Bubb, 2012: 1).

Championing managerialism

Second-tier bodies have also championed the cause of managerialism in the sector. Again, NCVO was in the lead. It followed the report of the Wolfenden Committee by setting up a working party under the chairmanship of a well-known management 'guru', Charles Handy, and, following its recommendation, established a Management Development Unit (MDU) in 1982. The MDU 'was an important catalyst' which 'generated a mixture of training courses and consultancy work throughout the sector' (Batsleer, 1996: 230). This development of management thinking and practice was, however, 'exploratory and multi-faceted' and did not lead to 'neatness and homogeneity'. It reflected the distinctive characteristics of voluntary organisations, which were 'pragmatic coalitions as well as principled missions', and helped organisations 'to operate in the twilight zone "beyond good practice", where what is desirable has to jostle with what is possible' and to live with 'ambiguity and imperfection' (ibid.: 243). Writing in 1995 on the eve of the publication of the Deakin Commission's report, Batsleer felt able to speculate that the lessons learned in applying management thinking to the complex and shifting circumstances in which voluntary organisations operated might provide lessons for a wider audience: 'There is a dawning realisation that managing in voluntary and non-profit enterprises may provide useful insights into the definition of generic management roles and competencies' (ibid.: 244).

This view of the distinctive nature of management in the voluntary sector began to change with the publication of Deakin's report and NCVO's response to it. Deakin went a good way further than Wolfenden in calling for improvements to the ways in which voluntary organisations were managed: as a quid pro quo for the better treatment the sector should be able to expect from government, voluntary organisations were expected to improve their managerial capacity and thus prove worthy partners in the delivery of services. They should engage in better planning (Recommendation 47: 127), monitor performance (Recommendation 50: 127) and develop appropriate quality measures (Recommendation 51: 128). One early response to this call was the establishment by NCVO of a Quality Standards Task Group (QSTG) chaired by Rodney Buse (whose background was in the corporate sector) in order to give effect to a specific recommendation by the Commission that voluntary organisations should 'engage with quality standards'. The QSTG was originally set up (in 1997) as a 'time limited project to act as a catalyst to help voluntary and community organisations (VCOs) to engage in quality improvement'. In the event it continued its work (hosted by NCVO but with 'semi-independent status') until 2004, when its role was overtaken by the performance hub set up as part of the ChangeUp, New Labour's capacity-building programme.

Deakin himself felt that the QSTG had been a valuable instrument for implementing his commission's recommendations: 'NCVO ran with the recommendations for reform in the voluntary sector and Rodney Buse's Task Force they hosted did good work on that agenda' (Jochum and Rochester, 2012: 9). What the QSTG did, however, was to begin to shift the agenda away from the 'exploratory and multi-faceted' approach of the MDU and the earlier ways of applying managerial ideas to the sector. Instead of looking to develop ways of addressing issues of performance and quality based on the distinctive challenges of managing voluntary organisations, it chose to adopt a system developed for and widely used by business corporations – the Excellence Model – and adapt it for use by voluntary organisations. This not only meant that one example of corporate managerial practice was widely adopted but also opened the door for the introduction of other techniques based on the same managerial principles.

Following the Cross-Cutting Review of the Voluntary Sector, 2002, New Labour launched an ambitious programme of capacity-building and infrastructure reform called ChangeUp. One important element in this strategy, which was announced in 2004, was the development of national 'hubs of expertise' to provide 'focal points for information, advice, direction and resources' in six areas where, it was felt, voluntary organisations lacked expertise. These hubs covered: performance; work-force development; governance; ICT; finance; and volunteer recruitment and development. They were to be hosted by 'partnerships of existing organisations' that included NCVO, VE and NAVCA together with other second-tier organisations (Home Office, 2004b). With the exception of the volunteering hub, these focal points disappointed the government's expectations, and they were replaced in 2008 by a set of National Support Services overseen by a new quango called Capacitybuilders, covering much the same areas of concern and entrusted in the main part to the same group of second-tier organisations. This second wave of top-down reforms came to an end in 2011, but not before the national intermediary bodies had become a major conduit through which the values, concepts and techniques of business-based management theory could be disseminated widely across the sector.

At local level, CVSs were also intimately involved with the ChangeUp programme. The 'bold but achievable' aim of the programme was 'that by 2014 the needs of frontline voluntary and community organisations will be met by support which is available nationwide, structured for maximum efficiency, offering excellent provision which is accessible to all' (Home Office, 2004b: 3). This would be achieved, first, by rationalising and developing local infrastructure organisations capable of meeting those demands and, second, through the development of expertise through the focal points provided by the national hubs. While the boldness of the aim was undeniable, it turned out to be far from achievable, and many local plans for infrastructure development were stillborn for lack of resources. On the other hand, the impact on CVSs was far from negligible: ChangeUp focused much of their attention and resources on the part of their work that involved providing support to front-line organisations and encouraged them to provide information, training and consultancy based on managerial theories that were designed to make them better able to secure and implement local authority contracts for the delivery of services.

Market values

The promotion of managerial approaches drawn from the experience of business by the intermediary bodies brought with it the adoption of many of the wider values and practices of the market. This process involved at least three different elements. In the first place, they transformed their organisations into facsimiles of businesses. NCVO, for example, required each of its constituent parts or 'cost centres' not only to cover the costs of their activities but also to achieve a margin or profit over and above these in order to make a contribution to the overheads of running the organisation as a whole, and activities were undertaken where they generated a return rather than where they met a need. ACEVO's organisational model is that of the AA or RAC, where members receive specified services in return for their annual subscription and a range of additional or optional products are also offered to them. The value of some of these products has been criticised: one commentator claimed, for example, that ACEVO's training and resources package on full cost recovery was 'significantly overpriced' and went on to make the telling comment that 'pricing the course according to the market inclination to pay is in itself no crime' ('Stolen', 2011). And VE's failure to develop sufficient income from the sale of services to replace the loss of central government funding was a significant factor in its decision to seek financial security through a merger with NCVO.

At local level, many intermediary bodies adopted a similar approach. The ChangeUp strategy not only encouraged them to see themselves primarily as providers of services to front-line organisations but also set them the aim of becoming 'sustainable' or no longer dependent on public funding for their activities. While some organisations and some kinds of provision might attract third party support, a key assumption of the ChangeUp strategy, bought into by the CVS movement, was that long-term sustainability could be achieved by recovering the costs of the services they provided from the front-line organisations that were their 'customers', despite any evidence that this was likely to be the case. The Conservative Party, even before they came to power in coalition with the Liberal Democrats, unsurprisingly also put their faith in a market-based approach: 'Wherever possible frontline organisations should be resourced and empowered to commission the support they need from Councils for Voluntary Service and other providers' (Conservative Party, 2008: 43).

In the second place, many intermediary bodies adopted new and aggressive approaches to marketing their services. Rather than see their purpose as identifying the needs of their members and developing ways of meeting them, they tended to offer a range of 'off the shelf' products borrowed from elsewhere. They developed marketing strategies that involve the 'segmentation' of their market to enable better targeting of specific services and the analysis of the strengths and weaknesses of their 'competitors', who might have been seen in the past as colleagues and collaborators. The aims of increasing 'market share' and reinforcing the position of an organisation in the market have also contributed to the growing number of mergers and takeovers in the voluntary sector that mirror the behaviour of the private sector.

In the third place, many intermediary bodies and their leaders collaborated and formed partnerships with the corporate sector. While the sponsorship of voluntary organisations by business has been a longstanding feature of the sector, this has been characterised mainly as a specific form of philanthropy. More recently, the relationship between the voluntary and the corporate sectors has changed and become more diverse. It is now common for voluntary organisations to 'out-source' some of their functions to private sector companies on the grounds of economy and efficiency. More significant, however, is the current that flows in the opposite direction; voluntary organisations have been enlisted as sub-contractors by corporate bidders seeking government contracts for delivering public services. There have been a number of concerns about how these arrangements have worked. On the one hand, there have been suggestions that voluntary organisations have been used as 'bid candy'; the only reason for their inclusion as 'partners' in a tender has been to make the bid more attractive and not as a serious commitment to sub-contracting important parts of the work to them. On the other hand, the private sector 'prime' contractors have been accused of 'creaming off' the provision of less demanding services and leaving the more complex and time-consuming cases to their voluntary sector sub-contractors. Overall, moreover, there are concerns about what sub-contracting means for the ability of organisations to define the nature and quality of the services they provide: not only do they have to meet the requirements of the public agency which has commissioned them, but they are also tied to specifications and systems laid down by the prime contractor.

The extent of sub-contracting has led NCVO to collaborate with SERCO – one of the largest private sector prime contractors for public services – to produce a code of practice for co-operation between the private and the voluntary and community sectors on the delivery of public services. Effective working between the two sectors, NCVO argues, 'has the potential to bring the specialist skills, dynamism, flexibility and innovation of the VCS together with the greater resources, scale, experience and wide ranging complementary skills of the private sector'. Its guidance – produced jointly with SERCO – 'is intended to provide best practice advice' in situations when 'government and other policy makers choose a public services model where large "prime" contracts are run by large organisations'. It accepts that 'public service reform is likely to lead to more contracting for the VCS directly with the private sector, and less with the state' and stresses the need to improve standards of sub-contracting (NCVO, 2012; see also Murdock, 2012).

Clearly, NCVO has accepted the norms of the market and sees no difficulty in principle in the engagement of voluntary organisations as sub-contractors: the only challenge is to manage the relationship, and the only consultation they have undertaken is aimed at making their draft code a more effective 'tool that will achieve what you need out there on the frontline'. NCVO is also happy with its choice of private sector partner, describing SERCO as 'an international service company that improves the quality and efficiency of essential services that matter to millions of people around the world' (NCVO, 2012) and glossing over its controversial history of providing services to the criminal justice system, where its management of detention centres and other facilities has been criticised (NCIA, 2012b). NCVO has also teamed up with Barclays Bank to provide 'a fantastic subsidised leadership programme that can really impact on the success of [the participants'] organisations' despite the bank's involvement in the activities that brought about a national financial crisis. In the past, voluntary organisations may have chosen their corporate partners with care for fear of reputational damage, but the wholesale acceptance of the logic of the market has led to a less selective approach, carrying a greater risk of reputational damage.

The rise of the chief executive

The second set of 'champions' of the new world of voluntary organisations were the chief executives. The lead given by the intermediary bodies in promoting the government's partnership agenda; accepting a greater role for voluntary organisations in the delivery of public services; adopting business-style managerialism; and embracing the values of the market were clearly key to the fundamental changes that took place in the character of the voluntary sector during the past two decades, but they were not the sole proponents of the new dispensation. Without more widespread support at the level of the individual organisation, the intermediaries might have not been so enthusiastic in their support for the changes, nor would their efforts have been so influential. The most important champions of change at this level have been the senior managers of voluntary agencies, who have almost universally acquired the title of chief executive – itself borrowed from the private sector – over the past 15–20 years.

In 1996 Batsleer (1996: 233) could characterise voluntary sector managers as 'self-effacing enablers' who were, nonetheless, expected to 'give clear – even charismatic – moral leadership to their organisation and strive to maintain the integrity and vitality of its value-base'. He could also claim that: 'The primary professional identities and allegiances of most paid managers still centre round the social concerns of their organisations rather than their roles and status as managers.' Today the picture has changed radically. Many voluntary organisations have grown and changed, with the result that their paid staff play a dominant role in performing their operational activities and they have developed a management structure with several levels. 'The rules of the game begin to change and associational principles have to co-exist with alien principles drawn from the private and public sectors' (Billis, 2010c: 60). The centre of gravity has shifted within the organisation and power has increasingly become located in its paid staff and – within them – in the hands of the chief executive, who is only too aware of the nature of his or her managerial functions. Compared with their predecessors, today's voluntary sector managers are much more likely to have undergone management training and are likely to see themselves as career managers who move from organisation to organisation in pursuit of greater responsibilities and higher salaries. And they may well have brought generic managerial skills with them from another sector or may use their experience in the voluntary sector as a basis for employment elsewhere.

The modern voluntary sector chief executive has been created in part by the changing environment in which the sector operates and partly by the dissemination of a business and managerial culture through the intermediary bodies. They have, in turn, become enthusiastic adopters of these values and norms and have contributed to their increasing grip on the sector. And the growing power and influence of the sector's senior managers are reflected in the way in which their representative body has been accepted as the voice of an important element within the sector. While ACEVO celebrated its silver jubilee in 2012, it is only since Stephen Bubb became its chief executive in 2000 that it has begun to make its presence felt. This is, of course, due in large part to the energy and chutzpah with which Bubb has pressed its cause and the extent of his personal and political networking. But it also reflects – and has reinforced – the higher profile and greater influence of its members in recent years.

Researchers, consultants and trainers

The third set of 'champions' who made a contribution to the growing consensus about the role of the voluntary sector and the ways in which voluntary organisations should be organised and managed consists of the growing numbers of academic researchers and teachers who found the sector a new area of interest and the organisational consultants and trainers who were quick to identify a new market for their wares. The earliest academic work (by David Billis at Brunel University and then at the LSE) sought to develop a theory of the voluntary sector that would explain why and how voluntary agencies differed from their counterparts in the public and private sectors and provide the kind of 'usable theory' on which effective ways of managing them could be based. Another early player in the field was the Voluntary Sector Management Programme at the Open University, which took part in 'the search for management processes deemed to be consonant with the broader social values and purposes of voluntary organisations' (Batsleer, 1996: 233). The small group of independent consultants and trainers who formed the Management Development Network in 1991 (see www.mdn.org.uk) were themselves products of the sector and tended to specialise in what Zimmeck (2000) has called (in the context of volunteer management) the 'home-grown' approach. This is a 'collectivist-democratic' model based on the accumulated experience of the leaders and managers of voluntary organisations which provides an alternative to the 'bureaucratic' or 'modern' approach based on the generic literature of organisational theory.

These early pioneers have been joined by a growing number of other researchers and consultants. The Voluntary Sector Studies Network (VSSN) – which has been the UK's specialist scholarly society in this field since 1995 – has a membership of 150 and sponsors its own journal, the *Voluntary Sector Review*. This growth has been fuelled in part by a substantial investment by the New Labour Government in the TSRC, based at Birmingham and Southampton Universities. And the field of consultants and trainers has become equally crowded: a number of specialist organisations such as the Charities Evaluation Services and the Institute for Fundraising have been established, consultancies with their roots in the sector have multiplied, and they have been joined by agencies from other sectors who have seen the voluntary sector as a new and growing market for their services.

The growth of academic interest in the sector has not, however, produced much in the way of additional 'usable theory' based on the need to understand the distinctive features and behaviour of voluntary organisations. Instead, interest has been focused on the role of the sector in social policy, on the one hand, or the application of generic organisational and management theories to voluntary organisations, on the other. While the size of the UK's voluntary sector academic community has grown, moreover, it is dwarfed by the number of scholars of the non-profit sector in the USA. The latter's focus on larger, more bureaucratic forms of non-profit organisation has had a significant impact on the development of the field of study in the UK, as elsewhere, and the study of non-bureaucratic voluntary action has been comparatively neglected. All too often UK scholars have accepted the discourse of partnership and the desirability of a greater role for the sector in service delivery, and assumed that there should be a widespread application of generic management approaches drawn from business to managing voluntary organisations. With a few honourable exceptions, they have failed to provide a critique of these developments.

The entry into the consultancy field of agencies with their roots in other sectors and applying analytical tools and prescriptions based on business models has already been noted. The large management consultancies in particular have been successful in competing for business with university-based units and 'home-grown' consultancies. At the same time, the existing and newer consultancies with voluntary sector roots have learned to use the language and approaches of orthodox managerialism to find their place in a growing market and, in the process, added their shoulders to the wheel of change.

Boundary crossers

The final category of 'champions' of the profound changes in the way voluntary organisations are understood and managed consists of the comparatively small number of people employed by national and local government bodies to promote their interests in voluntary action and manage their relationships with voluntary organisations. Many of these can be described as 'boundary crossers' – people who have been recruited because they have the relevant experience and expertise provided by a background of working in the voluntary sector (Little and Rochester, 2003; Lewis, 2010). This kind of emigration became commonplace during the New Labour years, either as 'part of a "big tent" inclusive policy-making process to stimulate new thinking on key social policy issues' or as a means of recruiting 'people with appropriate expertise and experience' (Lewis, 2010: 226).

Many of those who made the crossing saw themselves as 'critical friends' of the government who brought with them an understanding of the sector they were eager to share with civil service colleagues, but, as they became assimilated into the government machine, found themselves directing their critical friendship towards the voluntary sector (Little and Rochester, 2003). Little and Rochester (2003: 12) suggest that the 'answer to the question whether the voluntary sector leaders who have joined the government service are symptoms or causes of the co-option of the sector by government' was 'elusive and complex' and that the boundary crossers worked in 'the gap between the rhetoric of partnership and the reality of government-voluntary sector relationships'.

Less is known about the experience of emigrants to the local state, but there is anecdotal evidence to suggest that the process and the issues were similar. At national or local level, those who crossed the boundary found themselves in a kind of uncomfortable no-man's-land, and those who stayed tended to align themselves with their new statutory sector home. And they found it easier to influence the loosely connected and open institutions of the voluntary sector than to take on the impermeable and intransigent bureaucratic machinery of the state. Where they did have a role in shaping policy and policy implementation, this did not appear to involve 'changing the main thrust of government policy' but as mediation and building bridges between the sectors (Little and Rochester, 2003: 12). Given the imbalance of power between the sectors, it is easier to see the boundary crossers as smoothing the way for the sector's involvement with government on the latter's terms rather than challenging their course of action.

Conclusions

This section of the book has explored the influences and factors that have formed the current paradigm of voluntary action. This final chapter of the section has examined the ways in which different groupings within the sector have acted as 'champions' of the process. While the intermediary infrastructure organisations have played a key role in promoting the government's rhetoric of partnership and its policy of transferring the delivery of public services to voluntary organisations and in adopting the practices of generic managerialism and the values of the market, they have not acted alone. Other players have included the chief executives of individual agencies and their representative body; researchers, organisational consultants and trainers; and those who have crossed the boundary from the voluntary sector to work in national or local government. Individually and in combination they have been shaped by and helped to shape the forces that have moulded the voluntary sector as it appears today.

Overall, the processes that have produced the voluntary sector model for the twenty-first century have provided an example of the enduring explanatory power of two mainstays of the organisational theory toolkit – institutional isomorphism and organisational ecology. In their classic article on 'institutional isomorphism and collective rationality in organizational fields', DiMaggio and Powell (1983: 147) argued that 'bureaucratisation and other forms of organizational change occur as the result of processes that make organizations more similar without necessarily making them more efficient', a process that 'is effected largely by the state and the professions'. They distinguish between three kinds of isomorphic process, all of which can be seen to be at work in the formation of the contemporary vision of the voluntary sector in the UK. These are:

1. *Coercive isomorphism*, which is the consequence of pressure from other organisations on which organisations are dependent and includes formal and informal pressure from government, funding bodies and regulators.
2. *Mimetic isomorphism*, through which organisations respond to uncertainty in their environment in similar ways and which is transmitted by the movement of employees to new organisations and through the work of consultancy agencies.
3. *Normative isomorphism*, brought about by the increasing influence of professionalisation: a common background of education and training and a shared commitment to professional aspirations will produce similar responses to organisational challenges.

Population ecologists like Hannan and Freeman (1989) also offer explanations based on a unit of analysis that is wider than the individual organisation and based on a long-term perspective. They emphasise that new organisational forms are the product of a kind of natural selection: structures that are more efficient in the current environment eventually 'squeeze out' organisations with older, less efficient, forms, and their success leads to legitimacy in the overall population, which provides an incentive for the creation of similar organisational forms.

Institutional isomorphism and organisational ecology theories provide useful perspectives that help to explain the developments reviewed in this section of the book. They should not, however, be seen as the complete story. As well as the importance of the important role played by individuals and the significance of the choices made by key players, we need to look at some significant alternative perspectives that have been sidelined or ignored on the route to the homogenised voluntary sector of the twenty-first century. These are discussed in the next section of the book.

Note

1. As well as NCVO, ACEVO, NAVCA and VE, there were Charities Aid Foundation (CAF), Charities Finance Group (CFG), Welsh Council for Voluntary Action (WCVA), Big Society Capital, Institute of Fundraising, Locality, Northern Ireland Council for Voluntary Action (NICVA), Social Enterprise UK, Voice4Change and the Association of Charitable Trusts (ACF).

Part III

Alternative Perspectives

9
Governance, Ownership and Control

This is the first of five chapters that aim to provide a critique of and an alternative perspective on some of the key elements of the current understanding of the nature of voluntary action. It begins by revisiting some of the substantial body of academic and practitioner literature on governance and governing bodies in voluntary organisations and suggesting that its focus on 'what do boards do?' (Cornforth, 2003) diverts attention from the deeper issues of ownership and control that underlie arrangements for governance. The chapter goes on to explore the implications of Selznick's (1992: 290) argument that 'to govern is to accept responsibility for *the whole life* of the institution' and that 'governance takes account of all the interests that affect the viability, competence and moral character of an enterprise'. Such a responsibility, it suggests, is not borne by the members of the board alone; it is shared with a range of actors who may include present or past members of staff, volunteers, service users, supporters and other interested parties. Each organisation will have its own constellation of what Harris (1996) has called the 'Guardians' – the people who care whether the organisation lives or dies.

The chapter then discusses the extent to which these 'Guardians' are the equivalent of the 'principal owners' of for-profit organisations – the people who can exercise control over the key decisions that affect the destiny of the organisation. It argues that, in many voluntary organisations, ownership and control have increasingly become located in their staff rather than their boards (and the wider interests they may represent) and have tended to pass from the staff as a whole to their managers and especially to the chief executive. The chapter concludes by discussing some of the implications of these changes.

Governance and governing bodies

Much of the literature on governance focuses on what boards do – or what they should do. The starting point tends to be a belief that the governing bodies of voluntary organisations – boards, councils of management, trustees or executive committees – fail to carry out their functions or meet the expectations placed on them. The literature tends to follow a general pattern that involves: (1) defining the board's role; (2) demonstrating how and where governing bodies are failing to deliver; (3) suggesting explanations for the gap between theory and practice; and (4) prescribing ways of addressing the shortcomings of the board and its members.

Harris (1996) has identified a general agreement in the literature about four of the key responsibilities it has attributed to the governing body.

The first of these is to provide the point of final *accountability* for the activities and behaviour of the organisation. This function can be traced back to the initial requirement of charity law that a group of disinterested trustees take on the responsibility of ensuring that a trust's endowment was used for the purposes specified by the founder. By extension, a governing body came to be seen as the means of making sure that a charity's activities advanced its mission and helped it to meet its charitable objectives and of ensuring that it conformed to appropriate standards of behaviour. More recently, the role has been seen as taking responsibility for the conduct of staff and the quality of the services provided by the organisation.

The second commonly accepted key responsibility – to act as the *employer* of its staff – can be seen as closely related to the accountability function. While in many organisations the day-to-day conduct of recruitment and supervision of staff, monitoring of their work and, where necessary, invoking sanctions (which might include dismissal) for inadequate performance or unsatisfactory behaviour are delegated to managers, their actions are taken on behalf of the governing body and in line with rules and procedures set by the board.

The third responsibility is for setting the *policy* of an organisation. This involves 'determining how the mission, purposes and goals of the voluntary agency are set and, if appropriate, changing them in response to new circumstances' and 'in setting priorities, developing plans and monitoring outcomes' (Harris, 1996: 152).

The governing body's fourth key duty is to secure the *resources* needed by the organisation, not only in the form of money (which is generally seen as the principal need) but also in the shape of premises, staff and equipment.

A fifth responsibility, mentioned in some but not all of the studies reviewed by Harris, is to act as an *interface* – a link and/or a buffer between the organisation and its environment. 'On the one hand they are expected to represent the agency's activities and policies *to* the outside world; and, on the other, they are expected to bring in knowledge, pressures and opinions *from* the outside world' (Harris, 1996: 153).

This consensus about what governing bodies should be doing is matched by a widespread agreement in the literature that very few of them are living up to these expectations. Boards are characterised as lacking understanding of the mission of their organisation and how it is being pursued; ineffective and unable to discharge their functions to any great degree; increasingly dependent on their paid staff; and failing to focus their meetings on major issues rather than spending too much time on discussing matters of detail (Harris, 1993; Dartington, 1995; Harris and Rochester, 1996; Cornforth, 2003). It has been suggested that some boards do little more than 'rubber stamp' decisions taken by others (usually paid staff or managers) and add so little value that nothing would be lost if they were abolished (Knight, 1993).

More generally, critics offer two main sets of explanations for the ineffectiveness of boards. The first of these is the shortcomings of individual board members. In the first place, they are ignorant of the nature and extent of their responsibilities. Second, they lack commitment to the organisation and its cause and are unable to devote the necessary time or energy to their involvement with it. And, third, they lack the necessary skills and competencies required to be an effective trustee.

The second set of explanations is based on a perceived failure to define the board's role and the nature of its relationship to the rest of the organisation. At its simplest, this approach distinguishes between 'governance' – the role of the board – and management – which is undertaken by the organisation's staff and explains the ineffectiveness of governing bodies in terms of their failure to focus on their proper role and leave day-to-day management to those employed to undertake it. While this is a superficially persuasive answer (and one that has won widespread support), it has two major shortcomings. In the first place, it assumes that the boundary between 'governance' and 'management' can be clearly defined and generally respected, whereas in reality the line is fuzzy and its location is contested: as an apocryphal chair quoted by Chait (1993) quoted in Dartington, 1996: 214) pointed out, 'Whatever a trustee wants to discuss is policy and the rest is administration.' In the second place, the clear distinction of roles belongs with the traditional ABC model that divides organisations into three quite separate elements – 'owners', staff and users – and, as discussed in Chapter 7, is inappropriate and unhelpful as a means of understanding voluntary agencies. Just as we should not analyse the staff hierarchy of the agency in isolation, we cannot understand how the governing body (which is made up of or represents the 'owners') works without placing it in its complete organisational context.

The prescriptions suggested as remedies for the weaknesses identified by this diagnosis have been widely accepted and used as the foundations of a large number of handbooks and manuals, training courses and consultancy projects. Organisations are advised to recruit people with the necessary experience and skills (identified by a 'skills audit' of existing members) to take on roles and responsibilities that are clearly defined. They then need to provide the new recruits with appropriate induction, training and support to ensure that they can meet the demands of their position. Concentration on the performance of each individual should then be complemented by exercises undertaken by the board as a whole during an 'away day' or, in the USA, a 'retreat' through which it can clarify its role and reflect on how it should carry it out.

Despite a significant investment in these kinds of activity (by, for example, the Governance Hub and its successor service, the Leadership and Governance Work-stream, set up under the New Labour government's ChangeUp programme), there is little evidence of improvements in the effectiveness of governing bodies or in the levels of satisfaction in their performances. This suggests a need to look elsewhere for better explanations for the shortcomings in voluntary sector governance.

Some general theories of governance

Cornforth (2003) has summarised some of the main theoretical perspectives on organisational governance more generally, which can be used to help us understand what is going on within voluntary sector organisations. They provide us with a number of different models.

1. The 'default setting' for organisational theory based on the norms of the corporate sector is the *compliance* model. This is founded on *agency (or, more accurately, principal–agent) theory*. It assumes that the interests of the managers are not the same as those of the shareholders. As a result, the board needs to have non-executive directors to ensure that the managers do not pursue their own interests at the expense of the shareholders. Similarly, charity trustees are there to

ensure that the objects of the charity (or the wishes of the founder of an endowed trust) guide the work of the organisation.

2. A second perspective is the *partnership* model, derived from *stewardship theory*, and based on the very different assumption that the owners and managers of the firm have shared interests. The board is thus used not to obtain compliance but to improve organisational performance, and its members are selected on the basis of the kinds of expertise they can bring to bear on this function. Much of the 'how-to' literature on voluntary sector boards reflects this approach.

3. A third perspective – the *co-optation* model – is provided by *resource dependency theory*. This argues that organisations are dependent on others for key resources and have an over-riding need to manage the relationship with funders to ensure they maintain a flow of resources from outside. The board members are chosen because of the influence they have with external stakeholders.

4. A fourth perspective – *managerial hegemony theory* – leads to the 'rubber stamp' model. This emanates from the private sector and is based on the perspective that, while shareholders have formal control of the firm, effective control is in the hands of the managers. The board is of largely symbolic value and its role is to confer legitimacy on management decisions. The relevance to the voluntary sector is fairly clear.

5. A fifth and very different perspective is provided by the *democratic* model. Here the board is chosen by a larger or smaller electorate to which it is responsible and which it is seen to represent in some way. Its functions are to reconcile different interests, make policy and control the executives. Members are not expected to bring specific expertise to the role. This is, of course, the basic model of the membership association, and elements of it may continue to exist in some hybrid voluntary agencies.

6. A final perspective – the *stakeholder* model – has recently become influential in the corporate sector as well as in voluntary organisations. It is based on the idea that the organisation needs to take account of the requirements of a range of stakeholders who have different interests. The main function of the board is to balance these competing interests, and some of the board members may represent specific stakeholders.

These are, of course, *models*. None of them captures the complete reality of any governing body, while most boards live with the paradoxes of embodying more than one of the models and including members with very different views of why they are there and what the board is for.

Another approach

Another benefit of using this range of models to help explain the role(s) being played by boards is that they help to clarify the ways in which governing bodies relate to other elements in the make-up of the organisation and some of the features of its environment. In other words, they shift the focus from 'what boards do' to a concern with the way governance functions are performed in and by the organisation as a whole. Taking her cue from the suggestion of Kramer (1985) and others that the governing body role is 'contingent' and 'interdependent with the role of staff' and therefore 'not susceptible to implementation in isolation from other organisational roles', Harris (1996: 154) has developed two ways of understanding the relationship between boards and their organisational environment.

The first of these (Harris, 1993; Harris and Rochester, 1996) introduces an approach to managing the relationship between governing bodies and their staff that she called Total Activities Analysis (TAA). TAA assumes that the boundary between the work of the board and the work of the staff is not pre-ordained but needs to be negotiated between the two parties, and the distribution of responsibilities that results should be revisited at regular intervals and adjusted to changing circumstances such as different funding arrangements or changes to the kinds of services the organisation is providing. The use of TAA in one organisation:

> had thus identified the issues underlying the board's 'failure' to do its job and enabled the agency to address them. It is clear that they are not the kind of issues to which there is only one 'correct' answer. TAA clarified the choices the organisation needed to make and left it to make them on the basis of their preferred method of working and their perceptions of the distribution of skills and experience within their staff and committee members.
>
> (Harris and Rochester, 1996: 40)

Harris's second contribution goes beyond an analysis of the interaction between board and staff and beyond the ways in which functions might be allocated between them to look at the distribution of power within voluntary agencies. Her models involve four organisational elements, three of which are easily recognised. They are:

- The board
- The staff (paid and/or voluntary) and
- The users or beneficiaries of the organisation's activities.

The fourth of them, however, needs introduction and explanation. This consists of:

- The 'Guardians' – the founders of the agency or its successors as the people 'who have a positive concern for the long-term survival of the agency and its purposes'. The latter may include funders, former members or former clients (Harris, 1996: 155).

Harris sets out three models of the relationship between the four elements and the implications of each of them for the position of the governing body.

The first of these – the *traditional* model – can be represented in simple linear form. The guardians appoint (or are the same as) the board. This, in turn, employs the staff to deliver services to the agency's users or beneficiaries. This is the model on which philanthropic organisations have been established from the nineteenth century until the present day, and it provides a set of arrangements within which the board can undertake the functions discussed above.

In the second – *membership* – model the authority and role of the board are less straightforward. Here the guardians are the same as, or are drawn from, the organisation's users or beneficiaries. The board can easily be sidelined as a result of the close relationship between staff and guardians/users: 'where the two groups are in close and frequent contact, they can find ways of working that meet their own needs satisfactorily, but in which governing body involvement is seen as unnecessary or intrusive' (Harris, 1996: 158).

Similarly, the board's authority is seriously impaired in the third – *entrepreneur* – model, where the guardians are also the staff of the agency. If the organisation is 'owned' by the staff the board cannot exert control over the work of the agency and finds itself without a role, except perhaps as 'a support group for the staff'.

These two contributions from the work of Margaret Harris have shifted the emphasis from explaining perceived shortcomings in voluntary sector governance in terms of the personal inadequacies of the individual members of boards and a failure to understand the difference between 'steering' and 'rowing' to the analysis of underlying structural features. From this perspective the ways in which boards perform the functions ascribed to them is contingent on their relationship with other elements in the organisation and on the extent to which they have the authority to carry them out.

Governance and ownership

Harris (1999: 111) has also pointed the way towards the development of 'a theory of third sector governance' by highlighting the contribution of Philip Selznick to understanding the nature of governance. While not specifically addressed to voluntary sector organisations, Selznick's characterisation of governance provides a valuable starting point for further analysis. He makes a crucial distinction between the kind of commitment and kinds of activity needed to ensure the survival of the organisation and the integrity of its mission or governance, on the one hand, and the organisation of its work or management, on the other.

> To govern is to accept responsibility for *the whole life* of the institution. This is a burden quite different from the rational co-ordination of specialized activities (i.e. management). Governance takes account of all the interests that affect the viability, competence and moral character of an enterprise. The strategies of governance are basically political. They have to do with forming public opinion, accommodating interests, and determining what ends should be chosen and by what means those ends should be pursued.
>
> (Selznick, 1992: 290)

Clearly, this is a radically different approach from the perspective that governance is what boards do (or ought to be doing). While effective governing bodies can be at the centre of the organisation's efforts to meet the kind of responsibilities identified by Selznick, they will not take them on alone or unaided. Saidel and Harlan (1998) have drawn attention to the wider systems of governance which extend to advisory groups and similar bodies, while, as we have seen, Harris has shown how many of the board's functions are implemented in partnership with members of staff. It is a short step from these perceptions to the view that the broad functions of this conception of governance are performed by a number of players who include not only the members of the board but also other supporters of the organisation and a number of additional interested parties. To the extent that these disparate elements accept a share of the responsibility for the 'viability, competence and moral character' of an agency, they can be seen as its 'owners'. And the acceptance of responsibility will be accompanied by a claim to control or influence the conduct of its affairs.

Who 'owns' voluntary organisations?

The concept of 'ownership' is rarely applied to voluntary sector organisations. It has its origins in the world of the private sector firm, and it has been applied to public sector bodies, but it has been seen at best as of limited relevance to the study of the voluntary sector, even though it involves high levels of control over the destiny of an organisation. Those who own it can surely decide what kind of organisation it is; what it does and how it does it; whether it remains essentially the same or undergoes radical change; and, ultimately, whether it survives or is closed down. It is, therefore, important for us to be able to identify who those owners are. At the same time, there are constraints and limitations on the ability of those people to exercise the control we associate with ownership, and we need to be aware of these as well.

Much of what has been written about ownership has been provided by the economists who tend to assume that the 'normal' organisational form is the for-profit firm. At bottom, this is quite straightforward: the model is that of the joint-stock company where a number of private individuals jointly own an enterprise whose function is to provide them with a return on their capital investment in the form of profits. A slightly more sophisticated approach has been developed by economists who have noticed that public sector agencies, as well as voluntary or non-profit organisations, exist alongside the for-profit firm. Henry Hansmann, for example, suggests that, in addition to the receipt of 'residual earnings', ownership is also defined by the possession of 'ultimate control'. This typically means the 'power to elect the board of directors' (Hansmann, 1987: 28, quoted in Billis, 2010c: 49). And he makes a useful distinction (which we will return to) between 'formal control' (the arrangements set out in the constitution and other legal documents) and 'effective control' (which is what actually happens).

The basic 'shareholder' model of ownership is based on contractual theory. This views the firm as a nexus of contracts that enables people with economic assets to combine in order to get a higher return on them. But the contracting parties are not equal, and it is the shareholders who are most powerful. According to this theory, this is entirely beneficial both for the individual firm and for society as a whole. The assumption is that maximum wealth creation is the goal of business activity, and it follows that control should rest with those with the greatest incentives for pursuing this aim – the shareholders.

The development of the modern corporation has led to an alternative approach to understanding how it works. In place of the stockholder or shareholder model, we have been offered a model based on what has rather grandly been called stakeholder theory.

The stakeholder theory holds that the firm is operated – or ought to be operated – for the benefit not just of the shareholders but of all who have a stake in the company. Stakeholders are 'those groups who are vital to the survival and success of the corporation' or 'any group or individual who can affect or is affected by the achievement of the organization's objectives' (see Boatright, 2000: 356). These stakeholders will include employees, customers, suppliers and the local community.

> The corporation or firm is an organizational entity through which many different individuals or groups attempt to achieve their ends. A firm interacts continually with its stakeholder groups and much of the success of the firm depends on how well all of these stakeholder relations are managed.
>
> (Boatright, 2000: 357)

We have spent some time on this model because the practice as well as the literature of voluntary sector management increasingly uses the stakeholder term. But we need to be aware that the theory is not generally accepted by economists and other private sector theorists: many of them feel that these groups need to be satisfied only as a means of achieving the main purpose of making money for the shareholders.

While orthodox economists believe that the market is a perfect mechanism for ordering our economic lives, they have recognised from Adam Smith onwards that it does not meet all our needs. 'For a market to exist, a product or service has to benefit only the person who buys it. It cannot be available to everyone else free of charge' (Glennerster, 2003: 18). Activities which benefit the population as a whole, such as defence, clean air, policing and public health, are 'public' rather than 'private' goods which need to be provided collectively – by government – and paid for by all of us through taxation. But who 'owns' the governmental agencies which provide these public goods? Whereas the firm is owned by its shareholders, its statutory counterpart, the bureau, is – in principle – owned by the taxpayers.

In both cases, however, the exercise of control by their owners needs further discussion. Billis (2010c) goes beyond Hansmann's distinction between formal and effective control to suggest there are three levels of ownership:

- *The formal/legal owners* – the shareholders or taxpayers.
- *The active owners* – those who vote at company AGMs, on the one hand, or participate in the political process, on the other, even though their impact or influence may be slight.
- *The principal owners* – 'those who *in effect* can close the organization down... or change the fundamental boundary or mission of the organization through mergers or other actions. In the private sector it may be large pension funds or other major investors. In the public sector it is likely to be the elected representatives or a caucus of those representatives' (Billis, 2010c: 50–1).

The issues of ownership and control are thus comparatively straightforward in the for-profit and public sectors. In the voluntary sector, however, the concepts are less easy to apply.

The consensus among economists is that voluntary or non-profit sector organisations do not – cannot – have owners because the non-distribution constraint means that no one receives the residual returns. That is to say, the non-profit firm can make profits but cannot distribute them to its members. A number of writers have attempted to fill the gap with proxies for ownership – such as 'key stakeholders' who have the power to 'interpret the mission in controversial situations' (Speckbacher, 2003: 275–6, quoted in Billis, 2010c: 50). But for most economists voluntary agencies are anomalous; while privately owned bodies in the market sector produce private goods and publicly owned governmental agencies produce public goods, voluntary sector organisations are seen as privately owned producers of public goods.

Billis addresses this problem by suggesting that the ideal type of third sector organisation – to set alongside the private sector's *firm* and the public sector's *bureau* – is the *membership association*. In this organisational model, instead of shareholders or taxpayers, the owners are the members of the association and the threefold typology or ownership also applies:

> even in small, tightly knit groups, it is possible to differentiate between those (formal) members who stay in the shadows...; those who play an active part in committee and other activities; and a core group of those (principal owners) 'who everybody knows' will really be the key players in the defining moments of the group's history.
>
> (Billis, 2010c: 53–4)

While the association remains the most common organisational form in the sector, many voluntary sector organisations can be seen as 'hybrids' that have taken on some of the characteristics of one or both of the other sectors (discussed in more detail in Chapter 7). Here the identity of the owners, and especially that of the *principal* owners, is less straight-forward. They are very similar to Harris's Guardians – 'those who have a positive concern for the long-term survival of the agency and its purposes who may include founders, funders, former members or former clients'. In the 'shallow' form of the hybrid organisation the composition of this collection of owners could also include volunteers, members of the paid staff, or officers and staff of statutory agencies and other voluntary organisations working in the same field. These miscellaneous collections of interests tend, however, to be increasingly replaced or *dis*placed by an organisation's move into a more 'entrenched' form of hybridity. In some cases ownership can be transferred to external bodies such as funders and regulators. Housing associations are an extreme case: the Homes and Communities Agency exercises strict oversight of their activities and may even remove and replace board members if it deems this appropriate. More common, however, is the tendency for ownership and control to pass into the hands of the organisation's staff rather than their boards (and the wider interests they may represent) and to pass from the staff as a whole to their managers, and especially to the chief executive.

As a key component of the voluntary agency, its staff do, of course, have a part to play in its governance: many of them demonstrate a 'genuine commitment to organizational purposes through their freely given and un-coerced contributions to the operation and governance of the organization' over and above their paid work (Billis, 2010c: 62). But there is an important difference between making such a contribution alongside a range of other 'owners' and becoming the sole or principal proprietor of the organisation. We can identify three significant factors that have contributed to the concentration of power in the hands of the staff. In the first place, there has been a longstanding trend towards replacing volunteers with paid staff and generalist staff with specialists (see, for example, Billis and Harris, 1992) whose 'professional judgement' has become increasingly difficult to challenge. Second, funding relationships have become more complex: contractual arrangements require very detailed knowledge about provision and costings as well as the legal aspects of their terms, and this needs more time and possibly more expertise than part-time board members have at their disposal. And, finally, organisations have increasingly adopted a model of governance that sees board members as a source of expertise and people who can contribute to improving performance rather than challenge staff or question the organisation's 'direction of travel'. At the same time, the trend towards a focus on the delivery of highly specified outputs under very tightly drawn contracts has led to increasingly hierarchical and bureaucratic organisational forms that give managers more authority over front-line staff. The ultimate product of these trends has been the 'command-and-control' model outlined in Chapter 7.

Summary and conclusions

This chapter began by drawing attention to the widely accepted view that the boards of voluntary agencies are failing to perform their functions, the inadequacy of the programmes aimed at addressing these shortcomings and the contradictory nature of some of the main theoretical perspectives on governance. It has gone on to argue that the role of the governing body cannot be seen in isolation but that it is contingent on the activities of other key elements within the organisation. The chapter has then highlighted an account of governance that goes well beyond the activities of the board to embrace responsibility for 'the whole life' of the organisation and its 'viability, competence and moral character'. It has argued that, while the governing body ought to be at the centre of the organisation's efforts to meet these kinds of responsibilities, they cannot be expected to take them on alone or unaided. And those who do accept the responsibility will feel the need to control or influence the conduct of the organisation's affairs. This leads into a discussion of ownership and Billis's concept of the 'principal owners' who 'everyone knows' will be the key players in the defining moments of the group's history. The chapter then makes suggestions about the identity of these principal owners in different kinds of voluntary organisations and attempts to trace the shifting location of ownership in them.

Finally, we can attempt to draw out the implications of this analysis for our understanding of governance and ownership in voluntary organisations. It is simply not enough to address perceived weaknesses in the governance of an organisation by focusing on shortcomings in the awareness, knowledge and expertise on the part of individual board members, or on a failure of the board as a whole to understand the difference between 'steering' and 'rowing'. In the unambiguous voluntary association the match between those who have the formal responsibility for the conduct of its affairs and those with the real control or 'ownership' of the organisation is close enough for them to be treated as more or less identical. The situation in the 'shallow' hybrid form of voluntary organisation is more complex; the various interests who share – or compete for – ownership and who are therefore responsible for the life and death of the agency may or may not be adequately reflected or represented in its governing body. In these cases governance is more than 'what boards do'. And, in the 'entrenched' hybrid or more or less completely bureaucratic form of the voluntary agency, the control is exercised by principal owners – paid staff or managers – who are not members of its governing body, and the board is reduced to the status of a rubber stamp for decisions taken by others.

10
What Is Voluntary Action For?

Introduction

This chapter addresses questions that are rarely asked, let alone answered explicitly – what is the role or function of voluntary action in our society and why does it matter? It suggests that the implicit answers on which much of today's voluntary action is based are inadequate and misleading, and offers other explanations that provide a better basis for understanding and promoting it. The chapter pursues the argument on three levels. In the first place, it looks at the purposes or functions of voluntary organisations and argues that they are not purely instrumental – they do not exist simply to deliver certain services or activities – but are also expressive; they provide opportunities for behaviour that is intrinsically valuable. It takes the view that voluntary organisations should be seen as driven not by a set of goals but by the values on which they are founded. In the second place, it focuses on the individual volunteers and suggests that the value of their contribution needs to be assessed not simply on the basis of the amount and value of the unpaid labour it represents but also in terms of the wider social value it creates. And, third, it considers the role and significance of voluntary action in the aggregate by drawing on some of the discourse about 'civil society' to discuss its role as a vital intermediary between state and citizen and as a creator of social capital. The chapter concludes by suggesting ways in which the study of voluntary action and its practice might be shaped by a better understanding of 'what it is for'.

Voluntary organisations

Orthodox organisational theory demonstrates its origins in the study of manufacturing businesses by retaining a clear focus on the instrumental nature of organisations. They are seen – as Weber described them – as 'machines' that have been designed and built to secure the production of goods or the delivery of services and are to be judged on the efficiency with which they perform those functions, the delivery of the greatest number of goods or services of a specified quality at the lowest cost. The whole purpose of their management – of financial, physical and human resources and of performance and quality – is in the service of this single goal. And, increasingly, the expectations of voluntary organisations have been shaped by this template. As we have seen, they have been encouraged to adopt the most efficient form of organisational machinery – the bureaucratic model – and embraced the managerial techniques that come with it, including the application of business models to their management of performance and the orthodoxies of human resource management to the ways in which they recruit, supervise and support volunteers as well as paid employees.

But an instrumental purpose is not the sole reason for – and may not be the most important explanation of – the existence of voluntary organisations. The primary purpose of many voluntary organisations and groups is to provide opportunities for 'expressive' rather than instrumental behaviours; their activities are ends in themselves rather than the means to some external impact. Assessing their efficiency in producing goods or services does not, therefore, provide us with the only yardstick by which to judge their 'success'. The importance of the role played by 'the expressive dimension' has been explained by David Mason:

> How many bridge clubs, garden clubs, and churches exist solely as venues for playing cards, discussing flowers, and worshipping God? How many hospital board members, university alumni, and United Way workers function solely because of their concern for people's health, education or welfare? In addition to the ends just named, these organisations also provide direct personal gratification, satisfying activities and opportunities for cultivating friendships, having one's ego stroked, and socializing. People participate in and support both member-benefit and public-benefit entities some of the time because there is something they want to do (an expressive need) and some of the time because they want something done (an instrumental need). Voluntary sector organizations can accommodate either purpose.

And he adds:

> expressive action need not seek anything beyond itself for gratifica-
> tion; it needs no extrinsic reward, promotion or direct or indirect
> approbation...no extrinsic reward can substitute for the intrinsic
> rewards of the work itself.
>
> (Mason, 1996: 3–4)

The review of the history of the voluntary impulse provided in
Chapter 2 of this book identified the creation of opportunities for
expressive behaviours – and their close relatives, conviviality and sociability – as one of the neglected but important roots of voluntary action,
not only as an activity in its own right, as with the typical clubs
and societies of the eighteenth century, but also as one of a number of strands that came together to define a voluntary organisation
or group. Friendly Societies, for example, were aptly named because
they combined conviviality at their regular meetings with the provision of basic social insurance on a mutual basis, while some of the
later providers of social security among them started life as purely social
bodies. And, even the philanthropic charities of the late nineteenth century had an expressive dimension and a use for conviviality, both as a
means of strengthening the bonds between their workers and supporters
and as one form of the 'uplifting' activities that they provided for their
beneficiaries.

The general population of today's voluntary organisations is also
made up of a mixture of those whose sole or primary purpose is to
provide opportunities for expressive behaviour, those which are primarily instrumental and those which combine the two in a variety
of different configurations. Building on earlier attempts by Gordon
and Babchuk (1959), Warner and colleagues (1949) and Palisi and
Jacobson (1977), Mason has developed a typology that distinguishes
between organisations according to where they fall on these dimensions. It consists of four categories: expressive; expressive-instrumental;
instrumental-expressive; and instrumental organisations.

'Both the stated purposes and the routine activities' of the first of
Mason's types –*expressive organisations* – 'involve the doing of the thing
of interest itself'. They include 'social clubs that socialise, yacht clubs
that sail, fraternal organisations that fraternise, bowling leagues that
bowl, and other collectivities that help people who enjoy doing the
same things to do them better together' (Mason, 1996: 69). And, as well

as bodies which provide vehicles for their members' shared enthusiasms, expressive organisations also include among their number self-help or mutual support groups for people with a particular need or problem who can get together to provide one another with understanding and encouragement. The category has been sub-divided by Warriner and Prather (1965), who distinguish between three functions of expressive value – pleasure in performance, sociability and ideological symbolism. The first function is expressed by groups that engage in activities which their members enjoy performing, and include hobby clubs and those devoted to dancing or sports. The second function is characteristic of groups that provide opportunities for their members to interact, and include social clubs and dining societies. And the third function is characteristic of religious organisations and other groups that are defined by a shared value system and that provide opportunities for members to evoke or reaffirm their common beliefs.

Mason's second 'type', the *expressive-instrumental organisation*, serves expressive needs but may also deliver some instrumental outputs. People who have come together for friendship and sociability may find themselves engaging in instrumental activity either for their own benefit – such as repainting their clubhouse – or for the benefit of others, when, for example, a choral society may stage a concert to raise money for a local cause. Mason argues that the utilitarian culture of the USA and its Protestant work ethic mean that people are uncomfortable when involved in purely expressive behaviour and 'tend to influence participants in many purely expressive organizations to undertake instrumental activities and projects' (Mason, 1996: 72).

Mason's third type, the *instrumental-expressive organisation*, also serves expressive needs, but the delivery of instrumental outputs predominates. Nevertheless, the expressive element is vitally important to the health of the organisation: 'Board members, committee workers, fund drive solicitors, and service providers would not participate were it not for their organization's instrumental services; but, once involved, they are intrinsically motivated and expressively fulfilled.' People get involved in the first place for instrumental reasons but remain committed because of the expressive activities of the organisation. As Mason comments:

> When an organization by its instrumental objectives attracts someone who finds self-expression and fulfilment in the contribution he or she makes, that participant engages in a multiply rewarding activity. A major reason why the benefit of voluntary action is so great

and why it can be such a significant tool is its ability to motivate participants towards instrumental ends while the participants enjoy expressive rewards.

(Mason, 1996: 63)

Mason's final type is the *instrumental organisation*, which concentrates purely on instrumental outputs. Its 'purposes and activities... focus on its producing something of value for others outside the organization, and any expressive aspect is distractive' (Mason, 1996: 74). Despite a growing understanding of the importance of the expressive dimension in any form of work in any kind of workplace, the purely instrumental approach is at the heart of the kind of command and control managerial model that dominates the corporate world and has come to exercise a powerful influence in the voluntary sector (and is discussed in Chapters 7 and 11).

Another way of conceptualising the interaction between the expressive and instrumental dimensions of voluntary organisations is provided by the literature on associations, which draws a crucial distinction between activities that are of benefit to the organisation's members (which are generally expressive) and those that are of 'public' benefit (which are largely instrumental). There is a tendency to dismiss 'grassroots associations' as of minor interest because their activities are primarily directed inwards to meeting the expressive needs or desires of their members and not outwards towards some wider grouping. Lohmann (1992), however, has described them as 'mixed benefactories' and Harris (1998) has pointed out that many associations need to balance their member-benefit and public-benefit goals and activities: if they fail to satisfy their existing members, they will lose them, but, if they concentrate on their members' needs to the exclusion of the needs and interests of non-members, they will not be able to recruit new participants and will diminish and decline. Smith (2000: 115) argues that associations are largely member-benefit in nature but that they are 'partly public serving and not wholly member serving'. Organisations that are primarily expressive in purpose also have an instrumental dimension and, by the same token, those that are almost completely instrumental in their orientation may have an expressive component. The reality of associational life – and much of the experience of other kinds of voluntary organisation – is that they combine the expressive and the instrumental in one of the two combinations identified by Mason – the expressive-instrumental and the instrumental-expressive.

Another approach to the nature of the division between instrumental and expressive orientations is the distinction that has been made between organisations that are 'goal-oriented' and those that are 'driven by values'. Bureaucracies and other predominantly instrumental types of organisation are largely defined by their goals and success is measured by the extent to which those aims and objectives are achieved. Organisations in which values rather than goals drive the agenda are found most commonly – but by no means exclusively – in religious or faith-based organisations, which may be motivated by 'divinely ordained injunctions to simply care for neighbours and people in need' rather than propelled by concepts such as 'outcomes' and 'good practice' (Cairns *et al.*, 2007: 427). What this means for their management has been teased out by the reflections and conclusions made by Jeavons (1994: 211–18) on the back of his study of the 'management of Christian service organizations'. He puts forward ten 'principles or points of focus' which 'demand the attention of managers and board members of Christian service organizations' and include the following:

- A *focus on vocation* that involves asking questions like 'what is God's call on this organisation?' rather than 'what is its market niche?' or 'its greatest opportunity for growth?'
- A *focus on witness as well as service* that requires the leaders and members of these organisations to 'be consistently attentive to questions about *what statements are made and what messages are sent* as well as what practical needs are met by the work'.
- A *focus on means as well as ends*, not only in the ways in which services are delivered but also when it comes to the design and structure of the organisation itself. On the one hand, 'The manner in which services are provided, the relationships created between servers and served, and the relationship created among servers and resource providers and those served are all critical factors in shaping the message or witness.' And, on the other, 'Organizations that wish to emphasize the values of equality, the need for recognition of people's giftedness regardless of their status or background, and the need for genuine partnership in designing and engaging in ministry cannot achieve this through organizational structures that are essentially hierarchical, that separate personal qualities from the work to be performed, and that encourage competition rather than co-operation.'
- A *focus on servanthood* or 'genuine humility' that is 'related to the diminution of personal ambition, the absence of...any emotional and functional investment in hierarchy...and the presence of a

strong co-operative spirit' while 'Senior executives and board members should remember that their authority to manage or govern relates to their responsibilities, and the respect they have earned, not their rights.'

- A *focus on integrity* that has two dimensions. In the first place, it means being 'open and honest' and 'providing full disclosure in all financial matters' so as to meet the biblical injunction 'to take pains to do right not only in the eyes of the Lord but also of men'. In the second place, integrity means 'being what they claim to be', and this is of significant practical importance as well as crucial to the organisation's values: 'When there is a manifest disparity between what an organization claims to be and what it is, even when that disparity is not immediately evident to outsiders, a kind of dishonesty is present that will ultimately undermine the organization in many ways.'

For a glimpse of what these high-minded expressions of Christian values might mean in practice, we can turn to a study of a number of small charities providing emergency services for homeless people. While the lion's share of the resources available to voluntary organisations concerned with homelessness have been increasingly taken up by 'highly professionalised corporatist organisations... there remain myriad smaller and more traditional organisations' that depend on the contribution of volunteers to enable them to meet the 'basic needs for food and a place to sleep'. These are typically faith-based organisations, and it is clear that their Christian values underpin the work of the volunteers, who deliver their services and use their volunteering opportunities as a means of expressing their 'ethical citizenship' (Cloke *et al.*, 2007: 1098–9).

While the influence of values on organisational activities and behaviour can be seen most clearly in religious and faith-based organisations in which values are explicitly articulated on a routine basis, they can also be seen as central to the identity of many secular voluntary organisations. This is despite the major shift in recent years from 'traditional' to 'corporatist' organisational forms which has led, according to Cloke and his colleagues (2007: 1091), to 'the production and consumption of standardised welfare programmes and spaces'. Writing in 1983, David Gerard argued that an important reason why voluntary organisations were worthy of more attention was the central part played by values in voluntary activity, and that the study of those organisations might contribute a view of private and public sector institutions which encompassed their moral and social dimensions as well as their economic functions. Some 13 years later, Paton suggested that the values basis of voluntary organisations was revealed by the kinds of organisational conflicts that arose in them, which he called 'values issues'. These conflicts typically involved an appeal to higher values, had considerable significance both to the individuals concerned and to the organisation in which they worked, and which offered limited scope for resolution by means of a compromise. 'Thus', he concluded, 'as well as binding organisations together in shared commitments, values will also on occasion threaten to divide them bitterly' (Paton, 1996: 43).

The importance of a commitment to values as a core feature and guiding principle for the activities of voluntary organisations remains a significant part of the commonly accepted rationale for the existence of the voluntary sector and is quoted as evidence of its worth. At the same time, there is increasing concern that the historical values of the sector are under threat, not only from external forces but also from their neglect by those who manage and lead voluntary organisations. A recent report from Community Links, an innovative charity based in East London since 1977, has attempted to address these issues by *'encouraging boldness* in third sector organisations'. Through a process of collaborative inquiry it sought to identify a common set of values that together defined the sector and explained why people were committed to work in and through voluntary organisations; highlight the external threats to them from the nature of the relationship between government and the sector and from the nature of the funding environment; and encourage individual organisations to focus on their values and put them 'at the centre of every activity' (Blake *et al.*, 2006: 7).

Community Links' report is evidence not, as its authors intended, of the continuing vitality of the sector's values base but of its decreasing relevance in much of today's voluntary sector. The report argues that the combination of a number of common values provides the sector with a unique meaning or identity and that 'these values form an inseparable whole... in their practical delivery one value becomes the expression of another'. But the individual elements are, not surprisingly, couched in such general terms as to offer little in the way of clear and concrete guidance for action. They are: 'empowering people; pursuing equality; making voices heard; transforming lives; being responsible; finding fulfilment; doing a good job'; and 'generating public wealth' (Blake *et al.*, 2006: 19. And the recommendations for putting values at the heart of the activities of each organisation are equally bland. They take us little further than the advice offered by David Billis in

1993 when he cautioned voluntary agencies against an unplanned slide into change and suggested they needed to ask themselves some simple but fundamental questions about their mission and purpose (Billis, 1993b).

For an increasing number of voluntary agencies, values are simply no longer 'the beginning, the means and the end' as the Community Links report asserts. Much of this book has been directed towards explaining why and how this has come about. But values remain central to the purpose and activities of many secular as well as religious voluntary organisations. These will not, however, be announced in the mission statements, strap-lines or other kinds of 'branding' through which many agencies express their aspirations and which are increasingly similar to those used by private sector and governmental agencies. The evidence will be found in the way the leaders, staff and volunteers of an organisation can be seen to be trying to 'live' their values in their work and in the way they interact with users, colleagues and people outside the organisation. And it will be found in organisations and groups that, in the words of Cloke and his colleagues (2007: 1098–9), are 'marginalised' and 'outsiders' rather than those in 'that part of the voluntary sector which has been embraced by the state'.

Religious organisations have two features that help to ensure that values remain at the centre of their activities. In the first place, their primary purpose of coming together to worship is itself a kind of normative activity that reinforces the sense of shared beliefs and commitments. And, second, 'what is at the root of all religious organisations is the fact that, at every level, everyone can appeal to an authority structure outside the organisation itself... in God, mediated by sacred texts and traditions' (Torry, 2012: 113–14). Other organisations with a 'comparative advantage' in terms of values include those in the campaigning field whose goals of securing greater human rights and social justice tend to be reflected in their internal behaviour. And a much wider group of grassroots associations are held together by shared values: Smith (2000: 91) argues, for example, that 'by definition, all groups must guide their members to some extent regarding appropriate and acceptable thoughts (ideology), motives (desires), feelings (emotions) and actions (behaviours). The presence of a group goal and group style norms, among other factors, sees to this.' In the absence of strong incentives and sanctions such as salary increases, promotion and demotion or dismissal, this ideological consensus provides the 'internal guidance system' of the group as well as defining its goals and putting boundaries around its activities.

Volunteering

The second part of the attempt to explain the rationale of voluntary action moves the argument on from a focus on the functions of voluntary organisations to a consideration of the societal role of volunteering, and it argues that the more or less exclusive concentration on measuring its instrumental impacts needs to be broadened to take account of the expressive dimension. Approaches to assessing the impact of volunteering identify four main areas for measurement – the effect on the volunteers themselves; the contribution it makes to the welfare of users or beneficiaries; the value to the organisation through which the volunteer is engaged; and the community more generally (see, for example, IVR, 2004). The 'benefits' of volunteering – which reflect a view of its function or purpose (what it is 'for') – tend to be expressed in instrumental terms. The *IVR Impact Assessment Toolkit*, for example, looks at the impact on the volunteer in terms of personal development, acquisition of new skills and an increase in earning power; at the impact on users – and on volunteer-involving organisations – in terms of the quantity and quality of the services provided and the extent of the volunteers' contribution to them; and at the extent to which volunteers have improved the quality of life and the facilities and amenities of the local community. These measures are, however, set in a wider framework in which 'the major ways in which stakeholders can be affected are grouped into five types of "capital". The five are:'

> *Physical capital* – refers to outputs such as the number of trees planted or meals delivered by volunteers;

> *Human capital* – the acquisition of knowledge, skills and personal development by the volunteers and those they help;

> *Economic capital* – the effects that can be given a monetary value such as the unpaid work contributed by the volunteers which can benefit both organisations and communities and the development of marketable skills by volunteers and the people they work with;

> *Social capital* – contributing to the creation of a 'more cohesive community through building relationships, networks and bond of trust between people'; and

> *Cultural capital* – 'refers to assets such as a shared sense of cultural and religious identity, including language and heritage'.

(IVR, 2004: 14–15)

This framework captures much – but not all – of the constellation of roles and functions played by volunteering. And it encompasses all of the benefits of volunteering identified by the Commission on the Future of Volunteering (2008: 8–9) to support its assertion that 'volunteers do more than provide extra help and fill gaps in services.... Their contribution is distinctive and critical to how organisations are run and services are delivered'.

But, the line taken by VE and the other volunteering infrastructure bodies remains essentially an instrumental account that overlooks or ignores the importance of the expressive dimension. A recent study of 'how small groups can achieve big things' by Henry Hemming does full justice to the instrumental role of this kind of voluntary action: it is a means of getting things done, it contributes to the physical and mental health of group members and it contributes towards a sense of community. But he is also at pains to point out that participation in volunteer groups provides a sense of camaraderie and fellowship; a sense of belonging or an identity; and, above all, 'an excuse to escape' and 'an adult form of play'. 'These associations take us away from the monotony of daily life, leaving us refreshed and recreated. Without play we forget what it is to see through the eyes of a child and we shrivel up like raisins in the sun' (Hemming, 2011: 277).

In this he is echoing earlier authors like Adams (1981) and Smith (1973) as well as Mason (1996). Adams argued that 'Voluntary action is fun... [T]he undeniable fun of voluntary action seems to me a characteristic of this phenomenon almost entirely overlooked in the literature' (1981: 1, quoted in Mason, 1996: 66). The significance of the play dimension is also noted by Smith (1973: 12, again quoted by Mason, 1996: 66–7):

> To speak of the play element here is not to speak of something trivial and unimportant. As society becomes increasingly complex and as work activity is increasingly structured in terms of large bureaucracies, people's unsatisfied needs for play, novelty experience, and all manner of recreation tend to increase. The kind of easy interchange and blending of play and work that could be present in more traditional economies tends to be lost.

And, we might add, many of today's leisure activities reduce people to the role of spectator or consumer with little opportunity for active participation.

Both Adams and Smith have described volunteering as a combination of play and work. According to Adams, 'Volunteering is not work – you don't get paid for it – but it's not play either – it is, after all, serious; it's playful work, on the one hand, and serious play, on the other' (Adams, 1990: 3). For his part, Smith argues that some basic human needs are satisfied through both 'directly "expressive" ... groups whose aims are explicitly to provide fellowship, sociability and mutual companionship' and 'the sociability aspects of other kinds of collective and interpersonal forms of voluntary action' (Smith, 1973: 116).

As well as meeting the important need for fun and sociability, volunteering also provides a means of engaging in other forms of expressive behaviour. For many, it delivers the opportunity of finding 'pleasure in performance' (Warriner and Prather, 1965) through participation in the arts, sports and games and other forms of recreation, and can be exemplified by the idea of the 'amateur' who, rather than demonstrating the inexpertness associated with the pejorative view of the term, represents the ideal of pursuing an interest to the highest level out of love for the activity rather than financial reward. These kinds of pursuits also offer the possibility of escape from the stresses of everyday life. Hemming (2011: 277) quotes a member of the American Civil War Society who found relief in getting 'away from work, the telephone, the modern lifestyle' in favour of 'a simpler, stress free and slower lifestyle'. And, third, volunteering enables people to give expression to their most cherished beliefs through what Warriner and Prather (1965) term 'ideological symbolism' through churches and organisations like the Daughters of the American Revolution – to use Mason's (1996) example. This is the kind of expressive volunteering that underpins the 'ethical citizenship' displayed by the volunteers involved in the homelessness charities studied by Cloke and his colleagues (2007) and noted above.

The voluntary sector

For the third and final leg of this exploration of the rationale for voluntary action we change the focus again to look not at voluntary organisations, nor at volunteering, but at the field as a whole. A number of explanations have been advanced for the existence of a separate world of voluntary action or a voluntary sector. Three of these are based on utilitarian or instrumental considerations. They are that:

- It is the result of some limitations or deficiencies in the working of the otherwise all-powerful market. This is the view of US economists like Hansmann (1987), who argues that it is based on 'contract failure' theory. This is the view that 'nonprofits of all types typically arise in situations in which, owing either to the circumstances under which a service is purchased or consumed or to the nature of the service itself, consumers feel unable to evaluate accurately the quantity or quality of the service a form produces for them' (1987: 29). In those circumstances, consumers will opt for non-profit firms because they have greater confidence in organisations that have no incentive to take advantage of their customers.

- It is required by the shortcomings of the state. The non-profit form in the USA has been seen (by Weisbrod, 1977) as a provider of public goods which are beyond the scope of governmental agencies, whose provision is restricted by the willingness of the 'median voter' to support it. Non-profit organisations come into being to meet the demand that government is unable to satisfy. This explanation has some currency in the UK, where, for example, the government felt unable to respond to the HIV/AIDS epidemic in its early days and was content to let voluntary organisations meet the challenge. It has also been argued that some kinds of services – such as the provision of advice and information on welfare rights or advocacy on behalf of individual users of public services – are better provided by independent non-state actors.

- It provides us with a different way of doing things and a distinctive means of tackling social need. This view was advanced in the Wolfenden Committee's suggestion that voluntary action provided a kind of middle way – less formally organised than a statutory agency would be but more systematic than informal methods of care. And it is at the heart of Billis and Glennerster's (1998) concept of comparative advantage. The whole idea of 'welfare pluralism' or the 'mixed economy of welfare' depends on the perception that voluntary agencies have something to offer that is distinctive and of a different quality from provision made by governmental bodies or for-profit firms.

There is, however, a very different kind of rationale for the existence of voluntary action which is not so much rooted in economics on the one hand, or organisational theory on the other, but reflects an approach based on political science or sociology. Tony Marshall (1996) uses the idea of 'mediating institutions' advanced by Berger and Neuhaus (1977) to identify a principle that unites the heterogeneous elements that comprise the voluntary sector. Mediating institutions are 'groups or communities which are not so large that individuals cannot identify with them, nor have some meaningful and effective involvement in them, and which themselves link the individual to the nation-state'. They thus provide the means by which individuals may have a 'meaningful relationship' with the state and reduce the risk of anomie and alienation. The voluntary sector 'comprises those mediating institutions through which individuals can share in, and contribute to, meaningful association, the cultural stock of the nation, the material and psychological commonweal, and political action'. Moreover, 'the voluntary sector provides both the adhesive which holds [states] together and the solvent which enables them to change' (Marshall, 1996: 57–9). From this point of view, voluntary action is more than an alternative means of addressing social problems or a vehicle for expressive behaviour and conviviality; it has a vital role to play in social integration and the political process.

Conclusion

At all three levels of analysis – voluntary organisations, volunteering by individuals and the voluntary sector or voluntary action as a whole – the chapter has questioned the validity of the (largely implicit) ways in which the role of voluntary action is understood. It has argued that voluntary organisations have expressive as well as instrumental functions and discussed the ways in which the two elements may be combined. It has suggested that the importance of volunteering is not confined to the ways in which it contributes to service delivery, on the one hand, and personal improvement, on the other, but argues that its significance extends to the opportunities it provides for people to enjoy fun and sociability and escape from the workaday world; to pursue the enjoyment of performance; and to give expression to deeply held values and beliefs. And, finally, it has argued that, as well as offering a different and distinctive way of tackling social need, the voluntary sector has a wider and deeper function as a major part of the 'mediating institutions' of the ungoverned space between the state and the market.

The implications for the study of voluntary action and the formation of policy of this challenge to the instrumental view are far-reaching; they go beyond the addition of 'civil society' to the NCVO's strap-line or the renaming of the relevant part of the Cabinet Office as the Office for Civil Society to a radical change in the way we assess the value of voluntary action and the ways in which we promote and encourage its practice. These will be explored in later chapters of the present volume.

11
The Fallacies of Managerialism

Introduction

This chapter builds on the arguments advanced earlier in the book that voluntary agencies should not be viewed as bureaucracies but have distinctive, ambiguous characteristics (Chapter 7); are not driven by the norms and practices of the market (Chapter 6); and have purposes that go beyond the simply instrumental (Chapter 10). It argues that the approaches and techniques commonly used in the management of business (and adopted by statutory agencies) are not only unhelpful but also damaging when applied to the leadership and management of voluntary sector organisations. It begins by returning to the characterisation of the most common manifestation of the bureaucratic model which was introduced in Chapter 7 – command and control – to explain why it and the managerial approaches that flow from it are inappropriate ways of organising voluntary action. The chapter then looks in turn at the application of four specific managerial techniques – strategic planning, performance and quality management, marketing, and mergers and alliances – in voluntary sector organisations and concludes by suggesting an alternative approach to leading and managing in the voluntary sector.

The alternative to command and control

In a series of articles published in 2007 and 2008 the *Observer*'s former business editor, Simon Caulkin, developed a critique of an approach to management that he felt was becoming almost ubiquitous not only in the UK's corporate world but also in its public sector agencies.

In December 2007 he highlighted the findings of the Chartered Management Institute's 2007 *Quality of Working Life* report that:

> the most commonly experienced management styles in the UK are bureaucratic (the experience of 40% of respondents), reactive (37%) and authoritarian (30%) while just 17% of 1,500 managers polled experienced management as innovative, 15% as trusting and 13% as entrepreneurial.

These averages, he went on to say:

> hide huge differences in perception: what directors and senior managers saw as accessible, empowering and consensual, junior ranks judged bureaucratic (half the sample), reactive (38 per cent) and authoritarian (40 per cent).

And the situation was getting worse:

> Management is becoming more overbearing and controlling. Compared with three years ago, all three of the negative rankings have increased.
>
> (Caulkin, 2007a: 1)

Caulkin advances three reasons for the growing adoption of this command and control approach to management. The first explanation is that it is a response to the difficulty of recruiting staff of the right calibre: 'Many companies are operating with under-qualified, or at least inappropriately qualified staff: Square pegs in round holes don't produce good results, resulting in managerial browbeating or worse.' The second is that it is down to the fashionable importation of the business mores of the USA that produces a combination of 'robust' management methods and a pervasive insecurity of employment. This has been characterised by Cary Cooper of Lancaster Business School (quoted by Caulkin, 2007a: 1) as 'long hours, people as disposable assets, no psychological contract' and 'we'll pay you OK as long as you're delivering, but don't expect any employment commitment in return'. And, the third is that this approach to management is a function of the way in which the great majority of businesses and statutory agencies are structured as what are 'in effect, centrally planned dictatorships that are set up to take orders from the CEO rather than the customer' (Caulkin, 2007a: 2).

The command and control model remains the dominant form of managerialism in the UK and underpins many of the textbooks, 'how-to' manuals and training courses that are increasingly informing the way in which voluntary agencies are managed. It is based on a fundamentally pessimistic view of human nature that sees people as self-interested and prone to subvert the organisations in which they work for their own ends; only the strictest of controls on their freedom of action and ability to use their discretion will protect their employers from the damage they can cause. The readers of Caulkin's weekly columns have provided him with evidence that this approach does not work and that the fundamental belief on which it is based is not self-evidently true. In the first place, the organisations that espouse the command and control approach are frequently not very successful: 'These organisations', he says, 'don't work very well – they can't – and when push comes to shove, as it naturally often does, the knee-jerk reaction is to tighten the reins, not slacken them.'

Second, they have been out-performed by companies and agencies that adopt a very different management paradigm, ranging from the motor manufacturers Toyota to the long-established makers of Gore-Tex and the much newer products of the internet age like Linux and Google (Caulkin, 2007b: 2).

This alternative model of management is based on an optimistic view of human nature: while there need to be measures in place to ensure that employee performance does not fall below the standards required and that unacceptable behaviour is detected and stopped, successful organisations tend to work on the assumption that most of their staff want do a good job and gain satisfaction from doing it well. It also takes a sceptical view of the extent to which chief executives have a monopoly of wisdom and competence; a successful company harnesses the knowledge and expertise of the many rather than depending on the talents of one person. And it tries to ensure that what organisations do and how they do it are driven by the needs and wants of customers or beneficiaries rather than the prescriptions of top managers. Unlike the command and control model, this will give rise to organisations that are decentralised and organised as far as possible into small, self-managing teams; that have as few layers of management as possible – as well as comparatively modest gaps between the highest and the lowest paid staff; and that allow staff a significant amount of discretion about how they carry out their functions. This approach, argues Caulkin, is not 'soft and woolly', nor is it 'bottom-up anarchy': 'it is inside-out. If the organisation is built to face outwards, towards the customer rather than the chief executive, as at present, hierarchy becomes less necessary because it is the customer who exerts the discipline' (Caulkin, 2008: 2).

Since the 1980s voluntary organisations have increasingly been made aware of the need to take management seriously. As noted above, in 1983 NCVO set up a Management Development Unit in response to the report of a working party led by management guru Charles Handy (NCVO, 1981), and its first publication asked 'Can the salt of the earth be managed' (NCVO, 1983). Landry and his colleagues, in a classic study, graphically described the consequences of a failure to address the need for management in 'What a way to run a railroad' (Landry *et al.*, 1985). Unfortunately, the gap which these and other writers perceived has been filled by managerial approaches and techniques based on the 'command and control' model rather than what Zimmeck (2000), writing about the management of volunteers, has called a 'home-grown' alternative that might have resembled Caulkin's '*Observer*' model. It might, too, have provided the kind of organisational form that the Wolfenden Committee described as operating 'in the space between the loosely structured informal system and the more strictly organised statutory system' (Wolfenden, 1978: 29).

Strategic planning

The concept of strategic planning is a key characteristic of the command and control model and one of the ways in which chief executives exercise their top-down authority in organisations. It is no coincidence that the concept of strategy has been borrowed from the vocabulary of the army, where it is the preserve of field marshals or generals. But its use has not been restricted to authoritarian and bureaucratic regimes, and it is widely accepted as an essential means by which voluntary organisations can manage their relationship with their external environment. On the face of it, strategic planning offers some undeniable advantages; it encompasses the whole of an organisation's work; it is outward looking and involves developing strategies for action based on an understanding of what is going on in the outside world; and it looks forward to enable the organisation to plan how to pursue its mission five, ten or more years into the future. And the process through which it is undertaken appears reassuringly thorough and rigorous.

While the exact formulation of how to go about strategic planning varies from author to author (see, for example, Bryson, 1988; Courtney, 1996, 2002; Lyons, 1996), there is general agreement about the main features and stages of the process involved. These can be summarised as:

1. Review or revisit the *mission* or *basic purpose* of the organisation.
2. Undertake an *initial analysis* – scanning the environment for threats and opportunities and clarifying internal strengths and weaknesses.
3. Identify *strategic options* – formulate long-term aims and opportunities which would enable the organisation to achieve its basic purpose.
4. Develop an *operational plan* with concrete and measurable objectives to be achieved over a specified time-scale.
5. Identify the *resources needed* for implementation.
6. *Implement* the plan.
7. *Monitor progress* against the defined objectives.
8. Revisit the *mission* or *basic purpose* of the organisation and begin the process over again.

This general approach has the advantage of providing organisations with a clear and logical step-by-step process of identifying targets, developing the means of working towards them and assessing the 'distance travelled'. The ability of many voluntary sector organisations to translate the strategic planning model into practical action is, however, so limited as to make the approach of very little value to them. In the first place, they do not have the time or energy to commit significant amounts of time to the process of strategic planning, and they therefore risk making superficial and ill-considered responses to the questions it raises. Furthermore, those organisations with an inclusive approach to decision-making will need to apply a greater amount of energy to the process if they are to gain widespread 'buy-in' for the aims and objectives identified by it. In the second place, many organisations will find it unrealistic to invest their time and energy into long-term planning when their access to resources is essentially short-term 'hand-to-mouth' and they might well not have a future for which to plan.

At a more fundamental level, moreover, strategic management is based on some basic assumptions that may be true of private sector businesses but do not apply to many voluntary sector organisations. The first assumption is that the governing body and/or managers of the organisation have perfect control of their organisations so that implementation of any long-term planning is straightforward and unproblematic. Few organisations are simple machines staffed by 'desiccated automatons', and voluntary agencies have more than their share of mavericks who have their own very strongly held views about the mission and values of the organisation. Even agencies which have developed a strong command and control apparatus and a strict bureaucratic hierarchy turn out to be slow to respond to the helmsman's touch on the tiller. The second dubious assumption is that voluntary agencies can easily change or adapt what they do in the light of changes in their environment. While for-profit companies have the luxury of almost limitless choice – they can do anything legal to make a profit for their shareholders and can change the nature of their business as much or as often as they want to – voluntary sector organisations are constrained by their missions and founding values and, as a result, their leaders have comparatively limited room for manoeuvre.

On a more theoretical level, too, the strategic planning rests on foundations that are not altogether solid. It is a form of the kind of technocratic 'rational decision-making' which, although widely promoted, has been exposed as a naïve view of how organisations work and one which ignores the importance of the 'politics' of decision-making. And it is also based on a specific concept that a successful organisation is one that adapts readily to changes in its environment. Again this is widely asserted, but there is evidence that the experience of some bodies can be rather more complex and ambiguous than this. Milofsky and Hunter (1993) have argued, for example, that the original university settlement, Toynbee Hall, has been robustly healthy as an organisation throughout its long history despite having consistently failed to adapt to its environment.

Even if the strategic planning approach rested on more secure practical and theoretical foundations, there are other reasons why it might not be an appropriate technique for the management of voluntary sector organisations. The alternative methods of 'muddling through' and 'steering by the seat of one's pants' need not be a default position reflecting a lack of commitment to management but can have virtues of their own. In the first place, they locate the voluntary organisation in the complex and unpredictable reality of the world as they experience it rather than the simplified rational planning construct within which strategic planning takes place. And, in the second place, the absence of the constraints associated with 'five year plans' and strictly defined objectives means that they have an enhanced ability to adapt what they are doing and behave flexibly as they respond to the changing expression of their needs and demands by those they exist to serve.

The measurement of performance and quality

A second key characteristic of the command and control model is a focus on the measurement of an organisation's performance and 'quality'. 'Over the last decade various consultants, policy analysts, government bodies and the sector's own leaders have urged a range of performance improvement ideas upon the managers of voluntary agencies' (Paton, 2003: 9). These have embraced a variety of approaches including greater attention and better ways of measuring the outputs, outcomes and impacts of the work of voluntary organisations, including social impact measurement and social return on investment; improved financial reporting, including the use of the Statement of Recommended Practice (SORP) for charities; enhanced public communications; benchmarking and the identification of good practice; assessment of 'quality' drawn from the Quality Assurance School and commonly applied through the Practical Quality Assurance System for Small Organisations (PQASSO) system developed by the Charities Evaluation Service; standards based on human resource management like Investors in People; and the 'balanced scorecard' approaches which aim to give appropriate weight to a range of different ways of measuring performance. They have been assiduously promoted by consultants, especially those who have an interest in a specific approach; championed by enthusiasts who have enjoyed using particular tools; and frequently imposed on organisations by funders rather than spontaneously adopted by them.

What these managerial systems and methods have in common is the belief that it is both possible and desirable to identify a range of factors that provide robust indicators of successful activity that can be accurately measured. The techniques are all thus underpinned by the popular maxim of the business schools that 'if it can't be measured, it can't be managed'. They appeal to common sense: how can an organisation be clear about the extent to which it is achieving its aims and objectives without an attempt to measure progress, and how can it improve its performance without a systematic approach to assessing the quality of its work and the effectiveness and efficiency of its operations? And, as Paton argues, explicit and systematic attention to quality and performance issues can provide 'occasions where a range of people in the organisation could discuss the methods, take ownership of them and then play a part in relating them to the specific circumstances they faced' (Paton, 2003: 167). Their advocates also claim that these tools have demonstrated their effectiveness by improving the performance of many companies in the private sector and are, thus, of clear relevance and value to the managers of voluntary and public sector organisations that face very similar challenges. More specifically, they enable voluntary agencies to meet the need to demonstrate to their funders that the investment they have made in the organisation is being used as efficiently and effectively as possible.

On closer inspection, however, the case for applying to voluntary organisations techniques for measuring performance and enhancing quality developed in the business world is open to question. In the first place, the evidence that they have made a significant contribution to the effectiveness of private sector businesses consists largely of anecdotal accounts by practitioners who have adopted the approach and the claims of its proponents and is not supported by systematic research. According to Austin and his colleagues (1998, quoted by Paton, 2003: 37):

> Performance management has a chequered history even in the traditional manufacturing and bureaucratic settings ostensibly most conducive to measuring outputs and causally attributing outputs to individuals and organizational sub-groups. There are many more instances of dysfunction – instances where performance measures stimulate less than optimal or even counter productive behaviours – than there are instances of demonstrable success.

In a similar vein, Neely (1998: 1, again quoted by Paton, 2003: 41) argues that:

> As soon as performance measures are used as a means of control, the people being measured begin to manage the measures rather than performance.

In the second place, the extent to which the techniques of performance measurement developed for the corporate sector are applicable to and useful for voluntary agencies is questionable. As Einstein pointed out, 'not all that is important can be measured; not all that can be measured is important', and there are real issues about how performance and quality can be defined in voluntary sector organisations. There may be important and complex issues of cause and effect; to what extent can the impact of the organisation's work on its beneficiaries be isolated from other changes in the environment and other interventions? And, given that all the aspects of an organisation's work cannot be evaluated, on what basis can a choice be made about what to measure? In practice performance management tends to focus on what can be measured and what can be controlled rather than what is important. The tools can take over and replace rather than stimulate the kind of conversation about ends and means that should be taking place, By offering a schematic and simplified view of the complex reality of the fundamentally ambiguous voluntary agency the performance management approach may end up as a comforting but ultimately unrewarding ritual.

Paton concludes that 'measurement and other techniques are at their best when they support and inform dialogue around different concerns and conceptions of performance. They are least helpful when they are seen as an alternative to dialogue.... In short, communication and the people side of management remain fundamental' (Paton, 2003: 167). Thomas (2003) takes this line of argument a little further: he found that the half of the small organisations in his study which were using some kind of performance measurement tool were no better at address-ing issues of performance and quality than those that had not adopted this approach. In sum, while voluntary organisations benefit from con-tinuous reflection and discussion about how they can best go about their work, attempts to measure performance and quality are at best of limited value and, at worst, may detract from more open-ended consideration of the issues. Moreover, all but the most rudimentary – and therefore least useful – systems for measurement involve a considerable cost in terms of time and energy which voluntary organisations – especially the smaller ones – can ill afford to spare from their front-line activities.

Marketing

A third characteristic of the prevailing model is the adoption of 'a mar-keting approach'. Its origins in the corporate sector are revealed by the definition provided by the Chartered Institute of Marketing and used in one of the key texts: 'Marketing is the management process responsible for identifying, anticipating and satisfying customer require-ments profitably' (Sargent, 2005: 22). This form of words, according to Sargent, makes it clear that 'marketing is both a concept and a func-tion. At a conceptual level, marketing represents a philosophy...that places the customer right at the centre of everything that an organiza-tion does. At a functional level it may be regarded as that part of the organization which gathers research, helps design new services, prices them, distributes them and ultimately promotes them to the consumer.' Marketing as a concept can be reconciled with a fairly common way in which voluntary agencies see themselves (although the identity of their 'customers' can be problematic, as we shall see). But how useful is the business model of the marketing function to voluntary sector organisations?

Another popular book – Ian Bruce's *Successful Charity Marketing* – provides a guide to the key stages in the application of the 'fundamentals' of the marketing approach to the work of charities. Like strategic planning and performance measurement, this offers a smooth and logical step-by-step process that involves:

1. The identification of specific target groups or 'customers'; these include beneficiaries or service users, supporters (such as donors, volunteers and 'advocates'), stakeholders (including staff), funders and regulators.
2. Developing an understanding of the 'social and psychological factors that influence customer take-up behaviour'.
3. Carrying out marketing research: this means collecting data that can help the organisation understand the needs of its customers and beneficiaries using a variety of methods including personal experience, desk research, qualitative assessment by means of interviews and group discussions and the analysis of large data sets.
4. Segmentation: distinguishing between the different groups of customers so that specific products and services can be aimed at them.
5. 'Other-player' analysis: reviewing the activities, products and services of other providers (charities, statutory agencies and for-profit companies) and comparing their skills, resources and organisational effectiveness with your own.
6. Positioning: designing and adapting the organisation's products and services in the light of the views expressed by customers and the position of other players in the market.

(Bruce, 1998: 46–7)

Large voluntary organisations that appeal to large numbers of individual donors; run commercial subsidiaries which raise money by trading; and provide a range of services to a variety of beneficiaries will find this kind of approach helpful, but there are a number of problems involved in applying the approach to small agencies with less developed bureaucratic characteristics. The first problem is the identity of the 'customers' who are to be placed 'right at the centre of everything that an organization does'. This is not a problem in the commercial world where those who consume the products and services provided by the company also pay for them. Voluntary organisations, however, generally do not charge those who use their services, but raise the costs of providing them from other sources. To describe their relationships with both groups as providing products and services to 'customers' is to ignore the very different nature of the two sets of relationships and the tension between satisfying the needs of beneficiaries, on the one hand, and meeting the expectations of the funders, on the other.

Adopting the marketing management approach adds weight to the growing tendency of voluntary agencies to regard their funders as the customers to whom they need to sell their products rather than treating the users of their services as their principal consumers. In an earlier era, when the principal funding mechanism was grant aid, it was possible for organisations to put the service users at the centre of their concerns and look to the funder for the means through which their needs could be met. Successive waves of contracting and commissioning have changed the balance: organisations are increasingly required to compete for the approval of funding bodies to deliver services defined by the funders to people they have identified as being in need and who are increasingly relegated to the status of 'end-users'.

A second problem for voluntary organisations in using a marketing approach is the nature of the 'market', the acceptance of the idea that organisations are part of a market in which they compete with other voluntary organisations, social enterprises, commercial businesses and statutory agencies for contracts to deliver public services. In the past, some at least of these rivals would be seen as colleagues and collaborators that shared the same aspiration to meet the needs of specific groups of disadvantaged people. Information and expertise that might once have been used to improve the lot of beneficiaries are now likely to be treated as 'commercially sensitive' and deployed as a means of securing contracts.

Merger mania

The final – although rather different – key characteristic of the prevailing approach to management is the vogue for mergers and alliances between voluntary agencies. Much of this is externally driven. Governments – and, to a lesser extent, other funding bodies – have wanted to 'rationalise' the world of voluntary action since the end of the First World War (Penn, 2011), primarily for their own convenience. Ministers and civil servants alike are confused and irritated by what they see as the anarchic nature of the voluntary sector with its apparent duplication of functions and its plethora of intermediary or representative bodies. Above all, they are seeking an answer to what Nicholas Deakin has called 'the Kissinger Question', after the US Secretary of State was reputed to have asked: 'If I want to speak to Europe, who do I phone?' Governments believe they would gain from the consolidation of the sector's many organisations into a smaller number of larger entities. They would find it easier to manage their relationships with fewer bodies who could 'speak for the sector' and would be more at home with larger, more bureaucratic organisations that worked in a way they would find familiar. Wherever possible, governments have worked for this kind of rationalisation. They have promoted the transformation of federated organisations in which largely autonomous local groups have set up a national focus for representation and service into centralised national organisations with local groups which are subordinate to the central apparatus – as, for example, in the case of Victim Support. And organisations working in a similar field have been 'encouraged' to merge; the creation of VE from three very different organisations is one example at national level. And at local level the Coalition has pursued a policy of 'rationalising' local infrastructure by using its Transforming Local Infrastructure Fund as a means of consolidating local intermediaries with the aim of ensuring that there will be only one of them in each local authority area.

Mergers and alliances are not, however, promoted solely as a means of meeting governments' preferences; they are also held to offer a number of intrinsic advantages. The rational case is that they will create stronger organisations with wider support bases and a greater range of funding sources; they will result in economies of scale and the more efficient use of physical resources like buildings and equipment; they will enable organisations to achieve a higher profile and a stronger voice for their cause; and they will eliminate unnecessary and inefficient duplication of provision (Guthrie, 2000). But the research literature suggests that – in the voluntary sector as well as in the wider world of business – mergers are rarely driven by rational and strategic choices of this kind.

They are more likely to happen as the result of:

- a crisis or major 'disturbance' in the environment that presents a threat to organisational survival;
- the need to identify and occupy an organisational niche as a means of ensuring the organisation's survival;
- financial and other weaknesses;
- resource dependency; and/or
- a drive for growth and greater 'market share' (which is seen as a good in itself).

The process of merger also involves substantial costs and significant dis-advantages. It requires a high level of leadership and management as well as a major commitment of time and energy over a long period. And it can involve high levels of stress among those concerned, the disrup-tion of normal activities and a significant loss of efficiency in the short term. Successful mergers between voluntary agencies, moreover, may also have to overcome some major obstacles and barriers. In the first place, there may be differences in organisational structures to reconcile: the merger that led to the formation of VE involved an organisation with a centralised 'top-down' structure (the National Centre for Volun-teering); a federal body in which the central office was held accountable to its locally based members (Volunteer Development England); and a confederation of national organisations (the Consortium on Opportu-nities for Volunteering). In the second place, the organisational goals, values and cultures of the agencies involved may not be compatible. And, finally, some of an organisation's most valuable assets – the com-mitment of its volunteers, staff, supporters and donors – may not be transferable to a new structure.

These factors help to explain why there have been comparatively few successful mergers in the voluntary sector and why many of them are more correctly seen as acquisitions or takeovers than genuine mergers:

> A merger is the combination of two organisations into one. Merger is a high-stakes, high-risk, medium term strategy, requiring careful planning and management. The gains in terms of effectiveness and efficiency in the medium to long term must outweigh the short-term costs and risks. Takeovers are easier to manage and more likely to be regarded as successful than mergers of equals.
>
> (Guthrie, 2000: 23)

On the other hand, the evidence from the corporate world suggests that even takeovers rarely succeed: 'A 2004 study by Bain and Company found that 70% of mergers failed to increase shareholder value. More recently, a 2007 study by Hay Group and the Sorbonne found that more than 90% of mergers in Europe fail to reach financial goals' (Voight, 2009: 1). In the voluntary sector the definition of a successful takeover is not such an easy matter. The acquisition may well strengthen the stronger partner and can, to that extent, represent a gain in the sense that it can pursue its mission or cause with additional vigour. Against this, however, needs to be set the cost to the weaker partner. While it may be freed from the struggle to survive and the risk of closure, this might be at the expense of any sense of control over its future and the loss of its values and culture, that is to say, everything it has stood for. This can be seen as a loss to the diversity and strength of the sector as a whole.

Conclusion: Management or leadership?

Both the dominant command and control approach to management and the specific techniques of strategic planning, performance and quality measurement and management, marketing and the structural rationalisation through mergers and takeovers are taken from the theory and practice of the corporate sector and have been widely adopted and adapted for use in those voluntary sector organisations we have identified as 'entrenched hybrids'. There is evidence to suggest that their virtues have been exaggerated even on their 'home ground', and this chapter has argued that they are of dubious worth as the means of running genuinely ambiguous or hybrid voluntary agencies. And, if these approaches are unhelpful, it follows that voluntary organisations are not best led by people who have been trained in their application: in short, they do not need this kind of 'manager'. Instead, they need a type of leadership that is a more complete reflection of the complex nature of the voluntary organisation. The organisation's activities and behaviour will be determined not only by the exercise of the sanctioned power or authority vested in its bureaucratic dimension but also by the kind of leadership which is based in securing the willing consent of its constituents and is derived from its associational roots.

This kind of leadership needs some explanation. It is a far cry from the Napoleonic model of the visionary and all-powerful chief executive or the self-appointed leader of the sector who command attention in the sector's 'trade press'. In the first place, we can make a distinction between management and leadership. *Managers* co-ordinate the various functions of organisations and direct and supervise the work of subordinates. They tend to be seen as the key figures in the kind of organisation that can be conceived of as a machine and their work is based on the mastery of a collection of techniques. *Leaders*, by contrast, are seen as providing guidance and direction in organisations which can be viewed 'as societies or communities, rather than machines or warehouses' (Handy, 1988: 20). Their role is essentially political rather than technical. This is the kind of leadership which Kay (1996) has suggested as the approach which is most appropriate for voluntary sector organisations. His definition includes three important elements. In the first place, leadership is about taking people with you because they buy into a vision of how all those concerned can move forward together. Second, it involves creating and sustaining a number of meanings, such as the ethos of the organisation, the ways in which it should be working and a sense of the direction in which it is travelling. And, third, it is not necessarily exercised by an individual; it can be undertaken by a group. Indeed, the process of creating and sustaining meaning can involve a number of people, and the weight given to any explanation will be judged according to its merit rather than by the role or position of the person putting it forward.

12
Towards a 'Round Earth' Map of Volunteering

Introduction

The salient features of the 'dominant paradigm' of volunteering in the UK have been discussed in Chapter 4. The development of what has been called the 'volunteering industry' – which includes major volunteer-involving organisations; specialist national and local infrastructure bodies; and an emerging profession of volunteer management – is based on a number of widely accepted assumptions about the nature of individual voluntary action. These provide us with narrow definitions of volunteer motivation; the areas of social life in which volunteers are active; the organisational context within which volunteering takes place; and the ways in which volunteering roles are defined. In the process the dominant paradigm ignores or excludes a great deal of volunteer activity to leave us with a partial or, to use David Horton Smith's (2000) metaphor, a 'flat earth' map of the territory. This chapter sets out a more comprehensive or 'round earth' approach to volunteering by introducing two additional paradigms and combining them with the dominant model to create a three-perspective map which captures more fully some of the diversity of volunteering. This part of the chapter is based on the argument previously developed by the author and colleagues in Chapter 2 of *Volunteering and Society in the 21st Century* (Rochester *et al.*, 2010: 10–16). The chapter goes on to examine critically an attempt to capture the full range of global volunteering activity in typologies developed for the United Nations Volunteers before discussing some of the implications for theory and practice of these more comprehensive models of volunteering.

The dominant paradigm

In the UK, the USA and other Western 'developed' societies, volunteering is seen – by policy-makers, practitioners and researchers alike – through the lens of what Lyons and his colleagues (1998) have called the 'non-profit paradigm'. While the existence of other forms of volunteering has been acknowledged (by, for example, Musick and Wilson, 2008 and the Commission on the Future of Volunteering, 2007, 2008), this paradigm remains the 'default setting' for the analysis and discussion of volunteering in these societies. According to Lyons and his colleagues, research in particular is shaped by the interests of academics in the fields of economics, law and management studies while theory and practice are generally built on some basic assumptions about volunteers and volunteering.

The key elements of the non-profit paradigm are:

Motivation: in the first place, the non-profit paradigm assumes that the key motivation to volunteer is based on altruism. While there has been increasing recognition that people volunteer for a mixture of different kinds of reasons, the dominant view of volunteering is that it is essentially an act of philanthropy – a gift of time that can be treated as analogous to the donation of money. From this perspective people volunteer in order to help others who are less fortunate than themselves.

Areas of activity: in the second place, the paradigm assumes that volunteering takes place in the (broadly defined) field of social welfare. It contributes to the provision of advice, care and support for the benefit of people in need such as children, older people, people with disabilities or mental and physical health issues, and those living in poverty or social exclusion.

Organisational context: in the third place, it assumes that, in the normal course of events, opportunities for volunteering will be provided by large, professionally staffed and formally structured organisations. While these are most likely to be charities or voluntary sector organisations, they also include statutory agencies like hospitals, prisons or schools. Volunteers provide significant additional resources in the form of unpaid labour and are increasingly treated as 'human resources' that need formal and skilled management of a similar kind to that provided for paid employees.

Volunteer roles: finally, the non-profit paradigm assumes that the work to be carried out by volunteers is defined in advance by the volunteer-involving organisation. People are recruited for specific roles or tasks, and this may involve a more or less formal process of selection, induction and, in some cases, training. Roles are usually subordinate or supplementary – volunteers can take on routine tasks and enable paid staff to concentrate on the key operational activities of the agency – although some organisations, like Citizens' Advice Bureaux, deploy them in front-line roles. The contribution made by board members or trustees is frequently ignored in this view of volunteering and is seen as belonging to a different set of concerns labelled 'governance'.

The 'civil society' paradigm

A very different perspective on volunteering is provided by what Lyons and his colleagues have termed the 'civil society' paradigm, which is predominant in other parts of the world, including much of Europe and the developing countries of the global South. Unlike the 'non-profit' paradigm, it has its academic roots in political science and sociology and involves very different definitions of volunteer motivations; the areas of activity in which they are involved; the organisational context for their activities; and the kind of roles they play.

The key elements of the civil society paradigm are:

Motivation: in the first place, the civil society paradigm assumes that, rather than an altruistic or philanthropic impulse to help other, less fortunate, people, volunteers are motivated by self-help and mutual aid. Their activities are based on the ability of people 'to work together to meet shared needs and address common problems' (Lyons *et al.*, 1998: 52).

Areas of activity: in the second place, the civil society paradigm assumes, first, that the involvement of volunteers in social welfare takes the form of offering mutual support in self-help groups or campaigning for better provision rather than delivering care and other services. It also assumes that volunteer activities are not confined to the field of social welfare (however broadly defined) but that they are also involved in a whole range of other areas of public policy such as transport, planning issues and the environment.

Organisational context: in the third place, the paradigm assumes that, rather than being undertaken through voluntary or non-profit agencies with paid managers and staff, volunteering takes place in associations or self-help groups rather than voluntary or non-profit agencies with paid managers and staff. Recently there has been a greater degree of interest in the organisational forms referred to as 'grassroots associations' in the USA (Smith, 2000) and as constituting a 'community sector' in the UK (Rochester, 1997, 1998).

Volunteer roles: finally, the paradigm assumes that volunteers are members of associations and not only provide them with leadership but also undertake all of their operational activities, rather than being helpers who are recruited to play specific roles within organisations. The roles played by these member activists 'cannot be defined in advance' but 'will be developed over time in the light of experience, personal growth and reflection' (Rochester, 1999: 9).

This kind of voluntary action is sometimes referred to as 'horizontal volunteering' to distinguish it from the 'vertical' kind found in the dominant paradigm and can be characterised as activism rather than unpaid help. The scale and importance of this form of activity is generally underestimated in the UK and other places where the dominant paradigm holds sway. This low profile may be due in part to the small size of the individual organisations involved and the perception that they are run for the benefit of their members rather than for the public as a whole. But the number of grassroots associations, community groups and self-help groups is very high, and the contribution they make collectively to the quality of life and living conditions is very significant (Rochester, 1997).

Volunteering as serious leisure

By retrieving 'volunteering as activism' from out of the shadow of the dominant paradigm of 'volunteering as unpaid help or service', Lyons and his colleagues have made a major contribution to the development of a more rounded view of volunteering. We need, however, a third perspective – volunteering as serious leisure – to enable us to achieve a truly 'round earth' map of the territory. On the one hand, this perspective is simple common sense: volunteering is something we do in our leisure time and it has been identified as such by scholars for at least 30 years. Stebbins (2004), for example, cites work by Bosserman and Gagan (1972) and Smith (1975). On the other hand, this perspective has been largely neglected by scholarly writing on volunteering. This lack of interest may be explained by the association of leisure with frivolous activities that are at odds with the serious business of voluntary action and the pejorative connotations of words like 'amateur' and 'hobbyist'. More recently, however, the idea of volunteering as leisure has been explored in a series of articles by Stebbins (see, for example, Stebbins, 1996; Stebbins and Graham, 2004) which distinguished between three kinds of leisure volunteering:

- *Casual volunteering*, exemplified by 'cooking hot dogs at a church picnic or taking tickets for a performance by a local community theatre';
- *Project-based volunteering*, which is 'a short-term, reasonably complicated, one-off or occasional, though infrequent, creative undertaking' which might involve participation in the organisation of a sporting or cultural event; and
- *Volunteering as serious leisure*, which involves 'the systematic pursuit of...a hobby or a voluntary activity sufficiently substantial and interesting in nature for the participants to find a (non-work) career therein acquiring and expressing a combination of its special skills, knowledge and experience'.

(Stebbins, 2004: 5–7)

This last category provides us with a third paradigm with the following key elements:

Motivations: in the first place, the serious leisure paradigm assumes that volunteers are driven by essentially intrinsic rather than extrinsic motivations. Volunteers engage in serious leisure activities because of enthusiasm for the specific form of involvement and commitment to developing the expertise needed to practise it. For some, it can involve the use of 'free' time to create a substitute for the kinds of intrinsic satisfaction not available to them at work. For others, it represents a chance to express dimensions of their personalities that have no other means of expression.

Areas of activity: in the second place, the serious leisure paradigm focuses on volunteers in the fields of arts, culture, sports and recreation, where they form a large – and often unseen – part of the volunteering population. Activities include performance art such as theatre, music and dancing; the fine arts – painting and sculpture; archaeology, local history and heritage; ornithology and other aspects of natural history; the full gamut of organised sports; and recreational pursuits such as rambling and climbing.

Organisational context: in the third place, the paradigm addresses volunteering both within large and complex organisations and in small, community-based voluntary groups. Many local societies or clubs, such as sports clubs, are, moreover, connected to wider structures at regional and national level.

Volunteer roles: finally, the serious leisure paradigm assumes that volunteers play a great variety of roles. They may be performers or practitioners; conductors, directors, tutors or coaches; officials or administrators; or technical or maintenance workers. And there are frequent opportunities to move from one role to another.

A three-perspective model

Each of the three paradigms set out above captures a part of the phenomenon of volunteering; we can easily identify examples of volunteering opportunity as unpaid work or service; activism; and serious leisure. Separately, however, they do not adequately reflect the complexity of many volunteering experiences. If we take as a model from Billis (1993a) the use of overlapping circles to identify ambiguities and hybrid forms, the result is Figure 12.1.

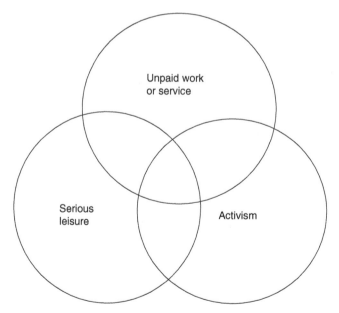

Figure 12.1 A three perspectives model

Alongside the unambiguous forms of volunteering as unpaid work or service, activism and serious leisure, we have identified four hybrid forms where either the nature of the organisation through which volunteering takes place or the combination of roles undertaken by the volunteer means that more than one perspective is required to understand the kind of volunteering involved. These hybrid forms are:

- Volunteering which can be seen as a combination of unpaid work and activism: this would include, for example, the kinds of activities undertaken by volunteers in bureaucratic or hybrid organisations whose main functions are campaigning rather than service delivery.
- Volunteering which can be seen as a combination of activism and serious leisure: this would include the work of people who dedicate much of their spare time to promoting social or small 'p' political causes in which they passionately believe and who develop both an expert knowledge of their field of interest and a set of skills in communications and public relations that enable them to exert an influence on the media and public opinion.
- Volunteering which can be seen as a combination of serious leisure and unpaid work: this would include volunteering by those whose involvement in the work of an organisation in the field of social welfare can involve the acquisition of the knowledge and skills that enable them to make a bigger or better contribution to its work.
- Volunteering which can be seen as a combination of all three elements: this would include volunteering by those who contribute unpaid work to an organisation which gives expression to their social or political aspirations and provides them with an activity substantial and interesting enough to provide them with a (non-work) career that often compensates for the lack of such satisfaction in their paid work.

Mapping by typology: The global reach of the UN

The development of a conceptual map of this kind is an important way of ensuring that any account of volunteering extends across the full gamut of the opportunities and activities through which it is expressed. But it is not the only way. Another valuable approach has been the creation of typologies that systematically separate out the various manifestations of voluntary action. Not surprisingly, given its global reach, it is the volunteering arm of the United Nations – United Nations

Volunteers (UNV) – that has produced some of the most comprehensive and detailed maps of this kind.

The first of three such initiatives was developed in advance of the UN's International Year of Volunteers (IYV) 2001. It provides a means of encompassing the full range of volunteering in all of its global diversity by identifying four broad, distinctive strands of voluntary action. These are:

> *Mutual aid or self-help*: probably the oldest form of voluntary action, in which people with shared problems, challenges and conditions work together to address or ameliorate them. Sometimes described as voluntary action 'by us, for us'.

> *Philanthropy and service to others*: what most people in the UK would identify as volunteering; typically involving an organisation which recruits volunteers to provide some kind of service to one or more third parties.

> *Participation*: the involvement on a voluntary basis in the political or decision-making process at any level from participation in a users' forum to holding honorary office in a voluntary sector organisation.

> *Advocacy or campaigning*: collective action aimed at securing or preventing change, which includes campaigning against developments seen as damaging to the environment and campaigning for better services – for example, for people with HIV/AIDS.
>
> (Davis Smith, 2000: 11–13)

Davis Smith's 'broad brush' approach is complemented by a second initiative, the detailed checklist of activities that was also developed as part of the preparations for the IYV. This was intended to provide a means of assisting people throughout the world to produce comprehensive surveys of the extent and nature of voluntary activity in their areas (Dingle, 2001). This long list was summarised by Rochester and his colleagues (2010: 27–9) as:

> *Children and youth*, which involves helping to set up or manage programmes that tackle problems affecting young people such as delinquency, neglect and abuse, helping to provide services to children and young people; helping to set up or organise a day-care programme, or taking care of children while their parents or carers are working;

Community activity, which includes helping to bring in the harvest and other resources that are vital for the community; removing rubbish or debris from public areas or making improvements to them; organising a collective response to a problem affecting a community; or drawing public attention to a problem faced by the community;

Promotion of commerce, which involves helping to improve or promote the production of goods, the exchange of goods and services and product safety, or setting up or managing a programme or organisation designed to promote these interests;

Community peacekeeping, which might involve helping organise members of the community to maintain order (e.g. patrolling public areas); taking part in direct action to investigate or prevent illegal or detrimental activity; helping to resolve a dispute between groups or communities; or helping to set up or organise a conflict resolution programme;

Culture, which involves helping to plan, set up, advertise, manage, provide technical assistance at, maintain order at, and clean up after a cultural event for public entertainment; or acting, performing music, singing, dancing, reading poetry, lecturing or displaying one's works of arts and crafts at a cultural event for public entertainment;

Data collection, which involves collecting specimens, reading scientific instruments, observing the weather for research or science; observing or interviewing people for research purposes; consulting archives and other documents for research purposes; or setting up or managing a programme or organisation designed to collect data for public information;

Economic justice, which involves helping to organise people to advance or protect their economic interests (e.g. setting up a union or campaign about working conditions); or participating in direct action, such as a strike, to protect the interests of working people;

Education, which involves teaching or training others to acquire new skills; or helping to set up or manage a school or other educational institution;

Emergency response, which involves such activities as helping to prepare for a natural disaster or eliminate its effects (e.g. building dykes or putting out fires), save victims of a disaster from immediate danger, provide comfort for victims of disaster or organise a response to a disaster;

Environment, which involves campaigning against threats to the environment or on behalf of endangered indigenous peoples;

Health care, which involves helping to disseminate information or organise a programme addressing health issues; helping to provide support services for health care institutions; providing health care or rehabilitation services; donating blood, bone marrow or organs; or setting up or managing a programme designed to provide health care, treatment or health education;

Human rights, advocacy and politics, which involves contacting and organising people to advance their political interests, such as encouraging people to vote or helping candidates; participating in direct action (such as a demonstration or march); supporting a social or political cause; helping to elect a candidate for political office; helping to set up or manage elections; or setting up or managing a party or other political organisation;

Law and legal services, which involves providing legal advice or legal representation on a *pro bono* basis; helping to promote a general understanding of the law and legal rights; or setting up or managing a programme to provide legal advice and representation on a *pro bono* basis;

Personal assistance, which includes providing counselling, emotional support or advice to friends, colleagues and neighbours, or helping to provide food or other necessities of life for them;

Promotion of knowledge, which involves disseminating knowledge or professional skills by giving public lectures, writing or editing articles or serving on the board of a professional association; helping to organise a public event aimed at disseminating knowledge or professional skills; setting up or managing an organisation aimed at representing professional interests; facilitating communication within professions; or disseminating information about them;

Recreation, which involves helping to plan, set up, advertise, manage, provide technical assistance at, maintain order at, and clean up after a sporting or recreation event for public entertainment; or taking part as a player, contestant, team member or participant in any of these events which were organised in support of a public cause rather than purely for one's own enjoyment;

Religious volunteering, which includes helping to organise a special event to celebrate a religious holiday or as an act of worship; promoting religious faith or values; participating in direct action to bring attention to a matter of religious intolerance; helping to set up or manage a church or other religious body; or helping to organise a funeral; and

Social assistance, which includes helping to provide immediate assistance to people in need (such as food, shelter and health care); helping to build structures to house or help people in need; or setting up or managing a programme or organisation to provide help for people in need.

More recently, in a third initiative, UNV has returned to the issue of classifying different types of volunteering as part of the process of reviewing developments in voluntary action during the decade following the International Year in 2001. In a series of so-far unpublished papers prompted by a brief to report on 'less recognised impacts of volunteering' for UNV, Jurgen Grotz has developed a further 'purposive typology' (Grotz, 2011; Smith and Grotz, 2011; Grotz, 2012). Having reviewed a number of existing typologies, he 'followed the tradition of his predecessors and created a typology to suit the task' (Grotz, 2012: 3). He used Rochester's tripartite conceptual map as a starting point, but this, like the four groupings proposed by Davis Smith, was too broadbrush for his purposes. At the same time, the detailed checklist of 18 different activities was too heterogeneous for his taste and he steered a course between them to produce seven categories or 'purposive' types. Some of the categories are familiar.

1. What Grotz calls the *traditional service type* is essentially the kind of volunteering identified in what Lyons and his colleagues have called the 'non-profit paradigm' and thus the dominant perspective in the UK. Grotz does, however, make a useful distinction within this category between the direct provision of help to people in need, on the one hand, and raising and administering funds to support the work, on the other.

2. Grotz's second category – *the mutual aid type* – is also based on the work of Lyons and his colleagues. It is sub-divided into different kinds of groups and their roles, including co-operatives which meet an economic need; friendly societies which provide social security and insurance; self-help groups which contribute to health and social welfare; and 'fraternities which provide companionship and favours'.

3. Like Davis Smith, Grotz categorises political engagement and activism as distinct or separate from mutual aid (these are conflated in Lyons and his colleagues' 'civil society paradigm'). And he then sub-divides them further. His third category becomes the *political and*

social engagement type, in which volunteers are involved, on the one hand, in supporting the work of the established political parties and, on the other, take on civic roles like school governor or magistrate.

4. Grotz's fourth category is the *activism type*. Unlike the *political and social engagement type*, this involves situations in which volunteers 'act outside the established political and public processes of government and governance' to pursue their objectives.

5. His fifth category – the *occupational support type* – is one of two kinds of activity which were represented in the long check-list but not mentioned in the more broad-brush groupings. Here people who work together or are in a similar occupation take collective action in pursuit of common goals. Grotz sub-divides them into trades unions; professional and scientific bodies; farmers' groups; and organisations of business people or trade associations.

6. The *religiosity type* – Grotz's sixth category – is the second of these two 'additional categories'. It includes all kinds of volunteering which takes place in a religious context, and this includes both activities in and for religious congregations and faith-based service organisations (although the latter might appear to be better located in the 'traditional service type').

7. Grotz's final category – *the leisure type* – then returns us to more familiar territory.

As we have seen, Grotz allows himself a wry comment on the way in which successive researchers have felt the need to devise individual typologies to shape their work and their conclusions. On one level, this is a perfectly sensible and defensible way of proceeding in the absence of a single, unifying theory of volunteering; each researcher crafts a typology that fits her or his needs. But, by the same token, the plethora of typologies is evidence of a substantial lack of consensus about volunteering and the variety of activities and purposes it encompasses.

Conclusions

This chapter has no ambition to fill the gap and present an overarching theoretical framework for the study of volunteering. It has not even discussed anything like the full range of ways in which volunteers and volunteering can be classified. It has not, for example, looked at 'typologies based on differences in the characteristics and attitudes of volunteers and the kind of involvement or relationship they have with the organisations through which they engage in voluntary action' (Rochester *et al.*, 2010: 29). Its purpose has been a good deal more modest. It has tried to expose the inadequacies of the 'dominant paradigm' as a means of describing what volunteering is and what forms it takes and to replace it with more of a 'round-earth' map of the terrain. As a map it is incomplete in places, lacks detail in many areas and is not necessarily to be trusted. On the other hand, it does indicate the existence of many of the key features of a landscape that are completely – and perhaps wilfully – ignored. At a minimum, it provides a guide to what exists beyond the dominant paradigm and an invitation to explore the wide world of volunteering in the hope that other travellers will follow the tracks we have sketched out and fill in the detail of some, if not all, of the many facets of voluntary action that have been comparatively neglected.

13
Dissenting Voices: The Case of the National Coalition for Independent Action

This chapter focuses on the dissenters who did not join the 'product champions' described in Chapter 8 but expressed concern and outright opposition to the trends dominating the recent history of voluntary action – and especially what was seen as the encroachment by the state on the independence historically enjoyed by voluntary organisations. It begins by discussing the initiatives taken by the Baring Foundation in developing its *Strengthening the Voluntary Sector* Programme and setting up an independent panel to monitor the state of sector independence. The main body of the chapter, however, focuses on the most active and least compromising of the critics of current trends – the NCIA – and reviews its foundation and development as an organisation; its assessment of the situation in which the voluntary sector found itself; and some of the activities it undertook to address the issues and problems identified by this analysis. This part of the chapter is based on the NCIA's internal documents. The chapter concludes by discussing the implications of the NCIA's analysis and experience for the theory and practice of voluntary action.

A new focus on sector independence

During 2006 and 2007, concern about the voluntary sector's relationship with the state was – briefly – high on the agenda for a number of bodies. In February 2007 the Directory of Social Change (DSC) published *The Interplay between State, Private Sector and Voluntary Activity: A Vision for the Future* (Wittenberg, 2007). Later that year, the Charity Commission presented the findings of its survey of the concerns expressed by registered charities about their participation in delivering public services, *Stand and Deliver: The future for charities providing public services* (Charity Commission, 2007) and Compact Voice published

Stronger independence, Stronger relationships, Better outcomes (Compact Voice, 2007). These three reports identified serious concerns about the way that the freedom of voluntary organisations to determine their own agendas was being eroded. The DSC report argued that 'the future of the sector is not for the government to determine' and that 'Involvement by the state should *enable* voluntary activity rather than seeking to control or harness it for particular purposes' (Wittenberg, 2007: 7, 11). The Charity Commission's survey of more than 3,800 charities found that only 26% of those that delivered public services felt free to make decisions without pressure to conform to the wishes of funders. And Compact Voice found that 69% of its membership said that funded groups feared that campaigning would affect their future funding, while 59% said that local public bodies were not demonstrating that they understood independence, despite the widespread adoption of local compacts which were expected to protect the rights of voluntary organisations to campaign and to criticise government policy 'irrespective of any funding relationship that might exist and to determine and manage its own affairs' (Compact Voice, 2007: 2).

It was against this background of concern that the Baring Foundation made the independence of the sector a new focus for its work. The Foundation has provided grants to voluntary organisations pursuing charitable purposes since it was established in 1969. In 1996 it set up a new grants programme called *Strengthening the Voluntary Sector* (STVS) that funded organisational development activities aimed at enhancing the efficiency and effectiveness of successful applicants.

> The programme excluded funding for services, with support being focused on strengthening the core systems, skills, structures and strategies that make up the infrastructure of an organisation. Consequently, the Foundation has supported a range of activities, from strategic planning to management training, from improving financial systems to strengthening user involvement.
>
> (Smerdon, 2006: 1)

Ten years later, in 2006, the Foundation gave this programme a new focus and invited organisations to apply for grants to support 'work that would help them to maintain or increase their independence from government' (Smerdon, 2006: inside cover). The new phase of the STVS programme was, moreover, to consist of more than opportunities for voluntary organisations to obtain funding for these kinds of activity; it also involved the publication of a series of papers aimed at drawing out 'the lessons learned through the grant-making'.

The first of these papers – written by the Foundation's Assistant Director, Matthew Smerdon, and entitled *Allies not servants: Voluntary sector relations with government* – set out the rationale for the new focus. It argued that government policies based on the assumption that voluntary organisations could and should play a bigger role in delivering public services imposed strains on them as well as offering wider opportunities and, in the process, might involve a risk to their independence. One way of responding to the threat to their autonomy was for organisations to develop and strengthen the organisational characteristics that would enable them 'to move towards a more productive relationship with government ... which can be summarised under two headings'. The first grouped together activities that enabled voluntary organisations to demonstrate their *legitimacy* – 'the justification for existing and having a seat at the table'. These included: effective user involvement in planning and management; better ways of collecting evidence of need; improved methods of assessing the quality and impact of what they did; and effective management and strong governance. The second theme was the *ability to act with confidence*, and this involved improving skills, capacity and expertise in negotiating and campaigning; better approaches to calculating costs and pricing services; and developing communication strategies and the skills needed to implement them (Smerdon, 2006).

A second paper reviewed the 515 applications received for the first round of funding under the refocused STVS programme and presented an analysis of the information they provided about what applicants saw as the nature of threats to their independence and the steps they could take to resist them. This study found that 'a diversity of organisations from across the whole voluntary sector' had experienced threats to their independence. The most common of these were the result of changes to funding criteria as the result of policy shifts and contracts which were focused on specific users or areas of work to the exclusion of support for the organisation's key activities. But more than a tenth of applicants to the programme reported that government was simply not prepared to listen to their views. Many applicants, however, felt that they could 'find ways of strengthening their independence' that would help them 'take control of their agendas'. The most common responses to the threat were 'developing confidence through extending skills' (62%) and 'creating confidence through organisational competence' (52%), while more than a third of the applicants claimed that they could 'strengthen independence through [the] greater legitimacy' associated with 'participative governance' (Pharoah, 2007: 8, 14).

These findings need to be assessed in the context of the objectives and limits of the grant programme from which these informants were seeking funding. STVS was founded on the assumption that 'organisations have a responsibility to ensure their own independence. They can be helped...but, in the end no one else will do it for them' (Smerdon, 2007: 6). As a result, applicants have focused on the extent to which the solutions to the problems they were facing were in their own hands. But the unaided efforts of individual organisations can only provide part of the response. Pharoah acknowledges that 'As the sector continues to grow and develop, it is important to ensure that it is shaped by policies which preserve and promote the very qualities which government is seeking when it commissions from sector providers and invests in sector capacity-building' (Pharoah, 2007: 1). And, arguably, an enlightened approach of this kind is more likely to occur as the result of collective pressure from the sector rather than the reaction of individual organisations.

The evolution of the STVS programme since 2006 has been shaped to some extent by the Foundation's realisation that it needed to do more than fund the enhancement of skills and systems in individual agencies. In the first place, it has narrowed the focus of its grant-giving to one area of voluntary action – the advice sector – so that the experience and learning of each grant recipient can be shared with its peers and promote action across the sector. Second, it has convened an 'Independence Summit' in 2009 which brought together a panel of speakers from foundations (Baring and Joseph Rowntree) and statutory bodies (the Charity Commission, the Commissioner for the Compact and the Office of the Third Sector) to introduce and stimulate a discussion about current initiatives to promote independence – what was being done, what was being learned – and about future challenges to independence and how these might be addressed. The 70 'practitioners, policy makers, funders and academics' who took part spent much of the day working in small groups and identified 'five priorities for action':

- Challenging the market model and commissioning;
- Increasing the scale and quality of campaigning;
- Ensuring independence is to the fore in the public perception of charities;
- Ensuring independence through governance; and
- Making use of the Compact (Baring Foundation, 2009: 3).

While the Foundation has retained its belief that 'the prime responsibility for maintaining independence rests with voluntary organisations themselves – trustees, staff and the people and communities they serve'

(Panel on the Independence of the Voluntary Sector, 2011: 6) – the summit's additional focus on the role of other players has been carried forward into its third major initiative – establishing and supporting the work of a Panel on the Independence of the Voluntary Sector. This has been set up 'to ensure that independence is seen as a top priority by the voluntary sector and those with whom it works, to monitor changes and make recommendations affecting all those involved' and 'to stimulate reflection, debate and action and make recommendations affecting all those involved' (Panel on the Independence of the Voluntary Sector, 2011: 25). Its main activity is 'to make a public statement on the state of voluntary sector independence' and the first of five of these was published in January 2012. The size of the task facing the Panel is revealed by the modest level of response to the consultative document on which the statement is based: 'around 35 written responses and consultation meetings were received and held, involving over 50 individuals and organisations'. The need for an initiative along these lines was underlined by the Panel's finding that '2011 was clearly...a year in which there were real risks to independence' (Panel on the Independence of the Voluntary Sector, 2012: 10).

The reasons for that concern were familiar – the nature of statutory funding models; the failure of government to listen to the experience and needs of the voluntary sector when making key decisions that affect them and their constituencies; the blurring of boundaries between the sectors; self-censorship and a climate that did not recognise independence of voice; threats to independent governance; and the limitation of existing safeguards and regulation. And the Panel's vision for addressing them – the 'key changes needed' – was couched in the most general terms: 'evidence of appreciation of the importance of independence'; 'recognition of the diverse needs of different parts of the sector'; 'a strong and distinctive voice for and within the sector'; 'compliance with effective safeguards; and self-audit by boards and trustees' (Panel on the Independence of the Voluntary Sector, 2012: 28). Revealingly, the only one of these prescriptions that clearly identifies an agent of change focuses once again on individual organisations and their governing bodies.

The National Coalition for Independent Action

One of the responses to the Panel's consultation document was submitted by the only other organised group to take up the issue of independence – the NCIA. NCIA felt that 'The idea of a Panel and an annual report on the state of the voluntary sector's independence' was 'a bold and useful initiative' but that 'the way in which the Foundation has gone about putting the idea into action' was 'deeply flawed'. It expressed doubts about the composition of a panel that was made up of the 'great and the good' rather than 'people with a more recent experience of working at the "sharp end" of voluntary action' and about the adequacy of its evidence base in the absence of bespoke 'systematic and rigorous research'. But its main concern was with the quality of the analysis on which the Foundation's initiative was based:

> Voluntary organisations have not lost their independence of thought and action simply through carelessness or the failure to assert themselves, but because successive governments have increasingly viewed them as instruments for achieving their policy objectives and have devoted themselves to ensuring that voluntary organisations are fit for that purpose.
>
> (NCIA, 2011d: 1)

While the Baring initiative can be seen as an enlightened form of 'top-down' philanthropy, NCIA has its roots in the 'bottom-up' self-help tradition and began life in the time-honoured way of so many voluntary organisations as a small group of people who decided to do something about a shared concern or interest. The prime movers were Andy Benson and Penny Waterhouse, independent consultants with substantial experience of working with voluntary organisations, who had become increasingly disillusioned with the ways in which many of their clients were losing control over the design and delivery of the services they provided under increasingly prescriptive contracts with statutory funders and under pressure to 'develop their capacity' by adopting bureaucratic and 'business-like' ways of managing their affairs. Worse still, in their view, was the supine way in which voluntary organisations – and their intermediary bodies – were embracing these new approaches or acquiescing in them rather than taking a stand against changes which threatened their independence of thought and action.

As a result of these – and related – concerns, Benson and Waterhouse embarked in March 2006 on what they originally called the 'Stop the Rot' campaign. This was a bid to promote and safeguard the historical role of voluntary organisations of challenging the status quo, influencing those in power and providing a means through which the voice of the grassroots could be heard. As well as gathering support from a handful of like-minded individuals, they attracted the interest of the New

Economics Foundation (NEF) think-tank and hoped to obtain funding from the new STVS funding programme announced by the Baring
Foundation, which they thought might be another possible partner.
NEF's involvement proved short-lived and hopes for working in collaboration with the Foundation remained unrealised. Nevertheless, the
number of people from across the sector who expressed interest in and
support for the campaign grew slowly but steadily. Nineteen of them
took part in an event held in October 2006 to 'discuss what could be
done to promote and safeguard independent action' at which participants 'met, discussed, complained, celebrated, imagined how things
could be different and came up with some proposals for action' (NCIA,
2006: 1).

One of the action points that commanded widespread support among
those who took part was the development of a manifesto around which
some kind of structure could be developed. The manifesto and an invitation to engage with the fledging organisation that had issued it duly
appeared in Spring 2007. By then the idea of a campaign to 'stop the
rot' had segued into a coalition to promote and protect voluntary and
community action that would involve building a 'larger group of people
and organisations' to 'begin the discussion and shape the action that is
needed'. At this stage the founders expected that this wider membership
would consist of 'local activists', 'second tier organisations' and 'other
individuals' committed to independent action. During 2007 they developed the coalition's organisational structure and began the search for
external resources.

Initially the organisation was led by a small planning group of committed individuals. Over time, and prompted in part by the need to
register as a Community Interest Company (CIC) in order to receive
external funding and be accountable for its use, a more sophisticated
structure began to emerge. This involved four constituent parts. At the
centre were the directors of the CIC, a small group whose role was 'to
make sure we're legal, financially viable and sane enough to do the
work'. They were also members of a larger body – the Planning Group –
that met bi-monthly and set the strategic direction of the coalition's
work. The work of the Planning Group was informed and supported
by a wider group of people – the Assembly – who were sympathetic to
NCIA's aims and activities and provided an opportunity for sharing stories, tips and inspiration as well as helping to define priorities for the
coalition's work. This met three times a year. Finally, the larger constituency from which members of the Assembly were drawn consisted
of those who had opted onto a general mailing and contacts list. By the

end of 2009 there were nine directors of the CIC, 15 members of the Planning Group, almost 100 members of the Assembly and some 500 contacts on the general mailing list.

This progress was due in large part to the decision of the Tudor Trust to provide the new organisation with the financial support it needed to reinforce the voluntary efforts of its founders and their early allies. The Trust was unique in its willingness to listen to, enter into a conversation with and then provide support for an untried organisation with a radical agenda. A series of carefully targeted and well-argued applications to other charitable trusts and foundations were turned down and, apart from a few small grants to support specific activities, NCIA has failed to obtain any other external funding. Tudor, moreover, has been consistent in its support: in 2008 it provided two years of initial funding and has followed this up with two further tranches on an increased scale in 2010 and 2012, a total of six years' support. It has also been more than a provider of funding; its staff and trustees have taken a critical interest in the coalition's ideas and its attempts to implement them over the past four years and contributed to its thinking as well as encouraging it to persevere in its efforts.

Taking stock in 2012, the directors of the CIC concluded that, while NCIA needed to carry on its work, it 'should not continue, in our present form, beyond 2015 and that we should actively plan to hand over our perspectives and materials to other agencies and initiatives'. The final tranche of Tudor Trust funding would enable the coalition to develop and implement an exit strategy that involved 'a legacy that will either remain after us or be able to be handed over to others'. This legacy has three main elements:

- Information about NCIA's supporter base: who they are and how their needs and aspirations can be reflected in 'future structures and handover arrangements after our demise';
- Identification of the coalition's organisational allies and the willingness and capacity of those who share NCIA's aims to take these forward in their work; and
- 'A body of work that properly documents the times we are living through and the oppositional analysis that underpins the work that we have undertaken'.

NCIA's critique

NCIA's original manifesto in 2007 started 'from the premise that the capacity of the Voluntary and Community Sector (VCS) to take independent action, to pursue divergent interests, and become actively engaged in dissent is already in jeopardy'. It argued that the VCS in the UK was a manifestation of the universal human right to freedom of association and spelled out what it meant by independent action and why it was so important to the VCS:

> Crucial to the role of the VCS is the freedom and capacity to take **independent action.** By independent action we mean the freedom and the means by which voluntary agencies, community and campaign groups decide for themselves, in conjunction with their users and communities, their interests, aspirations, objectives, priorities, methods and ways of working.
>
> (NCIA, 2007: 1)

The sector's freedom of action was being eroded – 'chiefly as a result of Government policy and action... aimed at creating the kind of sector that it wants to see' – and the response from the VCS itself was 'increasingly supine'. Furthermore, the legitimacy of campaigning activities – 'protest, dissent and opposition' – was under threat and those who were still prepared to engage in them were isolated and under-resourced. This was 'creating an emerging crisis for the VCS which must now be tackled' (NCIA, 2007: 2).

In a later report to the Tudor Trustees in 2011, Benson and Waterhouse restated their original vision:

> Our starting point back in 2006 was that the freedom afforded by voluntary action in a democratic society was not only virtuous in itself... but that it also brought many collective benefits, such as complementing state provision to meet needs, a capacity to hold other powerful or vested interests... to account, or to develop and articulate different and sometimes dissenting narratives of our world and the way in which it is viewed and organised. We felt that these values and benefits were being eroded, ignored or eliminated by the readiness with which voluntary and community groups allowed themselves to be drawn into fulfilling other people's agendas. Our gripe was with those involved in voluntary action and our call was for them to stop sleepwalking into being redefined in this way. Our argument was that this sapped the very life out of their purpose and the contribution they could make to our common wealth. Our core message was the need to 'defend ungoverned space' from co-option and enslavement.
>
> (NCIA, 2011a: 2)

They also reflected on the changes that had taken place in the landscape of voluntary action and the ways in which NCIA had adjusted to them. For its first four years the environment had been shaped by the New Labour project and the government's attempts to co-opt the voluntary and community sector by involving them in partnerships, investing in building their capacity and commissioning them to deliver public services. The arrival of the Coalition government in 2010 and its drastic programme of cuts to public expenditure changed the picture. NCIA was quick to attack what it saw as the 'fig leaf' of David Cameron's Big Society rhetoric and the smoke screen of the localism agenda that, in their view, promised but did not deliver greater opportunities for communities to shape local services. But the biggest shift in the environment was the wholesale adoption by the government of commissioning as a means of privatising public services and putting them in the hands of 'any willing provider'.

> Though voluntary agencies are again being invited to participate in these outsourcing programmes, it is becoming clear that the private sector is likely to be the main player, joined by large voluntary agencies that have turned themselves into private sector lookalikes. This time the offer to locally based small to medium sized voluntary agencies is to become sub-contractors to private sector primary contact holders.
>
> (NCIA, 2011a: 2)

In short, independent voluntary action was under threat not just from the state but also from the private sector.

In the new circumstances, Benson and Waterhouse rather optimistically declared that the argument about independence had been won:

> the damage done to independence is now widely acknowledged as are the new threats presented by the ConLib agenda. The main issues on which we now work are the demonstrable effects on voluntary action of privatisation and, in parallel to that, cuts to public services and the dismantling and destruction of the fabric of community through the fiction of the 'Big Society'.
>
> (2011a: 5)

In a later paper they reported that, while 'supporting community-based activism' and 'highlighting the ways in which "new managerialism" is changing voluntary agencies' remained priorities for NCIA, the 'main show' was the 'anti-privatisation focus...both because it is an issue of monstrous importance and because it connects together – ideologically and practically – a number of our concerns'. These included 'anti-cuts work, defence of accountable and mainstream public services, the impact of commissioning...and the increasing role of the private sector' (NCIA, 2012a: 2).

Ways and means

From the outset NCIA sought to build a constituency and a supporter base; encourage and assist activism at the local level; develop its analysis of the threats to independence and ways in which they could be resisted; and influence the wider world through a series of publications and the formation of alliances with other organisations. At an early stage it established an interactive website and a bi-monthly newsletter which have provided the means of communicating with its supporters and presenting the public face for the Coalition. The newsletter has presented a blend of widespread reportage of developments impinging on independence and critical commentary on the words and actions of key players in government and the voluntary sector. And the effort to produce it has been sustained over the long run; by the end of 2012 NCIA had published 30 issues of the newsletter.

Its attempts to promote local activism have been less successful. It has worked with advice agencies in Hackney and with a local CVS in West Sussex, but failed to build a wider programme in the absence of personal contacts of members of NCIA's Planning Group. An attempt to apply the experiences gained in Hackney to advice agencies in other areas proved to be problematic:

> It proved very difficult to find local areas within which to work and once we did the work has been slow and fragile.... There is a lot to do in building relationships, local understandings and joint interests before people are ready to take practical action together.
>
> (NCIA, 2010: 2)

The NCIA lacked the resources needed to make successful forays into the promotion of local action and had some serious reservations about the value of what could be seen as 'parachuting' into localities. It reconsidered its approach to promoting local activism, and this now consists of offering support to individual local agencies in the form of consultancy, modest amounts of money and brokerage that connects them to potential allies, on the one hand, and of gathering local intelligence and stories which will help to develop resources that others can use at a local level, on the other (NCIA, 2012a).

The newsletter has played a valuable role in developing and disseminating NCIA's analysis of the threats to the sector's independence, but the principal means of taking forward this element of its work has been the production of a series of publications. These have included leaflets and short 'position papers' dealing with specific topics such as commissioning, privatisation and managerialism as well as the general case for independence; resources like an 'independence audit'; and research studies and conference reports. At the same time its spokespeople – and especially Andy Benson, its co-founder – have appeared on variety of platforms to present NCIA's views to a range of audiences. And it has been able to reach new constituencies through building alliances with other organisations and organising joint conferences with them. NCIA has worked with the TUC and other partners on a major event about privatisation; with the London Voluntary Services Council on commissioning; and with National Community Activists Network (NatCAN) on the challenges facing local activists. These and other established and emergent alliances are, as we have seen, one of the ways in which NCIA is trying to build a legacy together with a comprehensive restatement of its take on 'what voluntary action is all about, and what we are trying to protect and promote' in the form of an 'NCIA manifesto for voluntary action' (NCIA, 2012a: 5) and an analysis of its supporter base that will enable their needs and aspirations to be addressed in the post-NCIA world.

Achievements and limitations

Looking back in the middle of 2011 over the NCIA's first five years' work, Benson and Waterhouse felt that it could lay claim to some significant successes (NCIA, 2011a: 4–5). In the first place NCIA had established its profile and taken the debate about independence into the mainstream: 'We may still be seen as "dangerous" (ridiculous as that seems) but we are no longer dismissed as irrelevant' and they had been described (by the chief executive of NAVCA) as 'the official opposition'. In the process they had helped to change the terms of the debate – 'we no longer have to make the argument about independence' – and the 'mood music – the assumptions that are made about the scene and the direction of travel'. In the second place, NCIA had 'built an extensive and national network of contacts' and 'created a safe home for people who share our perspectives and a forum for debate and critique' as well as developing alliances that enabled them to 'work with and through others'. And, third, NCIA held 'a body of knowledge and information that is extensive, distinctive and significant' and 'a valuable repository of evidence about the issues that concern us' and was about to 'be able to provide practical resources that will help supporters make the case or pursue their own agenda'.

On the other hand, Benson and Waterhouse were only too aware of the limitations of what had been achieved. Their original vision of launching a 'mass movement' had been abandoned at an early stage, but even the more realistic ambition of 'building a supporter base of actively involved individuals and organisations' had proved elusive. Similarly, NCIA lacked the ability to provide the kind of 'hands-on practical support' for local action it felt was needed. While it functioned as a fairly effective kind of 'think-tank' at national level, they believed that 'the essential differences will be made at local level' and their failure to combine the two levels of operation was frustrating.

Clearly NCIA has made an impact. It alone has articulated a reasoned critique of the ways in which voluntary action as it has been understood and practised has been pressed into the service of the state and radically changed in the process. It has encouraged and helped a small minority of voluntary organisations and those who work in them to resist the threats to their independence. And its influence is beginning to spread beyond its core constituency into the mainstream of the continuing debate. On the other hand, it has not halted the juggernaut of state and private sector hegemony, nor has it slowed its advance to any significant extent. NCIA may have won the argument, but it is losing the war. There has been no serious rebellion in the sector against those who have led voluntary organisations into 'partnership' with the state, and NCIA's supporters are numbered in the hundreds rather than the thousands. The muted response to its campaign may suggest that its analysis is flawed or, perhaps more probably, that its intervention came too late and that the damage to the independence of action enjoyed by voluntary organisations had already gone too far to be reversed.

Conclusions

This chapter has focused on the dissenters – those who have opposed the prevailing trends described in earlier parts of this book. It has looked at the experience of the two initiatives that have been taken to defend the independence of the sector from the embrace of the state and, latterly, its private-sector allies. We have seen how the Baring Foundation discovered that its initial assumption that the assertion of independence by individual voluntary agencies would be sufficient to prevent encroachment by government was not founded, and its establishment of an Independent Panel to monitor the situation across the sector. The chapter then focused on the efforts of NCIA to provide a 'wake-up' call for those voluntary and community organisations which were sleepwalking into getting their priorities and their ways of working redefined by the state and rouse them to a collective defence of their independence of thought and action. Given its modest resources, NCIA has made a significant impact, but its intervention may have come too late to defend the independence of many voluntary sector organisations.

Part IV

Conclusions and Implications

14
The Paradox of Sectorisation

This is the first of three concluding chapters that attempt to draw together the threads of the argument that has preceded them and identify some of its implications for the theory and practice of voluntary action in the future. It explores and tries to explain the paradox of sectorisation – how and why the creation of a voluntary sector identity and the development alongside it of institutions based on the idea that voluntary action was a distinctive and different kind of activity have led us to a situation in which, in 2013, voluntary organisations have come to be managed by the same rules and assumptions that apply to private sector businesses or public sector agencies.

Many who worked in and with voluntary organisations in the late 1970s enthusiastically embraced the concept of a 'sector' and proudly adopted it as a badge for their activities. They did so for a number of reasons. In the first place, the new identity raised the profile and enhanced the status of the voluntary organisations grouped under the banner: individually they were small and lacked influence, whereas together they could hope to gain a hearing from government at both national and local levels. Second, it provided managers of voluntary organisations with a rationale for getting together for mutual support and the exchange of information. And, third, it offered the possibility of developing a kind of 'critical mass' to support the development of professional practice, consultancy, education and training tailored to the specific needs of the sector.

All of these benefits flowed from an assumption of a common identity based on a distinctive set of organisational characteristics. While there were a number of ways in which they varied – such as size, scope, function and field of activity – voluntary organisations shared a constellation of defining features: the importance of values; governance by volunteer boards; complex and multiple accountabilities; human resources which included volunteers as well as paid staff; insecure funding; and the influence of charismatic founders and leaders (Harris, 1990). None of these characteristics was the exclusive property of voluntary organisations, but, it was argued, the presence of all or most of them was a unique feature of the organisations that constituted the voluntary sector. And it was the possession of these characteristics that created a sense of sector identity in those who worked in voluntary organisations.

These shared features were found across a diversity of organisational functions, sizes and organisational forms. Brenton (1985) identified four common functions carried out by voluntary organisations. Many of them provided a range of care, information and advice services for a variety of client groups and undertook activities aimed at improving the environment. Others promoted mutual aid between people who shared a health problem, disability or common interest. Yet others functioned as pressure groups in which the principal aim was to bring about changes in policy and practice by campaigning and lobbying policy-makers. Finally, 'intermediary' or 'second tier' organisations carried out resource and co-ordinating functions. This list is not exhaustive: voluntary organisations also engaged in individual advocacy to help people secure services to meet their specific needs (Kendall and Knapp, 1995), fund-raising for charitable causes, research and grant-making. Other important dimensions of diversity and difference included the scale and area of their operations; the legal and constitutional forms they had adopted; the kind of funding mix which supported their work; the nature of their relationship with the state; the degree of formalisation in their structures and operational arrangements; and the extent and nature of the contribution made by volunteers to the work of the organisation (Rochester, 1998).

The shared features listed above that cut across the heterogeneity of the voluntary sector were identified in a series of workshops, seminars, action-research projects and case studies involving hundreds of voluntary organisations that were undertaken by the Centre for Voluntary Organisation at the LSE and its predecessor, the Programme of Research and Training into Voluntary Action (PORTVAC) at Brunel University, during the period from 1979 to 1993. As well as identifying common features, these activities also highlighted the enduring nature of the shared challenges confronted by the participating organisations, many of which flowed from the distinctive nature of their defining features. The 'formidable list of issues' raised in the first workshop for voluntary sector directors and managers which was held in February 1979 were still preoccupying their counterparts who took part in a similar event 14 years later. These fell into three broad areas of concern. The first of these was 'aims and objectives' and included concerns about the impact of a changing environment on organisational values and culture. The second – 'work organisation' – focused on issues such as confusion over roles and internal structures and problems of internal accountability. And the third – 'governance' – included both the problems of relationships between paid staff and governing bodies and tensions between the national headquarters of federated organisations and their local units (Billis and Harris, 1996).

It was not, moreover, only those who worked within or with the sector who defined it by identifying the distinctive features of voluntary organisations (although without reference to the common challenges they faced). Successive governments have valued the sector not just as an additional set of resources that could be brought to bear on social problems but as a source of organisational responses that were qualitatively different from the ways in which the state was able to act. The Efficiency Scrutiny carried out by the Conservative government, for example, described the sector as 'an important force, which complements public services, and has the potential to do more'. In particular, it was 'able to get close to the customer' and 'innovative and able to respond to new needs' (Home Office, 1990: 6). New Labour's Compact was based on the 'shared vision' that: 'Voluntary and community groups... bring distinctive value to society and fulfil a role that is distinct from both the state and the market' and 'they act as pathfinders for the involvement of users in the design and delivery of services and often act as advocates of those who otherwise have no voice' (Home Office, 1998: paras 1, 2). The Cross-Cutting Review of the role of the third sector in social and economic regeneration (HM Treasury and Home Office, 2007: 5) began by stating:

> The third sector is a vital component of a fair and enterprising society, where individuals and communities feel empowered and enabled to achieve change and to meet social and environmental needs. The Government recognises the value of the diversity of organisations in the sector in providing voice for underrepresented groups, in campaigning for change, in creating strong, active and connected communities, in promoting enterprising solutions to social and environmental challenges and in transforming the delivery and design of public services.
>
> (HM Treasury and Home Office, 2007: 5)

It then went on to discuss the role of the third sector in 'transforming public services' in the light of an analytical framework for the potential benefits of its involvement first set out in the 2004 Spending Review (HM Treasury, 2005). These included:

- a strong focus on the needs of service users;
- knowledge and expertise to meet complex personal needs and tackle difficult social issues;
- an ability to be flexible and offer joined-up service delivery;
- the capacity to build users' trust; and
- the experience and independence to innovate.

(HM Treasury and Cabinet Office, 2007: 51)

The characterisation of the sector as innovative, flexible, close to the consumer and able to provide a voice for those who had not been heard has not been continued by the Coalition. In opposition the Conservative party had paid tribute to the sector's past record:

> Throughout history, many of the most pressing problems have been identified and tackled by voluntary action. Whether in education, public health, or the relief of poverty it has been voluntary groups which have been there first as pioneers; the first to notice a problem; the first to commit to resolving it; and the first to mobilise resources to deal with it.
>
> (Conservative Party, 2008: 6)

And it pledged to ensure that the flexibility and closeness to the user that had underpinned their past record should not be put at risk by the imposition or encroachment on them of bureaucratic measures or micromanagement by the state. In office, the Coalition's message was somewhat muted, wrapped as it was in the now discredited rhetoric of the 'Big Society'. But implicit in the description of the sector's role set out in David Cameron's introduction to the new government's version of the Compact is a view of its distinctive characteristics:

> Looking forward, the role of this sector has never been more important. Building the Big Society and getting citizens more engaged, involved and responsible for the communities around them will only be possible in partnership with the sector; improving and delivering better, more responsive public services can only be done with the help of the sector; and empowering communities can only

work where the skills, enthusiasm and commitment of the sector is harnessed.

(Cabinet Office, 2010: 3)

These approaches to identifying the distinguishing features of the sector were not, however, the only ways of defining voluntary organisations and the voluntary sector. One very significant influence was the 'structural-operational' definition developed by Salamon and Anheier (1992) for the Johns Hopkins Comparative Nonprofit Sector Project. This was an ambitious and extensive study of the sector in a large number of diverse societies, including the UK, where the research was undertaken by Kendall and Knapp (1996). For inclusion in the study, organisations had to meet the following criteria:

Formal. Only structured entities with constitutions or formal sets of rules... were included.

Independent of government and self-governing... with their own internal decision-making structures, and not directly controlled by a private (for-profit) entity or by the state.

Not-profit-distributing and primarily non-business. Organizations were ruled out if they were empowered to distribute net earnings to controlling persons... or had a commercial orientation which made them indistinguishable from for-profit firms.

Voluntary. A meaningful degree of voluntarism in terms of money or time through philanthropy or voluntary citizen involvement.

(Kendall and Knapp, 1996: 18)

Clearly this definition is rooted in the idea of a 'non-profit sector' that is the product of the USA. It replaces the rather loose and subjective bundle of characteristics used to explain the nature of voluntary organisations that we have explored above with a single clear defining principle, the 'non-distribution constraint' (Hansmann, 1980). It is, of course, true that the definition also calls for a 'meaningful degree of voluntarism', but, unlike the non-profit principle, this is open to interpretation and has in many cases come to mean, in practice, no more than the existence of a governing body composed of disinterested volunteers – as prescribed by charity law. The definition also excludes less formal arrangements for collective voluntary action, such as those

Smith (2000) calls 'informal associations' and Billis (1993a) terms 'unorganised groups'. And we should understand that the function of the 'structural-operational' definition is not to explain the distinctive nature of voluntary sector organisations but to enable researchers to measure 'the extent and nature of the sector's contribution to the UK economy and society' (Kendall and Knapp, 1995: 66) and in a way that enables them to be compared cross-nationally.

The attempt to arrive at a common definition that can be applied to very different societies has inherent difficulties and complexities, and Kendall and Knapp had to grapple with a mismatch between what was to be measured for purposes of international comparison and the widely held and culturally determined view of what comprised the UK's voluntary sector. They addressed this issue by excluding some of the organisations that were covered by the structural-operational definition – or what they termed the 'broad' voluntary sector – to create a narrow definition of the sector that would be acceptable within the UK. As well as recreational organisations, trades unions and professional and business associations, the exclusions included primary and secondary schools and higher education institutions (Kendall and Knapp, 1996: 24). On the other hand, the 'narrow' definition included institutions such as clinics and other health care agencies; theatres, galleries and museums; as well as housing associations, which were not commonly thought of as voluntary organisations. And, in pursuit of their aim of measuring the scale of the sector, Kendall and Knapp were most interested in the largest organisations, which accounted for the greatest amount of economic activity.

Researchers and policy-makers have taken two different approaches to understanding the nature of the 'loose and baggy monster' of the voluntary and community sector. On the one hand, there are writers who start from an observation of the characteristics that make voluntary organisations unlike other organisational forms. Their image of the sector is based on the kind of small to medium-size agency commonly found at local level, where the great majority of voluntary organisations are found. Their interests may include volunteer-led and staffed associations and community groups, but are less likely to extend to larger and more formal organisations. On the other hand, other commentators use the non-distribution constraint as the defining feature of the organisations they study. They have comparatively little interest in the 'little platoons' of the sector and none in the informal groupings on the opposite end of the voluntary sector spectrum from the biggest 'household name' charities. While the first group's approach was essentially about understanding the 'organisational grammar' of a distinct kind of organisational form and developing 'appropriate tools and theories' (Billis, 1993a: 136), the second body of people was more likely to be interested in applying generic organisational and management theory to an organisational sub-species.

The differences between the two intellectual groups were played out in the USA over the change of name and shift of emphasis through which the leading academic body in the field became the Association for Research on Nonprofit Organizations and Voluntary Action (ARNOVA) rather than the Association of Voluntary Action Scholars (AVAS) in 1990 and the subsequent development of a Community and Grassroots Section within ARNOVA (Smith, 2003). The change of name followed a shift in the centre of gravity of academic work in the USA and, given the numerical preponderance of American scholars in the field of non-profit and voluntary sector studies, in the wider world and especially in the UK, where the links with the USA were particularly well developed. The papers presented at ARNOVA's annual conferences and the articles published in its journal – *Nonprofit and Voluntary Sector Quarterly* – reflected the relative importance attached to studies of non-profit organisations, which were at best an imperfect match for the UK's voluntary sector because of the inclusion in the former of major institutions in the education, culture and health sub-sectors.

In the UK the divergence between the two areas of interest was less marked but could be discerned in the different approaches adopted by the growing number of universities that developed an interest in voluntary sector studies. The pioneering work by David Billis, initially at Brunel University and subsequently at the London School of Economics, was firmly in the first camp, and a similar focus was adopted at other universities, including East London, Roehampton and Birkbeck. The second approach was developed in a number of business schools such as those at City and London South Bank Universities. Of the two, the non-profit approach has outperformed the alternative. Postgraduate courses have continued to attract students at City and South Bank universities but have been discontinued at LSE and Roehampton and face a precarious future at Birkbeck. This is in large part due to the differences in their target audiences – those who work for larger agencies are more likely to have support from their employers – but also reflects the general direction of travel of the way we think about the sector.

Alongside the divergence of intellectual approaches among researchers and policy-makers, there have been a series of attacks on the idea that there is a single voluntary sector. The heterogeneity of the sector has, of course, been recognised from the start and was captured in the description of it by Kendall and Knapp (1995) as 'a loose and baggy monster'. But that is not the same as arguing, as a number of commentators have, that it includes organisations which are so different as to be incompatible and that it is a serious mistake to blur the differences between them and risk confusing one with another. One such commentator was Lord Dahrendorf, the distinguished philosopher, sociologist and political scientist, who revisited the points he had made in his Arnold Goodman Charity Lectures in 1983 and 2001 in his foreword to Jeremy Kendall's book on the Voluntary Sector:

> Increasingly it appears that 'the sector' is in fact two sectors: one genuinely voluntary, happily remote from government, hard-pressed to meet the charity tests of social usefulness – and the other linked to government as well as business, defined by its social objectives, subject to all sorts of controls and rules, and voluntary only in name. Sometimes the split runs right through the same organisation. Often, the old style voluntary organisations feel neglected and even underprivileged, whereas their new-style colleagues wonder why they do not have civil-service privileges since they have become quasi-governmental agencies.
>
> (Dahrendorf, 2003: xiv)

Ten years earlier, in 1993, Barry Knight had made much the same distinction in the CENTRIS report on Voluntary Action, funded and published by the Home Office, which, nonetheless, rapidly distanced itself from the report's conclusions in the face of criticism from the voluntary sector establishment. The focus of its ire was Knight's argument that the 'sector' idea yoked together two very different kinds of beast – on the one hand, 'the first force... authentic voluntary action, prophetic, vision led, reformist, independent of government' and, on the other, 'the third force... part of the wider social economy. It acts philanthropically on sub-contract from the state' which 'oversees performance and pays for work done'. 'It was unrealistic', he argued, 'to combine these types of action in a single organisation' (Knight, 1993: xvii–xviii). This was, however, exactly what the major voluntary agencies that dismissed his analysis out of hand claimed to do.

More recently, the DSC has argued that government policy has focused on the 2% of voluntary sector organisations with budgets of more than a million pounds a year which account for 70% of the sector's income. This represented 'a core grouping of around 2,000 organisations...that are more established, more powerful, and are addressing issues more closely aligned with government policy than the rest. Many of them deliver government policy under contract at national, regional or local levels.' Furthermore, 'the majority of this "top 2%"...are established, financially secure...and hold strong positions within their relevant spheres'. Their 'structural characteristics...are closer to those of established private sector companies than they are to the smaller groups of like-minded individuals that make up the rest of the voluntary sector, and as a result are far more accessible, understandable and closer to government' (Wittenberg, 2007: 7). These 2,000 or so organisations probably include the 'corporate national charities' identified by Andy Benson of the NCIA as competing against private sector companies for the contracts which are out of the reach of the great majority of small and medium-size organisations (NCIA, 2011b).

The debate about the extent to which the idea of a single voluntary sector stands up has been complicated by another fissure running through the heterogeneous collection of organisations that have been corralled within its boundaries. This is the distinction that has been made between the 'voluntary' and the 'community' aspects of the sector, which essentially mirrors the division made by David Horton Smith in the USA between 'paid staff nonprofits and voluntary groups' and 'grassroots associations' which were entirely dependent on voluntary effort (Smith, 2000). In the wake of the Deakin Report, a group of national organisations which provided a headquarters function or other services to local community groups had come together to form a Community Sector Coalition and made the case for the inclusion of their constituents on the policy agenda. Their efforts were rewarded by the adoption of the inclusive term 'voluntary and community sector' to describe the entity that negotiated the Compact with government and the recognition of a special place within the sector conferred by the development of a Compact Code for Community Groups (Home Office, 2003).

It is thus possible to distinguish not one but three voluntary sectors. Alongside organisations exhibiting the distinctive characteristics identified by Harris (1990) and listed at the start of this chapter are – on one side – the 'top 2%' 'corporate' agencies which are more like private sector companies and – on the other – community groups which are entirely dependent on the voluntary efforts of their members. The latter enjoyed only a brief period in the policy limelight, and their recognition as part of the sector was largely withdrawn by government in 2006 as a consequence of the rebranding exercise in which the 'third sector' became the preferred term as the New Labour government adopted a more instrumental approach to its dealings with voluntary agencies. On the other hand, the new terminology was intended to open the way for the acceptance of social enterprises – voluntary organisations which use commercial methods to finance their activities or businesses with a social or environmental mission – as part of the sector mix. For the government this involved 'the merger of responsibility for social enterprise and the voluntary and community sector in the new Office of the Third Sector, where the creation of a broader third sector beyond the voluntary and community sector focus of the 1990s was translated into institutional form'. For some of the other parties it has created 'a marriage of convenience' and a 'strategic alliance, based on the shared benefits to be accrued from a unified third sector policy discourse' (Alcock, 2010: 15).

Neither the widening divisions between different kinds of voluntary organisation nor the realignment of the sector's borders has had any marked impact on the widespread acceptance and use of the idea of a unified sector, which serves a number of interests.

> This overlying unity is a product of strategic alliances between practitioner representatives, policy makers, political actors and academic researchers. All contribute to the creation of the uncontested space ... as all have an interest in defending the unifying ideology of a third sector, from which political profile, policy support and financial backing for this broader sector can be extracted. All have an interest in promoting a discourse of unity as all may potentially benefit from its higher profile and greater social penetration.
>
> (Alcock, 2010: 19)

In the light of this explanation for the enduring strength of the idea of a unified sector, it is easy to understand why dissenting voices, including the NCIA and its allies, have been marginalised. It also provides us with the clue to unravelling the paradox of sectorisation.

Those who have benefitted most from the idea of 'voluntary sector unity' have been, on the one hand, the 'top 2%' of voluntary agencies and those like NCVO and ACEVO which promote their interests and, on the other, those in government bent on privatising public services. The biggest voluntary organisations have been given a more central role in the delivery of public services and gained substantial new resources as a result. Government has been able to implement its policies under the cloak of public esteem for charities and the argument that voluntary organisations have distinctive characteristics which give them unique advantages over statutory bureaucracies. Government rhetoric about the sector which has been swallowed whole by its most prominent elements has combined two largely incompatible messages: on the one hand, voluntary organisations offer greater flexibility, the ability to innovate and a highly developed responsiveness to their users and their needs while, on the other, they need to become better organised and more business-like in order to qualify for government contracts for service delivery. The first of these provides a rationale for the transfer of responsibility for public services from the state to voluntary organisations, while the second ensures that only the minority of 'corporate voluntary agencies' are able to win contracts to deliver them.

In other words, the promotion of a unified sector is a massive sleight of hand. The image of the informal, flexible and responsive alternative to the welfare bureaucracies of the state has been used to promote change, but the imposition of the organisational norms of bureaucracy and the culture and practices of the private sector has ensured that the real beneficiaries of a greater role for the sector have been the small minority of organisations that, far from fitting the image promoted by government rhetoric, most resemble the statutory agencies that have hitherto delivered public services and the private sector companies which are increasingly winning contracts under the commissioning regime.

15
Towards an Alternative Paradigm

The first chapter of this book introduced two narrow paradigms or taken-for-granted and implicit assumptions about voluntary organisations and volunteering that constrain so much of the thinking about the theory and practice of voluntary action. The first of these – the *voluntary organisation paradigm* – assumed that voluntary organisations were formally constituted agencies with hierarchical structures, controlled by professional managers who oversaw the delivery of services by paid staff to one or more kinds of user or beneficiary. The second – the *dominant paradigm in volunteering* – assumed that volunteers undertook unpaid work that needed to be managed and that was carried out in large, formally structured service-providing agencies. Subsequent chapters have explained how these two accounts of voluntary action have become so influential and have exposed their limitations and the way they constrain our understanding of a much more complex reality. This chapter outlines an alternative paradigm of voluntary action. Rather than viewing voluntary organisations as bureaucratic instruments for the delivery of services and volunteers as auxiliary human resources that need to be professionally managed, it draws on the separate literatures of volunteering and the study of voluntary organisations to argue that the essence or 'ideal type' of voluntary action is found in the activities and behaviour of 'unmanaged' volunteers within non-bureaucratic organisational settings.

Unmanaged volunteering

There are two major weaknesses in the volunteering literature: as well as focusing on volunteering as unpaid work, to the exclusion of a great deal of other kinds of activity, it rarely takes into account the organisational context within which volunteering takes place (Rochester, 1999b). Comparatively little attention has been given to the very large number of volunteers who are 'unmanaged' (Scott, 2010) or 'not biddable' (Kearney, 2001). Unlike those who are engaged in 'voluntary work', these volunteers do not slot themselves into pre-defined roles and submit to a process of selection, induction and, often, training, but exercise considerable autonomy over the scope and content of their volunteering activities. The process through which they become involved in volunteering may be informal, 'turning up' or 'dropping in' to 'lend a hand' without any preconceived ideas about the limits on their participation in the work or the way in which the organisation is managed. Their roles and responsibilities are negotiated with other people within the group or organisation and may change and grow over time in line with the interests and inclinations of the volunteer, on the one hand, and the needs and aspirations of the organisation, on the other (Rochester, 1992). Other unmanaged volunteers create the context for their activities by joining with others to form groups and associations based on shared needs or common aspirations. In both cases the relationship between volunteers and the organisation with which they are involved is deeper and more complex than the employer–employee relationship implied by the dominant paradigm. Volunteers may be the 'owners' of an organisation or significant 'members' or stakeholders who exercise significant influence over what it does and how it does it (Ellis Paine *et al.*, 2010).

The content of these relationships is shaped by the organisational arrangements within which volunteering takes place, but very little attention has been given by researchers to the variety of different contexts for volunteering. Major studies such as the national surveys of volunteering (1981, 1991 and 1997) and the Citizenship Surveys (2001–10) make a distinction between 'formal' volunteering undertaken in an organised setting and 'informal' volunteering carried out in the form of personal acts of service to others, but do not differentiate between variations in the 'organised setting' in which formal volunteering takes place. This lack of attention to this dimension of diversity may be explained by a view that 'volunteering is volunteering' and 'that what is being measured or described is essentially the same activity, regardless of context' (Rochester, 1999b: 10). It is more likely, however, that it is a consequence of the influence of the dominant 'non-profit paradigm' among researchers, policy-makers and practitioners and a reluctance to engage with the full complexity of the volunteering phenomenon. And we can go further: as well as the fundamental difference between the experience of 'managed' and 'unmanaged' volunteering, moreover, we can distinguish between various forms of collective voluntary action, including informal or 'unorganised' groups; associations; and shallow and entrenched hybrids. These differences shape the relationship between the volunteer and the organisation with which they are involved, but they also help to determine the nature of the volunteering activity itself, as well as the volunteer's relationship with other people involved in the organisation and the kind of 'reward' derived from the volunteering experience.

Non-bureaucratic voluntary organisations

The neglect of 'unmanaged' volunteers in the academic and practitioner literature is matched by a similar lack of interest in non-bureaucratic forms of voluntary organisations. One major exception has been the work of David Billis. In order to develop a theory to help us understand and explain the 'growing and increasingly significant role of "hybrid organizations" in the third sector' (Billis, 2010a: 3), he has argued that 'an ideal type of the third sector is best typified by the association' (Billis, 2010b: 53). This provides the third sector with a non-hybrid organisational form comparable to the for-profit sector's firm and the statutory sector's bureau but which, unlike them, is not bureaucratic:

> In this model people establish a formal organization in order to resolve their own or other people's problems. These members, through a process of private elections, elect committees and officers to guide the work of the organization. The organization may need additional voluntary labour to forward its policies. Other resources may also be sought and these are typically membership dues, donations and legacies. Work is driven neither by the need to make a profit nor by public policies but primarily by the association's own agenda. This approach differs from most prevailing theoretical approaches to the sector. The association, rather than being a rather peripheral component (as in the Johns Hopkins research), is now seen as the 'ideal model' and source of the distinctive sector attributes.
>
> (Billis, 2010b: 53)

This represents a major theoretical shift in understanding and explaining the key characteristics of voluntary organisations. It transfers the focus from the small minority of non-profit entities that command the great majority of the voluntary sector's income (and were thus of central importance to research conducted by Salamon and Anheier and others,

whose approach was rooted in economics) to the overwhelming majority of voluntary organisations and community groups. We do not have
reliable calculations of the size of this majority, but we can be fairly
confident that voluntary organisations that have annual incomes of
less than £10,000 – 54% out of the total of 180,000, according to the
NCVO (Clarke *et al.*, 2012) – are non-bureaucratic. And there is reason
to believe that the much greater number of what the NCVO calls 'civil
society organisations' – the NCVO estimates this population as num-
bering 900,000, but Elsdon (1995) has argued that it is in excess of a
million – will be overwhelmingly made up of associations and less formal groupings. And in the USA, Smith (2000) has calculated that there
are 'many millions' of grassroots associations and that this is many times
greater than the number of 'paid staff nonprofits'.

Not all of these non-bureaucratic entities, however, completely meet
the Billis definition of an association. In all, we can distinguish four
different types. Apart from the 'classic' or 'pure' association described
above, these consist of less formal or unorganised groups; micro
voluntary agencies; and self-help groups. The second of these categories – *less formal groupings* – have been variously described as 'informal or semi-formal associations' (Smith, 2000); 'transorganizations'
(Milofsky, 2008); and 'unorganised groups' (Billis, 1993a). Members
of less formal groups are united by a common purpose and a sense
of collective identity and they will have adopted a name, but their
'membership boundaries and leadership structures might remain vague'
(Smith, 2000: 77). The informal characteristics of such groups are based
on personal interaction, which means that they do not conform to
conventional ideas about organisations: 'organizational theory struggles
with these entities because it is not clear that they are "organizations"
as understood by contemporary students of nonprofit organization and
management' (Cnaan and Milofsky, 2008: 2). Milofsky suggests that this
might be because some of them 'tend to be embedded in larger community structures; they are part of, and in some fashion subordinate to, the
communities of which they are part' and that their systems 'span corporate, legal and economic ownership boundaries' (Milofsky, 2008: 5, 7).
For his part, Billis regards them as another form of hybrid: they have
their roots in the unorganised personal world but have adopted some of
the characteristics of the associational world.

The 'unorganised group' thus represents one form of non-bureaucratic
hybrid, as the 'rules' of the associational world are introduced into the
private world of family and friends. On the other boundary of the
association world can be found another example of hybridisation and
a third non-bureaucratic category – the *micro voluntary agency*. While

these bodies employ staff to carry out some of their operational work, they rely, like associations, on the voluntary efforts of the members of their governing body and, in some cases, other volunteers to undertake the tasks that the staff are unable to perform. A study of organisations with fewer than four full time staff or their equivalent suggests that they operate either as 'nascent bureaucracies' or on a largely non-bureaucratic basis. In the first case, they attempt to draw on principles and practices developed in bureaucratic settings despite the fact that their staff teams are simply too small to be organised into a fully blown bureaucratic structure with a clear hierarchy of authority and accountability and a high degree of functional specification. In the second case, they exhibit high levels of informality and trust and minimal differences in the status and role of management committee members, staff and volunteers (Rochester, 1998). Their organisational 'rules' have more in common with associations than with bureaucracies, and they can be seen as dipping their toes in the shallowest waters of hybridity.

The fourth example of non-bureaucratic collective voluntary action is the *self-help group*. These groups are composed of small numbers of people who typically share a problem or concern, such as a physical impairment or long-term medical condition; mental health issues; a life crisis like bereavement; or a status (like single parenthood) that might be stigmatised by society. The members of these groups come together for mutual support, to overcome problems of isolation or feelings of being marginalised, and to obtain information and advice about their situation (Wann, 1992). The key feature of these groups is the reciprocal nature of relationships, which is often characterised as 'by us, for us', although, as Richardson and Goodwin (1983) have suggested, such reciprocity is often serial; members benefit most at the beginning of their involvement and contribute more with growing experience and confidence.

Understanding non-bureaucratic voluntary action

Having introduced the concept of 'unmanaged volunteering' and outlined the types of non-bureaucratic organisational setting in which it takes place, we now need to make explicit the ways in which these organisations are fundamentally different from bureaucracies and how the behaviour of the volunteers who are involved in them diverges from that of the 'voluntary workers' of the dominant non-profit paradigm. This will be approached in three ways. In the first place, we identify the key features of formal, bureaucratic organisations and assess the extent to which these do not apply to less formal entities. In the second place, we move on from this essentially negative attempt at definition – what non-bureaucratic organisational forms are *not* – to explore ways of defining them positively by focusing on their distinctive characteristics. And, in the third place, we look at why and how volunteers become involved in these kinds of grouping, how their involvement is facilitated, supported and sustained, and the kinds of impact their activities may have.

Bureaucratic organisations and the limitations of conventional organisational theory

Conventional organisational theory is based on a set of assumptions about the nature of organisations that are rarely made explicit. These are drawn from one type of organisation – the corporate or for-profit bureaucracy – but increasingly applied to statutory agencies and voluntary sector organisations.

These assumptions can be summarised in a simple table:

Table 15.1 The conventional organisational model

Function and purpose	Seen in instrumental terms. Their purpose is to produce outputs (whether widgets or hours of care) and efficiency is measured in terms of the ability to make things or deliver services while using the minimum of resources.
Permanence	The assumption is that organisations are intended to exist for ever or, failing that, for as long as possible. One of the tasks of the board and chief executive is to ensure the survival of the organisation. Organisations are described as having a 'will to survive'.
Growth	Success is measured by the extent to which the business expands and the speed with which it grows.
Clear boundaries	Organisations have an existence that is separate or autonomous from the surrounding environment.
Unambiguous ownership	By a specific – and often quite small – group of people.
Authority and accountability	The owners of the business (the shareholders or their counterparts) delegate power to the board and staff to manage the organisation. Authority and accountability are clearly specified.
Structure	Essentially hierarchical. Each staff position is clearly defined in terms of the boundaries of the work to be performed and the extent to which the post holder has control over his/her own work and responsibility for the work of others.

Non-bureaucratic groupings are very different. In the first place, their purposes and functions are not solely or even primarily instrumental, but expressive: 'They often are more about the process than the products of their work or the tasks people seek to accomplish' (Cnaan and Milofsky, 2008: 2). As discussed in Chapter 10, Mason (1996) has argued that the 'expressive dimension' is the 'hidden power source of the non-profit sector as a whole' and it is in the grassroots association that the intrinsic value of an activity is most clearly seen to be at least as important as the delivery of outputs.

In the second place, non-bureaucratic groupings are unlikely to have ambitions to survive beyond the achievement of the aims that have brought them together: 'They may disappear when their signature problem is not present as a community concern only to reappear when a new crisis arises' and 'They may change character when new members join' (Cnaan and Milofsky, 2008: 2). There may, however, be variations in the life-span of non-bureaucratic organisations: 'In general [grassroots associations] tend to be short-lived even if successful, with some dissolving quickly, some lasting five to ten years and then dying, and others lasting longer.' These differences appear to be related to the nature of the issue or interest that led to their formation, but may also depend on whether the group is part of a wider movement with regional or national headquarters that provide sponsorship and support (Smith, 2000: 77).

In the third place, non-bureaucratic groupings tend to have permeable boundaries. In many cases the formal membership of those who have paid a subscription and committed themselves to the aims of the association does not define the group of people who play an active role in its affairs, which may also include supporters who are not 'paid up' members. And community groups are often 'settings or venues where community happens and as such are inseparable from the larger system that is this amorphous thing we call community' (Canaan and Milofsky, 2008: 2).

It follows that the ownership of the association is equally hard to pin down. For many groups it is the current membership that comprises the owners, but it is clear that the extent to which each of them exercises the authority and accepts the responsibility that follows from ownership varies. Billis distinguishes between 'those who stay in the shadows... those who play an active part in committee and other activities; and a core group of those ... "who everybody knows" will really be the key players in the defining moments of the group's history' (Billis, 2010b: 54).

In the kind of group highlighted by Milofsky and Cnaan and Milofsky, ownership may reside in the wider community, and the groups 'depend on relationships and history and the willingness of people to do what is needed when the time comes for work to be done. Their leaders may not be self-conscious entrepreneurs but rather may be citizens who are raised up by acclamation or by the needs of the moment' (Cnaan and Milofsky, 2008: 2). In these circumstances leaders either select themselves or are chosen by their peers; the extent of their authority will depend on their willingness to shoulder responsibility and the acceptance of their leadership by the rest of the active membership; and the way in which they provide leadership may vary over time and according to circumstances.

These three fundamental differences between less formal organisations and the bureaucracies of conventional organisational theory not only mean that organisational theories struggle to understand the non-bureaucratic world but also explain why attempts to apply conventional theories to them can be counterproductive:

> Organizations which are disorganized and that cannot draw on basic financial, group-leadership, and community mobilization skills are likely to sputter. These organizations are hurt further because the knowledge that their volunteers bring to the work often is inappropriate. People think they know how [to] build organizations from their experience with business organizations or large, bureaucratic non-profits, and they lack sourcebooks describing strategies that work for small nonprofits and associations.
>
> (Milofsky, 2008: 185)

Degrees of formality

There are, however, different degrees of formality within the overall population of non-bureaucratic organisations that it would be useful to identify at this stage of the argument. We can distinguish at least three dimensions: whether or not the group is part of a wider structure; its size; and the relative importance it attaches to instrumental and expressive behaviour.

'Polymorphic' groups, as Smith (2000: 80) terms those that are linked to a wider structure, are more likely to have a longer life-span than those that are completely 'free-standing'. These links offer the benefits of access to external resources but may bring with them a threat to the group's autonomy. Associations that aim to have complete autonomy 'will tend to have little or no access to the resources of other groups'

(Smith, 2000: 80). Those which are affiliated to other groups will have access to resources of various kinds – information and advice as well as physical resources such as meeting rooms and funding – but may pay a price in terms of their ability to choose their goals and the way they operate. The larger structures may include national or regional federations, or local institutions like a church, school or hospital, and links to them may involve formal requirements or informal pressures to use bureaucratic practices.

The second dimension is size. Grassroots associations are, for the most part, small (although there are significant exceptions). Smith draws on the work of Kanter and Zurcher (1973) to suggest that 'small size permits greater interpersonal contact and more fulfilling human interaction among participants, more pervasive interaction and more power sharing (less inequality)'. And he quotes Gummer (1988) to the effect that ' "small size by itself does not deter the growth of bureaucratic practices" but that it can permit a group to avoid bureaucracy if other factors are present, whereas large organizations inevitably are bureaucratic' (Smith, 2000: 78).

The third dimension is the relative importance the group attaches to instrumental or expressive behaviour – or to public-benefit or member-benefit activities. Many are, in the words of Roger Lohmann (1992), 'mixed benefactories' and deliver a combination of member and public benefits – although the balance between the two may vary to a large extent. Generally speaking, grassroots associations 'are very much more likely to be member benefit and member service orientated in goals, on the whole, than non member benefit and external service orientated in goals' (Smith, 2000: 114–15). But, as Harris has pointed out, many of them also provide public benefits, and a key challenge for them is to achieve a balance between focusing 'activities primarily on the needs of the immediate member' and taking 'a more outward-looking approach towards the needs of the community' (Harris, 1998: 32). For Smith (2000) this distinction between 'member-benefit' and 'public-benefit' activities runs along the same contours as the difference between expressive and instrumental purposes. Public-benefit goals involve instrumental purposes and a greater degree of formality, while member-benefit activities can be associated with expressive purposes and less formal ways of working.

Less formal organisations: A positive definition

Defining these organisational forms by what they are *not* – as non-bureaucratic entities – has its uses, but it is not as valuable as a positive definition. Roger Lohmann has pointed out the short-comings of a negative definition by arguing that defining voluntary organisations as non-profit was about as helpful as treating lettuce as non-animal:

> Lettuce is a non-fur-bearing, non-milk-producing, non-child bearing, and non-warm-blooded nonanimal. Further, as a mammal, lettuce is highly ineffective, being sedentary and not warm-blooded. All other mammals are much faster! Lettuce is also remarkably nonagile and fails to protect its young. On the whole, lettuce is a miserable excuse for a mammal!
>
> (Lohmann, 1989: 369)

Lohmann's unjustly neglected book on the Commons (1992) is a valiant attempt to provide a positive definition in place of 'negations and negative comparisons of voluntary action with the market or for-profit sector' (Lohmann, 1989: 367). He defines voluntary associations or, as he prefers to call them, the 'commons' as 'a social, economic and political space for un-coerced participation, sharing of resources and purposes, mutuality, and peer relations' and goes on to explain that 'Commons are social spaces outside the home and away from family and independent of political states and economic markets. They are found in many different cultures, locations and historical periods. We refer generally to participation in commons as voluntary association' (Lohmann, 1992: 272).

Lohmann locates the key features of voluntary association in the concept of *Koinonia*, which was used by the ancient Greeks to describe a set of relationships with five key characteristics:

> the ancient Greeks had five requisites for koinonia: (1) participation must be free and uncoerced; (2) participants must share a common purpose, whether major or minor, long term or short term; (3) participants must have something in common that they share such as jointly held resources, a collection of precious objects, or a repertory of shared actions; (4) participation involves *philia* (a sense of mutuality, often inadequately translated as friendship); and (5) social relations must be distinguished by *dikiaon* (fairness). This five-part definition encompasses all of the major elements sought by advocates of nonprofit, voluntary, independent, and third-sector terminology and does so in a simple and elegant manner.
>
> (Lohmann, 1992: 58–9)

He goes on to argue that a commons is a space 'in which associative communities create and reproduce social worlds' and that 'Associative social worlds are composed of the images, meanings and sense of reality shared by autonomous, self-defining collectivities of voluntarily associating individuals' (Lohmann, 1992: 59). Interaction in the social space that is the commons 'may be organized both informally, through use of common languages and a common worldview, and formally, through associations and other noncoercive groups' (Lohmann, 1992: 63).

How are they organised?

But how can the work of these non-coercive forms be organised in the absence of clearly defined instrumental goals, on the one hand, and a bureaucratic command and control structure, on the other? For Smith the answer can be found in the 'internal guidance systems' of grassroots associations. He suggests that 'all groups must guide their members to some extent regarding appropriate and acceptable thoughts (ideology), motives (desires), feelings (emotions), and actions (behaviours)'. And he argues that a group's guidance system consists of two elements – ideology, which 'spells out the goals and the reasons for them', and incentives consisting of a 'set of rewards and punishments for members that is manipulated by the group so as to attain group goals by accepted group means' (Smith, 2000: 91).

The importance of ideology to associations varies. Most of them need only what Smith calls 'moderate amounts of it':

> The limited ideology of a typical GA [Grassroots Association] asserts, implicitly or explicitly, the value of the specific GA and its goals, the value of its leaders and other active members ...; the importance of GA activities ...; the necessity of using GA-approved means to achieve its goals; the duty of members to participate in the GA and to support it financially; the importance of keeping present GA members while seeking additional ones as needed; and the necessity of resisting change in GA goals, structure and activities unless there are powerful reasons for such change.
>
> (Smith, 2000: 92)

There are, however, some kinds of associations that have more extensive ideological frameworks. These include some 'polymorphic' groups that are affiliated to bodies with highly developed ideologies, such as the Freemasons and other fraternities; social movements and campaigning bodies; faith-based organisations; and youth movements like the Boy Scouts and Girl Guides. Less conventional associations may need to develop an ideology which explains to members why the group does not conform to societal norms or why it espouses what is perceived by others to be radical change. On the other hand, 'GAs that mainly conform to societal norms and socially constructed "reality" ... do not need such elaborate ideologies to convince themselves and others that what they are thinking, feeling, wanting and doing makes sense and is right, good and just' (Smith, 2000: 95).

The behaviour of unmanaged volunteers

Having set out some of the key characteristics of non-bureaucratic forms of voluntary action, we turn to the reasons why people become involved in it. While these are similar to the incentives for any form of volunteering, the relative weight or importance of the different kinds of incentive tends to be different. Smith's (2000: 97–102) list of 'associational incentives' includes three main kinds of explanation for participation. The first is about *sociability* – satisfaction of the need for social interaction with other people. The second is about the satisfaction that comes from carrying out the work of the association: this includes *purposive* incentives (helping to achieve the association's goals); *service* incentives (providing services to one's fellow members or, more rarely, other people); and *lobbying* incentives (exerting influence on policy-makers). And the third is about *informational* or *developmental* incentives for the acquisition of knowledge and personal growth. While these are the main kinds of incentives, involvement in some groups may also be motivated by the *prestige* that accompanies membership of an elite body; the *utilitarian* motivation to join a minority of groups that offer professional or personal advantage; or the influence of the *charismatic* leaders of some organisations.

If we use Smith's list of 'incentives' as a framework, it is possible to rank what volunteers hope to achieve from their involvement according to the kind of organisational context in which it takes place. Bureaucratic and semi-bureaucratic organisations, for example, are most likely to provide service incentives; self-help groups tend to provide a blend of developmental, informational and sociability incentives; associations offer a mixture of sociability, informational and developmental incentives, on the one hand, and purposive and service incentives, on the other; and some associations and many less organised groups may provide lobbying and charismatic incentives.

The ways in which volunteers become involved in non-bureaucratic organisations are more easily differentiated from the experience of more formal bodies with their organised approach to recruitment, selection, induction and training. By contrast, grassroots associations, according to Smith (2000: 139–40), 'usually recruit new members informally by word of mouth' often at the invitation of friends or relatives. They tend to be 'rather simple to join, to participate in, or even to lead' and 'newcomers tend to be informally socialised' rather than undergoing training.

Many volunteers recruited by formal agencies continue to play the role for which they were selected throughout their involvement with the organisation. If they do change roles, it is the result of a formal appraisal of their suitability for the new position. By contrast, members of associations and volunteers in less formal organisations tend to have a more 'organic' or 'fluid' relationship with the organisation:

> There is no preconceived 'job' which they are requested to take on. Instead, the individual volunteer will explore the range of possible roles and choose one or more that he or she feels comfortable with. And, since what is on offer is a share in the ownership of the [project], the volunteers have opportunities to shape the future work of the project by sharing decision-making as well as helping to organise its activities and to maintain the organisation.
>
> (Rochester, 1992: 129)

In the least formal organisational types, different contributions are not associated with specified roles or offices. For them, the group meets as a whole to discuss and determine what it is going to do. There is no separate governing body and, for some, no 'business meetings' as opposed to its normal proceedings. One study of small groups in the USA found that, while 90% of them had recognised leaders, only 57% had elected officers (Wuthnow, 1994: 135, quoted in Smith, 2000: 110). And, where groups do have officers, it is not necessarily the case that the holders of key offices are its acknowledged leaders (Ockenden and Hutin, 2008). Formally acknowledged leaders gain their position partly because they have made themselves 'known to and respected by other members, especially current leaders. Volunteering to do various needed tasks in a GA seems to be a good entrée into subsequent leadership.' And 'making many social bonds with other members...also is important' (Smith, 2000: 155).

The involvement of volunteers in grassroots associations and simi-lar organisations is supported and maintained by their relations with other members of their group and by the work of the organisations' leaders. Given its emphasis on sociability incentives and its status as a serious leisure activity, associational volunteering puts a premium on the quality of relationships between members of the group. A priority for the induction of new members is to build relationships with existing volunteers rather than focusing on activities alone. And the relation-ship between leaders and the wider membership is key to maintaining commitment and getting the work of the group done. The associational norms of sociability and the leisure-time nature of the involvement mil-itate against tight supervision and sanctions are weak. 'Getting things done' will depend on the commitment of the volunteer to the ideology of the group and may be encouraged by polite enquiries about progress, while the only strong sanction may be to ask someone else to take on the responsibility for completing tasks.

The authority of leaders in informal organisations is thus derived essentially from their personal characteristics – an ability to embody the ideology of the association and their ability to communicate with their followers – rather than their position within a more formal struc-ture. There is something of a paradox here: leaders in non-bureaucratic organisations have a more important role to play, but have little or no power compared with those in bureaucratic agencies.

Some conclusions

This chapter has focused on the behaviour of unmanaged volunteers in non-bureaucratic voluntary organisations – or arrangements for collec-tive voluntary action. It has argued that the great majority of voluntary sector organisations are associations – or have strong associational fea-tures – and that most volunteers are not engaged as additional human resources or unpaid staff by service-providing bureaucracies. Following Billis, it has moved the association from the periphery to the centre of the world of voluntary action and identified four non-bureaucratic forms of collective action with associational features – the 'pure' associa-tion itself; hybrid 'unorganised groups' with their origins in the personal world of family and friends which have adopted some of the features of the association; micro voluntary agencies where the employment of staff has introduced elements of bureaucracy without undermining their associational foundations; and self-help groups. The chapter has not only shown how the non-bureaucratic forms differ from bureaucratic kinds of voluntary action, but also identified the defining features of the association and its variants and explored the behaviour of the unmanaged volunteers who are involved with them. The implications of this alternative paradigm of voluntary action will be discussed in the next and final chapter.

16
The Implications of Rethinking Voluntary Action

The starting point for this book was a concern that voluntary action as it has been understood and practised in the UK (and elsewhere) in the past was under threat and that there was a real and imminent danger that an important and distinctive part of our society would disappear. Rather than agitating for social change; identifying social needs and devising ways of addressing them; and providing arenas for conviviality, expressive behaviours and mutual support, voluntary organisations have been cast in the role of agents of the state whose essential role was to deliver public services on behalf of government in the form and on the terms laid down by statutory agencies. At the same time, volunteering has been seen as unpaid work that needed to be professionally managed and that was undertaken in large agencies concerned with social welfare rather than as the largely self-directed and autonomous behaviour of people engaged in a wide field of activity and active in a variety of organisational settings. The aims of the book have been to explain how this account of collective and individual voluntary action has come to be so widely accepted; to explore some of the consequences of the dominant paradigms; and to set out an alternative and more rounded view of voluntary action as a better guide to theory and practice. This final chapter will provide a brief reminder and review of the ways in which the book has addressed these goals before discussing the theoretical and practical implications of its argument.

Explanations

The first part of the book looked for explanations for the development of the dominant paradigms of the voluntary sector and volunteering in the history of voluntary action. It argued that the historiography of voluntary action had focused on a narrow range of activity and had given undue prominence to the history of philanthropy and the development of policy and practice in the field of social welfare. A more inclusive approach would also need to embrace activities based on conviviality, non-party political engagement and 'serious leisure'. It then looked in more detail at the ways in which the concept of the voluntary *sector* and the idea of the voluntary *worker* were invented and how they developed and gained influence over the way we thought about and practised voluntary action. This part of the book thus situates these two paradigms in context.

The second part of the book discussed the pressures and influences that have helped to shape the way the theory and practice of voluntary action are understood and discussed. It identified and explored the impact of three external forces – the growing influence exercised by successive governments over the work and conduct of voluntary agencies and volunteers; the permeation of the sector by the rules and values of the market; and the impact on the way voluntary action is organised by the predominance in our society of the bureaucratic model. The combined impact of these pressures on voluntary organisations has led to two separate but related consequences – a significant reduction in their independence of thought and action, on the one hand, and the steady erosion of their distinctive organisational features, on the other. A fourth chapter in this section looked at the 'pressure from within' and analysed the contribution of 'product champions' within the sector to the acceptance of basic assumptions about the inevitability of 'partnership' with government; the need to behave like businesses; and the adoption of purely bureaucratic organisational forms.

Challenging the dominant paradigms

The third section of the book challenged some of the orthodoxies of this consensus about the role and nature of voluntary action, and in the process made a case for the distinctiveness of voluntary organisations and volunteers. It looked in turn at:

Governance and ownership

Chapter 9 approached governance in voluntary organisations not as 'what boards do' but as 'responsibility for the whole life of the institution' which 'takes account of all the interests that affect' its 'viability, competence and moral character' (Selznick, 1992: 290). It sought to identify the 'principal owners' who exercised control over the key decisions that affect the organisation's destiny, assumed the ultimate responsibility for its governance and, as a result, defined its ethos and culture. In unambiguous voluntary associations ownership rested with an inner group of committed members; in shallow hybrids it might be located across a range of interests such as members, users, staff members and volunteers; and in the entrenched hybrid it could be seen as passing into the hands of the staff or the paid managers.

Purposes or functions

Chapter 10 provided a critique of the assumption that the sole or prime functions of voluntary action are instrumental. It argued that voluntary organisations do not exist simply to deliver certain services or activities but also to provide opportunities for behaviour that is intrinsically valuable. Similarly, it suggested that the value of the contribution made by the individual volunteer is not limited to the amount of unpaid labour it represents but has a wider social benefit. And, voluntary action in the aggregate has a vital role as an intermediary between state and citizen and as a creator of social capital.

Managerialism

Chapter 11 built on the critique set out in the previous chapter by arguing that the approaches and techniques used in the management of business (and increasingly adopted by statutory agencies) were not only unhelpful but also damaging when applied to voluntary organisations. It argued that the command and control model found in most businesses was totally unsuitable for organised forms of voluntary action that should be 'built to face outwards, towards the service user rather than the CEO' (Caulkin, 2007a: 2). After dissecting some of the specific examples of the misguided application of managerialism to voluntary organisations, it concluded by suggesting that voluntary organisations should be seen not as machines or warehouses needing technocratic management but as societies or communities requiring an appropriate kind of leadership.

A 'round earth' map of volunteering

Chapter 12 focused on volunteers and presented a three-perspective model as a means of developing a 'round earth' map that captured the full diversity of motivation to volunteer; the range of organisational contexts in which volunteering took place; and the variety of volunteer roles. In the process it has exposed the inadequacies of the dominant paradigm that defines volunteering essentially as unpaid work that needs to be managed and that takes place in formal organisational structures.

Dissenting voices

The final chapter in this section – Chapter 13 – focused on those who have 'swum against the tide' and featured the efforts of the NCIA to provide a 'wake-up call' to alert voluntary organisations from sleepwalking into allowing their independence of thought and action to be redefined by the state. In the process it has provided further evidence of the extent to which voluntary action as it used to be understood and practised has been eroded and the role of the sector's self-appointed 'leaders' in bringing this about.

An alternative paradigm

The final part of the book aims to move on from the negative to the positive. Having reviewed the events and pressures that have shaped the current perceptions of voluntary action and produced a critique of some of its consequences, it now turns its attention to the development of an alternative paradigm. Chapter 14 clears the way for this by addressing the 'paradox of sectorisation' and explaining how the stronger the voluntary sector's institutions have grown, the weaker its distinctive identity and ethos have become. The explanation was that the treatment of what had been regarded as a 'loose and baggy monster' as a single unified sector facilitated a remarkable sleight of hand. The advantages and defining characteristics associated with the voluntary sector – the ability of voluntary organisations to be responsive, flexible and innovative and to get close to the users of their services – has been transferred from the generally small-scale and less formal bodies where they are mostly found to the sector as a whole. As a result, the largest and most bureaucratic of voluntary agencies have been able to present themselves as appropriate bodies to take over the delivery of public services from the state despite the fact that in many ways they are organised and behave like the statutory agencies they have supplanted as delivery agents. For its part, government has been able to proclaim the virtues of the voluntary sector while entrusting its commissions to organisations that do not exhibit the features associated with the sector.

This understanding is the key that opened the door to the alternative paradigm set out in Chapter 15. Following Billis (2010c), it moves the voluntary association from the margins of the voluntary sector to its centre by recognising it as the sector's ideal organisational type and its equivalent to the private for-profit sector's firm and the public sector's bureau. It then defines what is different and distinctive about voluntary action in two dimensions; first, it is activity undertaken by unmanaged volunteers and, second, it takes place in non-bureaucratic organisational settings. The remainder of the current chapter will explore the implications of this view of the essential nature of voluntary activity for theory and practice.

A shift of focus

In the first place, the alternative paradigm involves a realignment of our map of the voluntary sector or, to use a different metaphor, a shift in the sector's centre of gravity. The dominant paradigm focuses on the largest and most formally structured organisations and assumes that their smaller and less bureaucratic counterparts need to learn from and emulate the way they are organised and managed. And organisations that are too small to be developed along these lines are seen as unimportant and rather contemptuously described as operating 'under the radar' (Soteri-Proctor and Alcock, 2013). If we map the sector's organisations on a spectrum ranging from the most to the least bureaucratic forms, then the degree of academic interest in each sub-species declines as we move from the largest and most formal to the smallest and least bureaucratic types. By contrast, the alternative paradigm focuses attention on the organisational forms that exhibit the organisational features that define the distinctive nature of voluntary action, and implies that we should be less – not more – interested in organisations as they become more like the bureaucratic forms that are also found in the private and public sectors.

At this stage it might be helpful to present a typology of the kinds of organisations that are found in the widest definition of the voluntary or third sector. This is set out in Table 16.1. It is based on the theory developed by Billis (1993a) that identifies three unambiguous 'worlds' of social action – the personal world of family and friends; the associational world; and the world of bureaucracy – and argues that there are ambiguous zones where they overlap. Where the personal world intersects with the associational world we find 'unorganised groups', while the intersection between the associational and bureaucratic worlds provides a space for 'ambiguous voluntary agencies'. The ambiguous status of many organisations corresponds broadly to the hybrid form Billis went on to discuss in a later work (2010). The typology begins with the

Table 16.1 A sector typology

Type	Features	Status
Unorganised groups	Have some of the features of associations but considerable ambiguity about who is/is not a member and how they organise their activities	Hybrid – personal and associational
Self-help groups	Small groups with a clear membership but little or no formal allocation of roles and responsibilities. 'For us by us' is the organisational maxim	Hybrid – personal and associational
Associations	Clear boundaries between members and non-members; arrangements for electing leaders and officers; rules governing how the organisations go about their activities; depend entirely on the efforts of their members to get their work done	Unambiguous
Micro agencies	Employ small number of staff (perhaps up to four Full Time Equivalent (FTE) on operational activities) but still depend on committee members and other volunteers to get their work done. Little distinction between roles and statuses of paid staff and volunteers	Shallow hybrid – associational with some bureaucratic features
Agencies with a lone manager	Employ enough staff to make it appropriate to appoint one of them as 'manager'. Some contribution from committee members and other volunteers to the work of the organisation	Hybrid – associational and bureaucratic
Federated organisations	Headquarters organisation may be an entrenched hybrid but local units may be associations or micro agencies. Clash of organisational cultures may help to create tensions between the centre and the periphery	Hybrid – associational and bureaucratic
Entrenched hybrids	Have sufficient staff to undertake their organisational activities with limited contribution from committee members and other volunteers. Hierarchical staff structure; specialisation of functions; senior management team rather than a lone manager	Bureaucratic with some residual associational features
Corporate voluntary agencies, social enterprises; and non-profit businesses	Complete hierarchical and functionally compartmentalised managerial and staff structure. Formal distinction between governance and management. Staff and especially senior managers become de facto principal owners with board as 'rubber stamp'	Unambiguous bureaucracies

four kinds of non-bureaucratic arrangements identified in Chapter 15 and proceeds via some hybrid types to unambiguous bureaucracies.

What the typology demonstrates is the key importance of understanding the 'organisational grammar' of associations, not only because the association is the ideal type and the numerically predominant form of voluntary organisation but also because the hybrid types of voluntary agency combine elements of the association with bureaucratic features in different ratios. Organisational theories based exclusively on the bureaucratic model cannot explain the complexity of many hybrid voluntary organisations.

Implications for the research agenda

Why do we study voluntary action and how do we go about it? Much effort has been devoted to measurement; researchers have asked how many voluntary organisations there are and what resources they command, or what proportion of the population is involved in volunteering and how much time they have given to it. Substantial resources were applied to the task of calculating the size and shape of the non-profit sector in a large number of countries by the Johns Hopkins Comparative Nonprofit Sector Project (Salamon and Anheier, 1992; and, for the British component, Kendall and Knapp, 1995, 1996) and there has been a series of major national surveys of volunteering (Field and Hedges, 1984; Lynn and Davis Smith, 1991; Davis Smith, 1998; Low *et al.*, 2007) as well as the Citizenship Surveys conducted by the Home Office (Attwood *et al.*, 2003; Home Office, 2004a; Kitchen *et al.*, 2006; Kitchen, 2009; Drever, 2010; DCLG, 2011; Cabinet Office, 2013). Mapping and measuring voluntary action – or 'building the evidence base' as it is commonly described – has also been a major focus for the work of the TSRC. And a great deal of often misdirected effort prompted by the ChangeUp programme has gone into studies of the extent and configuration of the voluntary sector and volunteering at local level.

Two other areas of interest that have continued to attract the attention of researchers in the UK and elsewhere are the relationship of voluntary or non-profit organisations with other sectors, and particularly with the state, and the internal workings of the governance and management of voluntary sector agencies. Both, in their different ways, have tended to concentrate on the larger and more formal parts of the sector. As the Community Sector Coalition pointed out in the wake of the Deakin Commission's report, voluntary organisations that are funded by government represent a small minority of the total population of the sector, and those in a relationship with national government are an even smaller proportion of the whole (Community Sector Coalition, 1996). Yet the relationship is a major preoccupation for voluntary sector researchers who approach the field from a social policy perspective. At the same time, the articles that fill most of the pages of *Nonprofit Management and Leadership* discuss governance and management issues from the point of view of conventional organisation theory rooted in the study of businesses and other bureaucratic forms. Many of the authors are based in business schools or the management departments of our universities, which have shaped the nature of their interest.

By contrast, some of the original concerns of the pioneers of non-profit and voluntary sector research have been largely neglected in recent years. Little, if any, attention has been given to the question of why voluntary organisations exist since the 1980s, when US economists like Hansmann (1987) and Weisbrod (1988) explained this in terms of the failure of the market and of government to provide all the public services that were needed. Similarly, the flurry of activity around the distinctive nature of voluntary sector organisations was largely confined to the 1990s, when Billis and Harris (1996) argued that a combination of common features and challenges defined the difference between them and organisations in the other sectors, the existence of which Knapp and his colleagues (1990) and Leat (1995) had doubted. Billis had already developed his 'worlds' theory to explain why voluntary organisations were different (1993a) and, with Glennerster (1998), to demonstrate how their distinctive organisational features give them a 'comparative advantage' in addressing specific kinds of social problems.

Qualitative research on volunteering has largely focused on three questions of interest to volunteer-involving organisations: motivation or 'why do they come?'; retention or 'why do they stay?'; and management or 'how can we best organise their work?'. The greatest volume of research outputs has been focused on motivation, as researchers look for the key to crafting the messages most likely to attract volunteers to particular organisations. These studies have served to qualify the simple assumption that volunteering was an act of unqualified altruism by showing that most volunteers get involved as the result of a cocktail of motivations, including the selfish and the instrumental as well as the philanthropic and social, and that the nature of the relationship between volunteers and causes is more in the nature of an exchange than a gift. On the other hand, they have been interpreted in a way that supports an almost cynical approach to volunteer recruitment that has largely removed altruism from the equation. Studies of retention have suggested a range of explanations for why volunteers leave or stay. On the one hand, they can point to dissatisfaction with the way the volunteering opportunities are organised and suggest that 'volunteer management' is the key to retention. On the other, they suggest that the intrinsic value of the activity itself may be the reward that keeps volunteers committed. The third question has been answered in two ways – by the adoption of the techniques of human resource management as applied to the management of paid staff, and by the use of bespoke approaches that take account of the different status and motivation of volunteers (Willis, 1993; Davis Smith, 1996; Zimmeck, 2000).

What all three of these discussions have in common, however, is the basic assumption that volunteers are involved in comparatively large and formally structured organisations that have the capacity to devise and implement systems for the recruitment, induction and management of volunteers who will carry out specific tasks. The focus is, therefore, on just one of the kinds of organisational setting or context in which volunteering takes place. A second limitation of the scope of this kind of research is the definition of the questions to be addressed: motivation is emphasised at the expense of the opportunities available to potential volunteers through their personal networks and communities; retention is discussed largely in terms of personal satisfaction rather than the achievement of collective goals; and management is seen as a means of getting maximum value out of the volunteer's involvement. One study that can be seen as an attempt at a broader approach – Jone Pearce's *Volunteers: The Organizational Behaviour of Unpaid Workers* published in 1993 – started from the premise that 'Systematic research has tended to focus on surveys of volunteers' motives, to the virtual exclusion of attention to what volunteers actually do in organizations and how volunteers might more effectively work together.' The author went on to describe her work as exploratory and to express the hope that it would 'spur attention' in the form of 'research as well as counter argument' (Pearce, 1993: 182–3), but this hope seems to have been illusory and the work has sunk with little or no trace.

The alternative paradigm and the typology to which it has led provide the basis for a different kind of research agenda and a different set of priorities for study. The key features of the new agenda can be summarised.

1. In the first place, we need to shift the *focus* from the idea of a 'sector' and, within that, attention to the management of

non-profit businesses to concentrate on the activities and behaviour of unmanaged volunteers involved in non-bureaucratic organisational settings. As well as discarding the 'sector' metaphor, this focus means that the common distinction between the study of voluntary organisations and research on volunteering can be ignored.

2. Second, the *overall aims* of research on voluntary action can be redefined as (a) identifying the ways in which it is different from other forms of collective activity and (b) understanding how non-bureaucratic voluntary groups are organised and managed.

3. Third, we can identify a broad *agenda* that involves (a) a better understanding of voluntary associations; (b) an exploration of how the principles of associational working inform and are applied to the organisation of other non-bureaucratic forms of collective action – unorganised groupings, self-help groups and micro agencies; and (c) an attempt to understand how associational principles influence the workings of hybrid organisations and the extent to which they can be reconciled or combined with the bureaucratic features of these organisations.

4. Within that broad agenda we need to understand the impact of organisational goals on the way groups operate. In particular we need to look at the balance – or tension – between expressive aims (or member benefit) and instrumental aims (or public benefit) and to distinguish between organisations that promote greater social comfort and those that exist to achieve social change.

5. More specifically, we need to explore why and how people join non-bureaucratic groups; what influences their degree of commitment and length of involvement in the organisation; how the relationships between participants are structured; how organisational aims are determined; how the 'work' of the group is organised; and how leadership is exercised.

6. We need to accept that we cannot pursue this agenda by quantitative methods aimed at collecting evidence but need to take it forward by qualitative studies with a view to developing 'usable' theories to explain 'how things work'.

A research agenda based on the alternative paradigm set out in Chapter 15 and which takes account of the argument that has led up to it would not, of course, begin with a blank sheet of paper. David Horton Smith (2000), for example, has gathered together a formidable body of evidence about voluntary associations; Roger Lohmann (1992) has developed a theory of non-bureaucratic organisations that could underpin further study; and Carl Milofsky (2008) has looked in detail at some of the more informal ways in which people act collectively. While slight in comparison with the general literature on volunteering and the voluntary sector, this provides a valuable framework on which we need to build and some important theories that we need to refine if we are to develop our understanding of the essential nature of voluntary action.

Implications for practice

Adopting the alternative paradigm has implications beyond a restructuring of the research agenda. In the first place, the current institutional framework that is based on the idea of a 'unified sector' needs rethinking to reflect the distinction between non-bureaucratic, hybrid and bureaucratic entities. Infrastructure organisations at national and local levels need to be reconfigured to align their work with one or more of these very different types of organisation rather than to persist with the tacit claim that they represent all of them. NCVO should, for example, concentrate on what it does best – acting as a trade association and training school for the 'corporate' charities whose main purpose is to act as contractors and deliverers of services. At the other end of the spectrum, support for associational and less formal activities needs a different kind of home, possibly in a new agency based on the work of the Community Sector Coalition. The hybrid forms may need a third kind of national focus in which the importance of their bureaucratic elements can be recognised without an assumption that these represent a more 'normal' or valuable way of doing things and that the natural and inevitable organisational trajectory is towards fully fledged bureaucracy. And, at local level, CVSs would need to recognise that many of their members are hybrid organisations that need support to operate as they are rather than to be transformed into bureaucracies. For their part, local volunteer centres need to reconsider whether their role is simply to help organisations recruit and manage unpaid workers or whether it might involve promoting voluntary action more generally.

In the second place, the alternative paradigm requires a change in our approach to the provision of advice, consultancy, support and training for 'capacity-building'. As we have seen, treating informal organisational forms as if they were bureaucracies is not only inappropriate but can be actively harmful. A different set of approaches, concepts and other tools is needed to nurture healthy and effective associations, and these need to be developed, tested and disseminated. Similarly, the standard organisational theory textbook provides only some of the guidance needed by those who lead and manage hybrid organisations, and insights from associational life also inform their endeavours. Zimmeck (2000) argued that there were two broad approaches to the management of volunteers based on two different organisational models. 'Modern management' based on the bureaucratic model was gaining support for an increasingly formalised and professionalised approach. There was a risk that it would supplant the 'home-grown' style with its roots in a collectivist–democratic organisational model and a more sensitive, flexible, dynamic and effective approach to managing volunteers. What was true for the management of volunteers is equally true for managing hybrid voluntary organisations; codifying and disseminating a 'home-grown' or more appropriate style is the key to the management of the hybrid voluntary organisation. In contrast to the present model of 'capacity-building', moreover, we need to acknowledge the importance of the experiential wisdom of experienced practitioners rather than rely on the teaching of 'experts' who base their instruction on inappropriate models and theories. The challenge is to harness the collective knowledge and understanding that already exists within the world of voluntary action rather than import ideas from elsewhere.

And, third, acceptance of the alternative paradigm has implications for the ways in which we look at funding and accountability. The current funding model focuses on rewarding the instrumental function; payment is made for the delivery of a specified level of service. The view of voluntary action presented in this book, however, emphasises the fact that the purpose of many voluntary organisations is largely expressive and their contribution to the well-being and the quality of life of their members and beneficiaries cannot be measured simply in terms of outputs. In the past, charitable trusts and statutory agencies were happy to provide financial support to organisations that they saw as providing social value without needing to prescribe the kind and level of outputs they expected from them. This kind of funding has been dismissed as 'gift-giving' and is deeply unpopular in the contemporary funding world, but it has its place alongside other modes of funding in which the funding body increasingly defines the methods as well as the aims of the programmes it is prepared to support.

Unorganised groups and voluntary associations do not, of course, depend on external bodies for the resources they need, and their leaders are accountable for their actions to the other members. In hybrid organisations, accountability is multi-faceted, and there may be a number of different interests that have a legitimate interest in what the organisation does and how it does it. In the shallow hybrids it is the

inner core of active members who, as the 'principal owners', have ultimate responsibility for the key decisions that have to be made and for
managing the tension between the aspirations and needs of its constituents and the requirements of its funders. The more bureaucratic
entrenched hybrids and the unambiguous corporate agencies do not
have to grapple with this kind of tension: their staff (or their managers)
have become the principal owners, the survival of the organisation
and its financial health have become the overriding considerations,
and the requirements of the funders are the necessary conditions for
achieving them.

Last words

In the last 30 years or so, governments in the UK have conducted a sustained and energetic campaign to transfer many of the functions of the
state from the public sector to the voluntary and for-profit sectors. They
have used the idea of a unified voluntary or third sector as a significant
means of bringing this about. In the first place, the concept of a sector has allowed governments to contrast the 'flexibility, responsiveness,
innovation and closeness to service users' of voluntary sector organisations with the rigid, unimaginative and bureaucratic character of the
statutory agencies they will replace. This is, however, an illusion: the
small minority of voluntary sector organisations that have been trusted
with the new role are unrepresentative and have more in common with
the agencies they have supplanted than they have with the bulk of the
organisations that comprise the sector and provide the evidence for the
characteristics featured in government rhetoric. And, second, the sector
has been used as a stalking horse and its taking on the role as a provider
of public services can be seen as a prologue to the main event, which is
the wholesale out-sourcing of the state to the private sector.

In the process the idea of 'voluntary action' as an independent
and distinctive sphere of activity has suffered a great deal of collat-
eral damage. The trajectory of the 'voluntary sector' juggernaut has
diverted attention away from the voluntary associations that are the
'ideal type' of voluntary sector organisation and obliterated the associational elements that contribute to the hybrid nature of many voluntary
organisations by concentrating our eyes on their bureaucratic dimensions. In the process, many voluntary organisations have lost sight of
their original purposes and functions; have surrendered much of their
independence of thought and action; have been 'captured' by their
staff or their senior managers; have failed many or all of their users or

beneficiaries; and, apart from not distributing their profits or surpluses as dividends, are indistinguishable from private sector companies.

In this book I have tried to explain how and why the idea and practice of voluntary action have come under attack and to explore some of the implications of the ways in which the concept of a unified voluntary sector has been used to promote ideas of 'partnership' with government; a major role as a provider of public services; and a bureaucratic approach to effectiveness and capacity that run counter to the key characteristics of organised voluntary action. I have then tried to define what is distinctive about voluntary action in its 'pure' and hybrid forms and explored some of the implications for research and practice of restoring the voluntary association to its central position as the sector's 'ideal type' and shifting the focus of attention from the bureaucratic and semi-bureaucratic end of the spectrum to more distinctive forms of voluntary activity. Rethinking voluntary action in this way would involve a radical revision of the research agenda and equally significant changes in the way in which the institutions of the sector should be configured; in our approach to improving organisational effectiveness and capacity; and for funding relationships and arrangements for accountability. This prescription is unlikely to find favour with those who have acted as product champions of the unified sector and all it has stood for, but I hope and believe it may encourage and assist those who are less complacent about the current state of voluntary action and its future prospects in a hostile economic and political environment.

References

6 P and Leat D. (1997) 'Inventing the British voluntary sector by committee: from Wolfenden to Deakin', *Non-Profit Studies* 1(2): 33–47.

Active Community Unit (2003) *Voluntary and Community Sector Infrastructure: A Consultation Document*, London: Home Office.

Adams, D. (1981) 'Why is volunteering fun? Some notes on play work and voluntary action', Paper presented to the meeting of the North Central Sociological Association, Ohio State University.

Adams, D. (1990) 'Issues and ideas in the culture of American voluntarism', Paper prepared for the meeting of the American Sociological Association, Washington, DC.

Adur Voluntary Action and National Coalition for Independent Action (2010) *The Local State and Voluntary Action in West Sussex: The Results of Exploratory Qualitative Research*, Lancing and London: Adur Voluntary Action and National Coalition for Independent Action.

Alcock, P. (2010) 'A strategic unity: defining the third sector in the UK', *Voluntary Sector Review* 1(1): 5–24.

Attwood. C., G. Singh, D. Prime and R. Creasey (2003) *2001 Home Office Citizenship Survey: People, families and communities – Research Study 270*, London: Home Office.

Austin, R., P. Larkey, J. Royo, A. Neely and D. Waggoner (1998) 'Measuring knowledge work: pathologies and patterns', Paper presented to the first international conference on performance measurement, Cambridge: Centre for Business Performance, Cambridge University.

Aves, G. (1969) *The Voluntary Worker in the Social Services: Report of a Committee Jointly set up by the National Council for Social Service and the National Institute for Social Work Training*, London: Bedford Square Press and George Allen and Unwin.

Barrett, G. (1985) *Blackfriars Settlement: A Short History 1887–1987*, London: Blackfriars Settlement.

Batsleer, J. (1995) 'Management and organisation', in J. Davis Smith, C. Rochester and R. Hedley (eds) *An Introduction to the Voluntary Sector*, London: Routledge.

Berger, P. and R. Neuhaus (1977) *To Empower People: The Role of Mediating Structures in Public Policy*, Washington, DC: American Enterprise Institute for Public Policy Research.

Beveridge, W. (1942) *Report of the Inter-Departmental Committee on Social Insurance and Allied Services*, London: HMSO, Cmnd6404.

Beveridge, W. (1948) *Voluntary Action: A Report on Methods of Social Advance*, London: Allen and Unwin.

Billis, D. (1993a) *Organising Public and Voluntary Agencies*, London: Routledge.

Billis, D. (1993b) *Sliding into Change: The Future of the Voluntary Sector in the Mixed Organisation of Welfare*, Centre for Voluntary Organisation Working Paper 14, London: London School of Economics and Political Science.

Billis, D. (2010a) *Hybrid Organizations and the Third Sector*, Basingstoke: Palgrave Macmillan.

Billis, D. (2010b) 'From welfare bureaucracies to welfare hybrids', in D. Billis (ed.) *Hybrid Organizations and the Third Sector*, Basingstoke: Palgrave Macmillan.

Billis, D. (2010c) 'Towards a theory of hybrid organizations', in D. Billis (ed.) *Hybrid Organizations and the Third Sector*, Basingstoke: Palgrave Macmillan.

Billis, D. and H. Glennerster (1998) 'Human services and the voluntary sector: towards a theory of comparative advantage', *Journal of Social Policy* 27(1): 79–98.

Billis, D. and M. Harris (1992) 'Taking the strain of change: British local voluntary agencies enter the post-Thatcher period', *Nonprofit and Voluntary Sector Quarterly* 21(3): 211–25.

Billis, D. and M. Harris (1996) 'Introduction: enduring challenges of research and practice', in D. Billis and M. Harris (eds) *Voluntary Agencies: Challenges for Organisation and Management*, Basingstoke: Macmillan.

Blake, G., D. Robinson and M. Smerdon (2006) *Living Values: A report encouraging boldness in third sector organisations*, London: Community Links.

Boatright, J. (2000) *Ethics and the Conduct of Business*, Upper Saddler River, NJ: Prentice Hall.

Bosserman, P. and R. Gagan (1972) 'Leisure and voluntary action' in D. Smith ed., *Voluntary Action Research*, Lexington MA: D.C. Heath.

Brenton, M. (1985) *The Voluntary Sector in British Social Services*, London: Longman.

Brewis, G. (2011) 'Challenging narratives: towards an understanding of the history of volunteering', Paper presented at the NCVO/VSSN Researching the Voluntary Sector Conference, 7–8 September.

Briggs, A. and A. Macartney (1984) *Toynbee Hall: The First Hundred Years*, London: Routledge and Kegan Paul.

Brostomer, M. (2006) *Volunteering England Annual Return for Volunteer Centres 2005–6*, London: Institute for Volunteering Research.

Bryson, J. (1988) *Strategic Planning for Public and Nonprofit Organizations*, San Francisco, CA: Jossey Bass.

Bruce, I. (1998) *Successful Charity Marketing: Meeting Need*, 2nd ed., London: ICSA Publishing/Prentice Hall.

Bubb, S. (2012) Bubb's Blog, 23 November at http://bloggerbubb.blogspot.co.uk, accessed January 2013.

Butler, P. (2012) 'Thatcher's outsourcing fantasy fails in reality', *Guardian*, 16 October.

Byrne, P. (1997) *Social Movements in Britain*, London: Routledge.

Cabinet Office (2010) *Business Plan 2011–15: Cabinet Office*, London: Cabinet Office.

Cabinet Office (2013) *Community Life Survey: Q2 2012–13 (August–October 2012) Statistical Bulletin*, London: Cabinet Office.

Cairns, B., M. Harris and R. Hutchison (2007) 'Sharing God's love or meeting government goals: local churches and public policy implementation', *Policy and Politics* 35(3): 413–32.

Carmel, E. and J. Harlock (2008) 'Instituting the "third sector" as a governable terrain: partnership, procurement and performance in the UK', *Policy and Politics* 36(2): 155–71.

Caulkin, S. (2007a) 'Command, control... and you ultimately fail', *The Observer*, 16 December.

Caulkin, S. (2007b) 'A refreshing tip for 2008: tear up the textbook', *The Observer*, 30 December.

Caulkin, S. (2008) 'Thank you readers. I couldn't have done it alone', *The Observer*, 6 January.

Chait, R. (1993) *How to Help Your Board Govern More and Manage Less*, Washington, DC: National Center for Nonprofit Boards.

Charity Commission (2007) *Stand and deliver: The future for charities providing public services*, London: Charity Commission.

Chesterman, M. (1979) *Charities, Trusts and Social Welfare*, London: Weidenfeld and Nicolson.

Clark, P. (2000) *British Clubs and Societies 1580–1800*, Oxford: Oxford University Press.

Clarke, J., D. Kane, K. Wilding and P. Bass (2012) *The UK Civil Society Almanac 2012*, London: National Council for Voluntary Organisations.

Clarke, R. (2004) 'Social reformer and local councillor who challenged the Merseyside police over the Toxteth riots', *Guardian*, 29 July.

Cloke, P., S. Johnsen and J. May (2007) 'Ethical citizenship? Volunteers and the ethics of providing services to homeless people', *Geoforum* 38(6): 1089–1101.

Club and Institute Union (1927) *A Short History of the Working Men's Club and Institute Union*, London: Working Men's Club and Institute Union.

Cnaan, R. and C. Milofsky (2008) *Handbook of Community Movements and Local Organizations*, New York: Springer.

Commission on the Future of the Voluntary Sector in England (1996) *Meeting the Challenge of Change: Into the 21st Century*, London: National Council for Voluntary Organisations.

Commission on the Future of Volunteering (2007) *Call for Evidence*, London: Commission on the Future of Volunteering.

Commission on the Future of Volunteering (2008) *Manifesto for Change*, London: Commission on the Future of Volunteering.

Community Sector Coalition (1996) *Rooting for the Community Sector*, London: Community Sector Coalition.

Compact Voice (2007) *Stronger Independence, Stronger Relationships, Better Outcomes: Report Drawing on a Local Compact Voice Survey Conducted for Local Sector Independence Day, 4th July 2007*, London: Compact Voice/National Council for Voluntary Organisations.

Conservative Party (2008) *A Stronger Society: Voluntary Action in the 21st Century*, Responsibility Agenda, Green Policy paper No. 5, London: Conservative Party.

Cornforth, C. (2003) *The Governance of Public and Non-Profit Organisations: What Do Boards Do?* London: Routledge.

Courtney, R. (1996) *Managing Voluntary Organisations: New Approaches*, London: ISCA Publishing.

Courtney, R. (2002) *Strategic Management for Nonprofit Organisations*, London: Routledge.

Craig, G., M. Taylor, N. Carlton, R. Garbutt, R. Kimberlee, E. Lepine and A. Syed (2005) *The Paradox of Compacts: Monitoring the Impact of Compacts*, Home Office Online Report 02/05, London: Home Office.

Crowson, N., M. Hilton and J. McKay (2009) *NGOs in Contemporary Britain: Non-State Actors in Society and Politics since 1945*, Basingstoke: Palgrave Macmillan.

Dahrendorf, R. (2001) *Challenges to the Voluntary Sector:* The 18th Arnold Goodman Lecture, London: Charities Aid Foundation.

Dahrendorf, R. (2003) 'Foreword' to J. Kendall *The Voluntary Sector: Comparative perspectives in the UK*, London: Routledge.

Dartington, T. (1995) 'Trustees, committees and boards', in J. Davis Smith, C. Rochester and R. Hedley (eds) *An Introduction to the Voluntary Sector*, London: Routledge.

Davis Smith, J. (1995) 'The Voluntary Tradition: Philanthropy and Self-help', in J. Davis Smith, C. Rochester and R. Hedley (eds) *An Introduction to the Voluntary Sector*, London: Routledge.

Davis Smith, J. (1996) 'Can Volunteers Be Managed?', in D. Billis and M. Harris (eds) *Voluntary Agencies: Challenges for Organisation and Management*, Basingstoke: Macmillan.

Davis Smith, J. (1998) *The 1997 Survey of Volunteering*, London: National Centre for Volunteering.

Davis Smith, J. (2000) 'Volunteering and social development', *Voluntary Action* 3(1): 9–23.

Davis Smith, J. (2001) 'Volunteers: making a difference?', in M. Harris and C. Rochester (eds) *Voluntary Organisations and Social Policy in Britain: Perspectives on Change and Choice*, Basingstoke: Palgrave.

Deakin, N. (1996) 'What Does Contracting Do to Users?,' in D. Billis and M. Harris (eds) *Voluntary Agencies: Challenges for Organisation and Management*, Basingstoke: Macmillan.

Deakin, N. (2001) 'Public Policy, Social Policy and Voluntary Organisations', in M. Harris and C. Rochester (eds) *Voluntary Organisations and Social Policy in Britain: Perspectives on Change and Choice*, Basingstoke: Palgrave.

Della Porta, D. and M. Diani (2006) *Social Movements: An Introduction*, Malden, MA: Blackwell.

Department for Communities and Local Government (2008) *Communities in Control: Real People, Real Power*, London: Department for Communities and Local Government, Cm7427.

Department for Communities and Local Government (2011) *Community Action in England: A Report on the 2009–10 Citizenship Survey*, London: Department for Communities and Local Government.

Department of Health (1989) *Working for Patients (NHS Reforms)*, London: HMSO.

Diani, M. (1992) 'The Concept of Social Movement', *Sociological Review* 40(1): 1–25.

Dimaggio, P. and W. Powell (1983) 'The Iron Cage Revisited: Institutional Isomorphism and Collective Rationality in Organizational Fields', *American Sociological Review* 48: 147–60.

Dingle, A. (2001) *Measuring Volunteering*, Washington, DC: Independent Sector and United Nations Volunteers

Drever, E. (2010) *2008–09 Citizenship Survey: Volunteering and Charitable Giving Topic Report*, London: Department for Communities and Local Government.

Durning, J. (2006) *Review of ChangeUp National Hubs: Final Report*, Birmingham: CapacityBuilders.

Ehrenreich, B. (2007) *Dancing in the Streets: A History of Collective Joy*, London: Granta.

Ellis Paine, A., N. Ockenden and J. Stuart (2010) 'Volunteers in Hybrid Organizations: A Marginalized Majority?', in D. Billis (ed.) *Hybrid Organizations and the Third Sector*, Basingstoke: Palgrave Macmillan.

Elsdon, K. (1995) *Voluntary Organisations: Citizenship, Learning and Change*, Nottingham: NIACE.

Field, J. and B. Hedges (1984) *A National Survey of Volunteering*, London: Social and Community Planning Research.

Fuller, L. (1969) 'Two Principles of Human Association', in J. Pennock and J. Chapman (eds) *Voluntary Associations*, New York: Atherton.

Gaskin, K., R. Hutchison, M. Hutin and M. Zimmeck (2008) *The Commission on the Future of Volunteering; Results of the Public Consultation*, London: Commission on the Future of Volunteering.

Gilchrist, A. and M. Taylor (2011) *The Short Guide to Community Development*, Bristol: The Policy Press.

Glennerster, H. (2003) *Understanding the Finance of Welfare: What Welfare Costs and How to Pay for It*, Bristol: The Policy Press.

Gordon, C. and N. Babchuk (1959) 'Typology of Voluntary Associations', *American Sociological Review* 24: 22–29.

Gosden, P. (1974) *Self Help: Voluntary Associations in Nineteenth Century Britain*, London: Batsford.

Griffiths, H. (1981) *The Development of Local Voluntary Action: An Interpretative Account of a Conference Held at Swanwick, Derbyshire, on 23–25 January 1981*, Berkhamsted and London: Volunteer Centre UK, National Council for Voluntary Organisations and Voluntary Services Unit, Home Office.

Grotz, J. (2011) *Less Recognised Impacts of Volunteering, Unpublished Report Prepared for the State of the World's Volunteerism Report*, Bonn: UN Volunteers.

Grotz, J. (2012) 'A Review and Discussion of Classification Systems for Volunteering', Paper presented at the 18th NCVO/VSSN Researching the Voluntary Sector Conference, 10–11 September, University of Birmingham.

Gummer, B. (1988) 'The Hospice in Transition: Organizational and Administrative Perspectives', *Administration in Social Work* 12: 31–43.

Guthrie, M. (2000) *Mix, Match, Merge: Issues and Options for Considering Mergers and Other Partnerships*, London: VOLPROF, City University.

Hadley, R. and S. Hatch (1982) *Social Welfare and the Failure of the State*, London: Allen and Unwin.

Hall, P.D. (1992) *Inventing the Nonprofit Sector and Other Essays on Philanthropy, Voluntarism and Nonprofit Organizations*, Baltimore and London: The Johns Hopkins University Press.

Hannan, M. and J. Freeman (1989) *Organizational Ecology*, Cambridge, MA: Harvard University Press.

Handy, C. (1988) *Understanding Voluntary Organisations*, Harmondsworth: Penguin.

Hansmann, H. (1987) 'Economic theories of nonprofit organization', in W. Powell (ed.) *The Nonprofit Sector: A Research Handbook*, New Haven, CT and London: Yale University Press.

Harris, B. (2004) *The Origins of the British Welfare State: Society, State and Welfare in England and Wales, 1800–1945*, Basingstoke: Palgrave Macmillan.

Harris, B. (2010) 'Voluntary action and the state in historical perspective', *Voluntary Sector Review* 1(1): 25–40.

Harris, M. (1990) 'Working in the UK voluntary sector', *Work, Employment and Society* 4: 125–40.

Harris, M. (1993) 'Exploring the Role of Boards Using Total Activities Analysis', *Nonprofit Management and Leadership* 3(3): 269–82.

Harris, M. (1996) 'Do we need governing bodies?', in D. Billis and M. Harris (eds) *Voluntary Agencies: Challenges for Organisation and Management*, Basingstoke: Macmillan.

Harris, M. (1998) *Organising God's Work: Challenges for Churches and Synagogues*, London: Routledge.

Harris, M. (1999) 'Voluntary Sector Governance: Problems in Practice and Theory in the United Kingdom and North America', in D. Lewis (ed.) *International Perspectives on Voluntary Action: Reshaping the Third Sector*, London: Earthscan.

Harris, M. (2001) 'Voluntary Organisations in a Changing Social Policy Environment', in M. Harris and C. Rochester (eds) *Voluntary Organisations and Social Policy in Britain: Perspectives on Change and Choice*, Basingstoke: Palgrave.

Harris, M. and C. Rochester (1996) 'Working with governing bodies', in S. Osborne (ed.) *Managing in the Voluntary Sector*, London: International Thomson Publishing.

Harris, M., C. Rochester and P. Halfpenny (2001) 'Voluntary organisations and social policy: Twenty years of change', in M. Harris and C. Rochester (eds) *Voluntary Organisations and Social Policy in Britain: Perspectives on Change and Choice*, Basingstoke: Palgrave.

Hatch, S. (1986) *Developing Local Voluntary Action*, Occasional Paper 86/6, London: Policy Studies Institute.

Hedley, R. and J. Davis Smith (1992) *Volunteering and Society: Principles and Practice*, London: Bedford Square Press.

Hemming, H. (2011) *Together: How Small Groups Achieve Big Things*, London: John Murray.

HM Treasury (2005) *2004 Spending Review New Public Spending Plans 2005 – 2008 Stability, Security and Opportunity for All: Investing for Britain's Long-term Future*, London: Stationery Office.

HM Treasury and Cabinet Office (2011) *Corporate Governance in Central Government Departments: Code of Good Practice 2011*, London: Stationery Office.

HM Treasury and Home Office (2007) *The Future Role of the Third Sector in Social and Economic Regeneration: Final Report*, London: Stationery Office, Cm7189.

Home Office (1990) *Efficiency Scrutiny of Government Funding of the Voluntary Sector*, London: Home Office.

Home Office (1998) *Compact on Relations between Government and the Voluntary and Community Sector in England*, London: HMSO, Cm4100.

Home Office (2000) *Funding Code of Good Practice*, London: HMSO.

Home Office (2003) *Community Groups Compact Code of Good Practice*, London: HMSO.

Home Office (2004a) *2003 Home Office Citizenship Survey: People, Families and Communities – Research Study 289*, London: Home Office.

Home Office (2004b) *ChangeUp: Capacity Building and Infrastructure Framework for the Voluntary and Community Sector*, London: Home Office.

Howlett, S. (2010) 'Developing Volunteer Management as a Profession', *Voluntary Sector Review* 1(3): 355–60.

Institute for Volunteering Research (2004) *Volunteer Impact Assessment Toolkit*, London: Institute for Volunteering Research.

Jacques, E. (1976) *A General Theory of Bureaucracy*, London: Heinemann.

Jeavons, T. (1994) *When the Bottom Line is Faithfulness: Management of Christian Service Organizations*, Bloomington and Indianapolis, IN: Indiana University Press.

Jochum, V. and C. Rochester (2012) 'An interview with Nicholas Deakin', *Voluntary Sector Review* 3(1): 5–13.

Jones, S. (1986) *Workers at Play; A Social and Economic History of Leisure 1918–1939*, London: Routledge Kegan Paul.

Kane, D. and J. Allen (2011) *Counting the Cuts: The Impact of Spending Cuts on the UK Voluntary and Community Sector*, London: National Council for Voluntary Organisations.

Kanter, R. and L. Zurcher (1973) 'Evaluating Alternatives and Alternative Valuing', *Journal of Applied Behavioral Science* 9: 381–97.

Kay, R. (1996) 'What Kind of Leadership Do Voluntary Organisations Need?,' in D. Billis and M. Harris (eds) *Voluntary Agencies: Challenges for Organisation and Management*, Basingstoke: Macmillan.

Kearney, J. (2001) 'The Values and Basic Principles of Volunteering: Complacency or Caution?', *Voluntary Action* 3(3): 63–86.

Kendall, J. (2003) *The Voluntary Sector: Comparative Perspectives in the UK*, London: Routledge.

Kendall, J. and M. Knapp (1995) 'A Loose and Baggy Monster: Boundaries, Definitions and Typologies', in J. Davis Smith, C. Rochester and R. Hedley (eds) *An Introduction to the Voluntary Sector*, London: Routledge.

Kendall, J. and M. Knapp (1996) *The Voluntary Sector in the UK*, Manchester: Manchester University Press.

Kitchen, S. (2009) *2007–08 Citizenship Survey: Volunteering and Charitable Giving Topic Report*, London: Department for Communities and Local Government.

Kitchen, S., J. Michaelson, N. Wood and P. John (2006) *2005 Citizenship Survey: Active communities topic report*, London: Department for Communities and Local Government.

Knapp, M., E. Robertson and C. Thomason (1990) 'Public money, voluntary sector: whose welfare?', in H. Anheier and W. Seibel (eds) *The Nonprofit Sector: International and Comparative Perspectives*, Berlin and New York: de Gruyter.

Knight, B. (1993) *Voluntary Action*, London: Home Office.

Kramer, R. (1985) 'Towards a Contingency Model of Board-Executive Relations', *Administration in Social Work* 9(3): 15–33.

Krugman, P. (2007) *The Conscience of a Liberal*, New York: W.W. Norton.

Landry, C., D. Morley, R. Southwood and P. Wright (1985) *What a Way to Run a Railroad: An Analysis of Radical Failure*, London: Comedia.

Lansley, J. (1976) *Voluntary Organisations Facing Change: The Report of a Project to Help Councils for Voluntary Service Respond to Local Government Reorganisation*, London: Calouste Gulbenkian Foundation.

Last, J. (2012a) 'Acevo Report Warns of £5.5bn Sector Cuts', *Civil Society Finance*, 5 March.

Last, J. (2012b) 'Crown Representative for Voluntary Sector Is Appointed', *Civil Society On-Line*, 18 June.

Leat, D. (1993) *Managing across Sectors*, London: City University Business School.

Lewis, D. (2010) 'Encountering Hybridity: Lessons from Individual Experiences', in D. Billis (ed.) *Hybrid Organizations and the Third Sector*, Basingstoke: Palgrave Macmillan.

Lewis, J. and H. Glennerster (1996) *Implementing the New Community Care*, Buckingham: Open University Press.

Little, A. and C. Rochester (2003) 'Crossing the Great Divide', Paper presented at the 32nd Annual Conference of the Association for Research on Nonprofit Organizations and Voluntary Action (ARNOVA), Denver, Colorado, 20–22 November.

Locke, M., P. Robson and S. Howlett (2001) 'Users: at the Centre or the Sidelines?', in M. Harris and C. Rochester (eds) *Voluntary Organisations and Social Policy in Britain: Perspectives on Change and Choice*, Basingstoke: Palgrave.

Loewenberg, F. (1992) 'The Roots of Organised Charity in the Ancient World', Paper presented at a meeting of the Voluntary Action History Society, London.

Lohmann, R. (1989) 'And Lettuce is Non-animal: Towards a Positive Economics of Voluntary Action', *Nonprofit and Voluntary Sector Quarterly* 18(4): 367–83.

Lohmann, R. (1992) *The Commons: New Perspectives on Nonprofit Organizations and Voluntary Action*, San Francisco, CA: Jossey Bass.

Low, R., S. Butt, A. Ellis Paine and J. Davis Smith (2007) *Helping Out: A National Survey of Volunteering and Charitable Giving*, London: Cabinet Office.

Lynn, P. and J. Davis Smith (1991) *The 1991 National Survey of Voluntary Activity in the UK*, Berkhamsted: Volunteer Centre UK.

Lyons, M. (1996) ' "On a Clear Day" ... Strategic Management for VNPOs', in S. Osborne (ed.) *Managing in the Voluntary Sector*, London: International Thomson Publishing.

Lyons, M, P. Wijkstrom and G. Clary (1998) 'Comparative Studies of Volunteering: What Is Being Studied', *Voluntary Action* 1(1): 45–54, reprinted in J. Davis Smith and M. Locke (eds) (2007) *Volunteering and the Test of Time*, London: Institute for Volunteering Research.

Macadam, E. (1934) *The New Philanthropy*, London: George Allen and Unwin.

McCord, N. (1976) 'The Poor Law and Philanthropy', in D. Fraser (ed.) *The New Poor Law in the Nineteenth Century*, Basingstoke: Macmillan.

McKay, J. and M. Hilton (2009) 'Introduction', in N. Crowson, M. Hilton and J. McKay (eds) *NGOs in Contemporary Britain: Non-State Actors in Society and Politics since 1945*, Basingstoke: Palgrave Macmillan.

Marshall, T. (1996) 'Can We Define the Voluntary Sector?', in D. Billis and M. Harris (eds) *Voluntary Agencies: Challenges for Organisation and Management*, Basingstoke: Macmillan.

Marx, K. (1852) *The Eighteenth Brumaire of Louis Napoleon*, New York: Die Revolution.

Mason, D. (1995) *Leading and Managing in the Expressive Dimension: Harnessing the Hidden Power Source of the Nonprofit Sector*, San Francisco, CA: Jossey Bass.

Milofsky, C. (2008) *Smallville: Institutionalizing Community in Twenty-First Century America*, Hanover, NH and London, University Press of New England.

Milofsky, C. and A. Hunter (1993) 'The Force of Tradition at Toynbee Hall: Culture and Deep Structure in Organizational Life', Paper prepared for presentation at a special meeting of the Voluntary Action History Society, London, January.

Morris, S. (2006) 'The Greatest Philanthropic Tradition on Earth? Measuring the Extent of Voluntary Activity in London, 1874–1914', Paper used as basis for presentation at a meeting of the Voluntary Action History Society, London.

Murdock, A. (2012) 'Transferring the Compact Principle? Exploring the Emergence of a Code of Practice between the Private and Third Sector', Paper presented at a VSSN Day Conference, Cardiff University, 4 December.

Musick, M. and J. Wilson (2008) *Volunteers: A Social Profile*, Bloomington and Indianapolis, IN: Indiana University Press.

National Association for Councils of Voluntary Service (2004) *Changing Lives: CVS Making a Difference for Local People*, Sheffield: National Association for Councils of Voluntary Service.

National Association for Voluntary and Community Action (2012) *Joint Letter to the Economic Secretary of the Treasury*, 24 October at http://www.navca.org.uk/, accessed December 2012.

National Coalition for Independent Action (2006) *Taking Voluntary and Community Action: An Event to Discuss What Can Be Done to Promote and Safeguard Independent Action October 5th 2006*, London: National Coalition for Independent Action.

National Coalition for Independent Action (2007) *Promoting and Protecting Voluntary and Community Action*, London: National Coalition for Independent Action.

National Coalition for Independent Action (2010) *What We've Learnt So Far and Where Next for NCIA: A Report to the Tudor Trust (and Everyone Else)*, London: National Coalition for Independent Action.

National Coalition for Independent Action (2011a) *NCIA – Plans and Progress 200811; A Report to Tudor Trustees*, London: National Coalition for Independent Action.

National Coalition for Independent Action (2011b) *The Devil That is Commissioning*, London: National Coalition for Independent Action.

National Coalition for Independent Action (2011c) *The Baring Foundation's Panel for the Independence of the Voluntary Sector: A Response from the National Coalition for Independent Action*, London: National Coalition for Independent Action.

National Coalition for Independent Action (2012a) *Refunding Proposal to the Tudor Trust – June 2012*, London: National Coalition for Independent Action.

National Coalition for Independent Action (2012b) *Newsletter 27*.

National Coalition for Independent Action (2012c) *Newsletter 30*.

National Council for Voluntary Organisations (1981) *Improving Effectiveness in Voluntary Organisations: Report of the Charles Handy Working Party*, London: National Council for Voluntary Organisations.

National Council for Voluntary Organisations (1983) *MDU Bulletin 1*, London: Management Development Unit, National Council for Voluntary Organisations.

National Council for Voluntary Organisations (2012) *Code of Practice for Private-Voluntary Sector Relationships*, London: National Council for Voluntary Organisations.

National Council for Voluntary Organisations and Charities Aid Foundation (2006) *UK Giving 2005/06: Results of the 2005/06 Survey of Individual Charitable Giving in the UK*, London, National Council for Voluntary Organisations and Charities Aid Foundation.

Neely, A. (1998) *Measuring Business Performance*, London: The Economist/Profile Books.

Ockenden, N. and M. Hutin (2008) *Volunteering to Lead: A Study of Leadership within Small Volunteer-led Groups*, London: Institute for Volunteering Research.

Owen, D. (1964) *English Philanthropy 1660–1960*, London: Oxford University Press.

Palisi, B. and P. Jacobson (1977) 'Dominant Statuses and Involvement in Types of Instrumental and Expressive Voluntary Associations', *Journal of Voluntary Action Research* 6(1–2): 80–8.

Panel on the Independence of the Voluntary Sector (2011) *Voluntary Sector Independence*, London: Baring Foundation and Civil Exchange.

Panel on the Independence of the Voluntary Sector (2012) *Protecting Independence: The Voluntary Sector in 2012*, London: Baring Foundation and Civil Exchange.

Paton, R. (1996) 'How are values handled in voluntary agencies', in D. Billis and M. Harris (eds) *Voluntary Agencies: Challenges for Organisation and Management*, Basingstoke: Macmillan.

Paton, R. (2003) *Managing and Measuring Social Enterprises*, London: Sage.

Pearce, J. (1993) *Volunteers: the Organizational Behaviour of Unpaid Workers*, London: Routledge.

Penn, A. (2011) 'A social historical approach to understanding organisational issues in voluntary action', in C. Rochester, G. Gosling, A. Penn and M. Zimmeck (eds) *Understanding the Roots of Voluntary Action*, Eastbourne: Sussex Academic Press.

Pharoah, C. (2007) *Sources of Strength: an Analysis of Applications to the Baring Foundation's Strengthening the Voluntary Sector – Independence Grants Programme*, London: Baring Foundation.

Popple, K. (2008) 'The First Forty Years; the History of the Community Development Journal', *Community Development Journal* 43(1): 6–23.

Prochaska, F. (1988) *The Voluntary Impulse: Philanthropy in Modern Britain*, London: Faber and Faber.

Public Administration Committee (2011) *Oral Evidence on Smaller Government: Bigger Society*, 5 July, London: House of Commons, HC 902v.

Pugh, D. (1990) *Organization Theory: Selected Readings*, 3rd ed., Harmondsworth: Penguin.

Reading Committee (1967) *The Place of Voluntary Work in After-Care: Second Report of the Committee Chaired by the Dowager Marchioness of Reading*, London: HMSO.

Ramsay, N. (2012) *Annual Return of Volunteer Centres 2011*, London: Institute for Volunteering Research.

Rehnborg, S. (2005) 'Government Volunteerism in the New Millennium', in J. Brudney (ed.) *Emerging Areas of Volunteering*, Indianapolis, IN: ARNOVA.

Richardson, A. and M. Goodwin (1983) *Self-help and Mutual Care: Mutual Aid Organisations in Practice*, London: Policy Studies Institute.

Rimmer, J. (1980) *Troubles Shared: The Story of a Settlement 1899–1979*, Birmingham: Phlogiston Publishing.

Rochester, C. (1992) 'Community Organisations and Voluntary Action', in R. Hedley and J. Davis Smith (eds) *Volunteering and Society*, London: Bedford Square Press.

Rochester, C. (1997) 'The Neglected Dimension of the Voluntary Sector: Measuring the Value of Community Organisations', in C. Pharoah (ed.) *Dimensions of the Voluntary Sector*, West Malling: Charities Aid Foundation.

Rochester, C. (1998) *Social Benefits: Exploring the Value of Community Sector Organisations*, West Malling: Charities Aid Foundation.

Rochester, C. (1999a) *Juggling on a Unicycle: A Handbook for Small Voluntary Agencies*, London: Centre for Voluntary Organisation, London School of Economics and Political Science.

Rochester, C. (1999b) 'One Size Does Not Fit All: Four Models of Volunteer Management', *Voluntary Action* 1(2): 7–20, reprinted in J. Davis Smith and M. Locke (eds) (2007) *Volunteering and the Test of Time*, London: Institute for Volunteering Research.

Rochester, C. (2008) 'Exploring the Roots of Voluntary Action: the Role of Conviviality', Paper presented to the International Conference on the History of Voluntary Action, University of Liverpool.

Rochester, C. (2009) 'A decade of Civil Society under New Labour', Lecture given at the British Academy, February.

Rochester, C. (2012) 'Councils for Voluntary Service: the End of a Long Road?', *Voluntary Sector Review* 3(1): 103–10.

Rochester, C., A. Ellis Paine and S. Howlett (2010) *Volunteering and Society in the 21st Century*, Basingstoke: Palgrave Macmillan.

Rochester, C., G. Gosling, A. Penn and M. Zimmeck (eds) (2011) *Understanding the Roots of Voluntary Action*, Eastbourne: Sussex Academic Press.

Rochester, C., J. Harris and R. Hutchison (1999) *Building the Capacity of Small Voluntary Agencies*, London: Centre for Voluntary Organisation, London School of Economics and Political Science.

Rochester, C. and M. Torry (2010) 'Faith-based Organizations and Hybridity; A Special Case?', in D. Billis (ed.) *Hybrid Organizations and the Third Sector*, Basingstoke: Palgrave Macmillan.

Rochester, C. and M. Zimmeck (2013) *The Case for Statutory Compacts between Welsh Local Authorities and the Third Sector: Summary Report and Recommendations*, Social Research Report 8/2013, Cardiff: Welsh Government.

Saidel, J. and S. Harlen (1998) 'Contracting and Patterns of Nonprofit Governance', *Nonprofit Management and Leadership* 8(3): 243–60.

Salamon, L. (1998) Letter to the Editor, *Nonprofit and Voluntary Sector Quarterly* 27(1): 88–9.

Salamon, L. and H. Anheier (1992) 'In Search of the Voluntary Sector I: The Question of Definitions', *Voluntas* 3(2): 125–51.

Sandel, M. (2012) *What Money Can't Buy: The Moral Limits of Markets*, Harmondsworth: Allen Lane.

Sargent, A. (2005) *Marketing Management for Nonprofit Organisations*, 2nd ed., Oxford: Oxford University Press.

Scott, D. (2010) 'Understanding Volunteering', Paper presented to the 'Volunteering Counts' Conference, Manchester, March.

Scott, D. and L. Russell (2001) 'Contracting: the Experience of Service Delivery Agencies', in M. Harris and C. Rochester (eds) *Voluntary Organisations and Social Policy in Britain: Perspectives on Change and Choice*, Basingstoke: Palgrave.

Seebohm, F. (1968) *Report of the Committee on Local Authority and Allied Social Services*, London: HMSO, Cmnd3703.

Selznick, P. (1992) *The Moral Commonwealth: Social Theory and the Promise of Community*, Berkeley, CA: University of California Press.

Sheard, J. (1992) 'Volunteering and Society 1960–1990', in R. Hedley and J. Davis Smith (eds) *Volunteering and Society: Principles and Practice*, London: Bedford Square Press.

Siederer, N. (2006) *Change Up Programme: Infrastructure Investment Plans: Collation and Analysis of Data: Report for Capacity Builders, Section 2: Main Report Including Aims, Summary and Recommendations*, London: Good Foundations Consultancy.

Smerdon, M. (2006) *Allies not Servants: Voluntary Sector Relations with Government: A Discussion of the Thinking behind the New Focus of the Baring Foundation's Strengthening the Voluntary Sector Grants Programme*, London: Baring Foundation.

Smerdon, M. (2007) *Submission to the Inquiry on Commissioning Public Services from the Third Sector Public Administration Select Committee*, London: Baring Foundation.

Smerdon, M. (2009) *Mission, Money, Mandate: Report of the Independence Summit, Held at the Baring Foundation, Wednesday 8 July 2009*, London: Baring Foundation.

Smith, D.H. (1973) 'Dimensions and Categories of Voluntary Organizations/NGOs', *Journal of Voluntary Action Research* 2(2): 116–20.

Smith, D.H. (1975) 'Voluntary Action and Voluntary Groups', *Annual Review of Sociology* 1: 247–70.

Smith, D.H. (2000) *Grassroots Associations*, Thousand Oaks, CA: Sage.

Smith, D.H. (2003) 'A History of ARNOVA', *Nonprofit and Voluntary Sector Quarterly* 32: 458–72.

Smith, D.H. and J. Grotz (2011) 'A Conceptual Map of Volunteering: Main Purposive Types', Unpublished paper, Chestnut Hill, MA: Department of Sociology, Boston College.

Soteri-Proctor, A. and P. Alcock (2013) 'Micro-mapping: What Lies beneath the Third Sector Radar?', *Voluntary Sector Review* 4(1): 379–98.

Speckbacher, G. (2003) 'The Economics of Performance Management in Nonprofit Organizations', *Nonprofit Management and Leadership* 13(3): 267–81.

Stebbins, R. (1996) 'Volunteering; a Serious Leisure Perspective', *Nonprofit and Voluntary Sector Quarterly* 25(2): 211–24.

Stebbins, R. (2004) 'Introduction' to R. Stebbins and M. Graham (2004) *Volunteering as Leisure/Leisure as Volunteering: An International Assessment*, Wallingford: CABI Publishing.

Stebbins, R. and M. Graham (2004) *Volunteering as Leisure/Leisure as Volunteering: An International Assessment*, Wallingford: CABI Publishing.

Stiglitz, J. (2012) *The Price of Inequality: The Avoidable Causes and Invisible Costs of Inequality*, London: W.W. Norton.

Stolen (2011) Comment on the Guardian's *Voluntary Sector Network Blog* 13 April

Tarrow, S. (1994) *Power in Movement*, Cambridge: Cambridge University Press.

Taylor, M. (2011) *Public Policy in the Community*, 2nd ed., Basingstoke: Palgrave Macmillan.

Taylor, M. and J. Kendall (1996) 'History of the Voluntary Sector', in J. Kendall and M. Knapp (ed.) *The Voluntary Sector in the UK*, Manchester: Manchester University Press.

Thomas, B. (2003) *The Practicalities of Performance Management in Small Voluntary Agencies*, Unpublished MSc dissertation, University of Roehampton.

Tilly, C. (2004) *Social Movements, 1768–2004*, Boulder, CO: Paradigm Publishers.

Torry, M. (2012) 'Is There a Faith Sector?', *Voluntary Sector Review* 3(1): 111–18.

van der Feen, S. (2011) *The Big Squeeze: the Squeeze Tightens: The Economic Climate, Londoners and the Voluntary and Community Groups that Serve Them, Phase 3, July 2011*, London: London Voluntary Services Council.

Voight, K. (2009) *Mergers Fail More Often than Marriages, CNN.Com Business World*, 22 March, accessed at http://edition.cnn.com/2009/BUSINESS/05/21/merger. marriage/index.html, accessed January 2013.

Wann, M. (1992) 'Self-help Groups: Is There Room for Volunteers?', in R. Hedley and J. Davis Smith (eds) *Volunteering and Society: Principles and Practice*, London: Bedford Square Press.

Warner, W. and others (1949) *Democracy in Jonesville: A Study in Quality and Inequality*, New York: Harper and Brothers.

Warriner, C. and J. Prather (1965) 'Four Types of Voluntary Associations', *Sociological Inquiry* 35: 138–48.

Weisbrod, B. (1977) *The Voluntary Nonprofit Sector*, Lexington, MA: D.C. Heath and Co.

Weisbrod, B. (1988) *The Nonprofit Economy*, Cambridge, MA: Harvard University Press.

Willis, E. (1993) 'How to Manage Volunteers and Maintain Your Values as Well', *Volunteers* 102, Berkhamsted: Volunteer Centre UK.

Wittenberg, B. (2007) *The Interplay between State, Private Sector and Voluntary Activity: A Vision for the Future*, London: Directory of Social Change.

Wolfenden, Lord (1978) *The Future of Voluntary Organisations*, London: Croom Helm.

Wuthnow, R. (1994) *Sharing the Journey: Support Groups and America's New Quest for Community*, New York: Free Press.

Young, N. (2012) 'Volunteer Centre Network "Will Fragment" under Council Cuts', *Civil Society Online*, 2 May.

Zimmeck, M. (2000) *The Right Stuff*, London: Institute for Volunteering Research.

Zimmeck, M. (2013) *The Case for Statutory Compacts between Welsh Local Authorities and the Third Sector: A Literature Review*, Cardiff: Welsh Government.

Zimmeck, M. and C. Rochester (2013a) 'Something Old, Something New, Something Borrowed, Something Blue: Governments' Approach to Volunteering in England since 1997', in G. von Schnurbein, D. Wiederkehr and H. Ammann (eds) *Volunteering between Freedom and Professionalisation, Papers from the European University for Voluntary Service, 31st August – 3rd September 2011, Basel, Switzerland*, Zürich: Seismo.

Zimmeck, M. and C. Rochester (2013b) 'Not Meeting the Challenge of Change: Government, the Voluntary and Community Sector, Recession and the Compact in England, 1997–2012', in R. Laforest (ed.) *The Voluntary Sector and the Recession: Taking Stock of Evolving Relationships*, Toronto: McGill-Queen's University Press.

Zimmeck, M., C. Rochester and B. Rushbrooke (2011) *Use It or Lose It: A Summative Evaluation of the Compact*, Birmingham: Commission for the Compact.

Index

NOTE: Names of organisations and bodies are given in full in the index; for expansion of abbreviations see the list on pages x–xi.

academic research and teaching, 1
  and alternatives to dominant
    paradigm, 235, 237–41
  and changes in voluntary
    organisations, 5–6, 113, 124–6,
    127
  courses in voluntary sector studies,
    50, 51, 125, 211
  and dominant paradigm of
    voluntary action, 66, 235
  lack of critical analysis of
    management practices, 51,
    125–6, 239
  and motivation, 238–9, 240
  and non-profit sector in USA, 45–6,
    126, 209–10, 211
accountability
  and alternative paradigm, 242–3
  and bureaucratic model, 100, 102
  and governing bodies, 134
Active Community Unit (ACU), 48, 76
activism, 179, 181–2
  activism type volunteering, 187
  see also campaigning activity;
    grassroots associations;
    National Coalition for
    Independent Action
Adams, D., 157, 158
advocacy role of voluntary action,
    86, 185
  see also campaigning activity
affiliated orders, 23, 31
affiliation of non-bureaucratic groups,
    224–5, 226–7
agency theory and governance, 136–7
Alcock, P., 214
Alcoholics Anonymous, 23
altruistic motivation, 177, 238–9
Alzheimer's Disease Society, 23

amateur interests and volunteering,
    158, 180
ambiguous voluntary organisations,
    107–8, 109, 110–11, 235–7
Ancient Order of Foresters, 23, 31
Anheier, H., 218–19, 237
anti-social behaviour and
    volunteering, 54–5
archives of voluntary organisations, 15
arts
  clubs and societies, 33
  culture and voluntary action, 184
  volunteering as serious leisure, 180
Association of Chief Executives of
    Voluntary Organisations
    (ACEVO), 39, 82, 112, 118, 214
  market-based values, 121
  prominence and government
    influence, 96, 114, 115
  and rise of chief executives, 124, 127
  and service delivery role, 116–17
Association for Research on Nonprofit
    Organizations and Voluntary
    Action (ARNOVA), 45, 211
Association of Voluntary Action
    Scholars (AVAS), 211
Association of Volunteer Managers, 65
associational charities, 104
  historical context, 19–20, 24, 33, 34
associations
  and incentives, 227
  as organisational form, 99, 104–6,
    218, 229, 241–2; and
    ambiguous voluntary agencies,
    107–8, 109, 110–11, 235; and
    expressive–instrumental
    interaction, 151, 224; and
    hybridised voluntary
    organisations, 109, 144, 218,

229, 241–2; as ideal third sector
form, 105, 110, 218, 234–5;
membership association, 143–4,
218, 222
research requirements, 240
and typology of alternative groups,
235, 236
see also associational charities;
grassroots associations;
non-bureaucratic organisations
authority
and associations, 106
and bureaucratic model, 99–100,
102
autonomy. *see* independence of
voluntary sector
Aves Committee and Report, 53, 54,
55–66
function of volunteers, 56–8
organisation and management of
volunteers, 59–62, 65
significant impact on volunteering,
62–5

Barclays Bank, 123
Baring Foundation, 2, 189, 190–3,
194, 195, 202
Barrow Cadbury Foundation, 51
Batsleer, J., 118, 123–4, 125
beer and mutual aid in Middle Ages,
22, 31
benefits, conditionality and unpaid
work, 81
Benson, Andy, 76, 194, 197, 198,
200–1, 213
Berger, P., 159
Beveridge, William, 16, 17–18, 21
Big Society agenda, 198, 208
Billis, David, 5, 50, 125, 145, 154–5,
159, 211
'ABC division', 101–2
alternative group typology,
235–7
ambiguity and hybridisation,
106–9
hybrid organisations, 218–19
membership association model, 99,
104–5, 124, 143–4, 218, 219,
222, 229, 234–5

unorganised groups, 210, 219,
235
'worlds' theory, 106–7, 109, 238
Birkbeck College, London, 211
Blair, Tony, 48, 79, 88
Blake, G., 154
boards and governance, 133, 134–8,
139, 145, 178
Boatright, J., 142
'boundary crossers', 115, 126–7
Brenton, M., 206
Brewis, G., 53–4
British Association of Settlements
and Social Action Centres
(BASSAC), 4
Brophy, Michael, 38
Brown, Gordon, 79, 88
Bruce, Ian, 170
Brunel University, 50, 211
Programme of Research and
Training into Voluntary Action
(PORTVAC), 206
Bubb, Sir Stephen, 96, 116–17, 118,
124
bureaucratic model and organisational
form, 70, 77, 99–111, 112, 148,
232
'ABC division', 101–2, 104,
135–6
and alternative perspectives of
volunteering, 182, 216–30;
implications of alternative
paradigm, 235–44; and
limitations of organisational
theory, 221–3; non-bureaucratic
organisations and action,
216, 218–30, 234–44; typology
of alternative groups,
235–7
and ambiguity and hybridisation,
99, 106–9, 233; ambiguous
voluntary agencies, 107–8, 109,
110–11, 235–7; hybridisation
and organisations, 108–9, 110,
144, 146, 174, 219–20, 229,
233, 235–7, 241–3; unorganised
groups, 104, 107, 109–10, 111,
219, 229, 235

bureaucratic model and organisational
    form – *continued*
    associational form, 99, 104–6,
        107–8, 110–11, 218, 234–5;
        membership associations,
        143–4, 218, 222
    and challenge of voluntary
        organisation, 102–4, 161–4,
        215, 239
    characteristics of, 99–104
    domination of command and
        control approach, 161–4,
        233
    and governance, 145
    and incentives, 227
    and instrumental organisations,
        152, 221
    and size of group, 224
    see also 'business' model and
        voluntary organisations
Buse, Rodney, 75, 119
business
    corporate partners for voluntary
        organisations, 122–3
    and non-profit sector in USA,
        42–3, 44
    see also command-and-control
        organisations; market-based
        approach to welfare
'business' model and voluntary
    organisations, 26, 50, 51, 70, 77,
        85–6, 94
    Excellence Model and quality
        standards, 119
    promotion by intermediary bodies,
        119–20
    and treatment of volunteers and
        staff, 95
    see also bureaucratic model and
        organisational form
Byrne, P., 27, 28

Cairns, B., 152
Cambridge House, Camberwell,
    3–4
campaigning activity
    and alternative perspectives on
        volunteering, 182
    and civil society paradigm, 178

exclusion from New Labour's policy
    agenda, 77
historical context, 16, 17, 29–30,
    37–8; community groups, 30;
    social movements, 27–9, 34
ideology and guidance, 226–7
NCIA critique of voluntary sector,
    196–9, 234
and UN global typology, 183
and values, 155
capacity building
    and alternative paradigm, 241–2
    and market-based approach, 96
    and New Labour, 75–7, 84, 119–20
CapacityBuilders initiative, 50–1, 120
capital framework and volunteering,
    156–7
careers and bureaucratic model, 100
Carmel, E., 52
carnival, conviviality and voluntary
    action, 30
casual volunteering, 180
Caulkin, Simon, 102–3, 161–4
CENTRIS Report on Voluntary Action,
    212
'champions' and changing
    perspectives, 112–13
ChangeUp programme, 50, 77,
    119–20, 121, 136, 237
charismatic authority structures, 100
charismatic leaders as incentive, 227
charitable trusts, 19, 24, 26, 33, 34,
    134
Charitable Uses Acts, 19
charities
    historical development, 19–21
    see also associational charities;
        charitable trusts
Charities Aid Foundation (CAF), 38
Charities Evaluation Services, 125, 167
Charity Commission, 189, 190, 192
Charity Organisation Society (COS),
    20–1
Chartered Institute of Marketing, 169
Chartered Management Institute, 162
Chartism, 28–9
Chicago School of economics, 87

chief executives, 112, 114, 115, 123–4, 127
and dominance of command and control model, 162, 163
children and voluntary action, 183
Christian service organisations, 152–3, 155
'church-ales', 22, 31
Citizenship Surveys, 237
City University, London, 211
civic roles and volunteering, 187
Civil Service and public sector reform, 91–2
civil society, 2, 37, 52, 147
'civil society' paradigm, 178–9, 186
see also voluntary and community sector
Civil Society (on-line journal), 117
civil society organisations, 219
Cloke, P., 153, 155, 158
Club and Institute Union (CIU), 32
clubs and societies
conviviality and voluntary action, 30–3, 34, 149
as expressive organisations, 149–50
Cnaan, R., 110, 222, 223
Coalition government
and 'civil society', 37
and distinctive nature of voluntary sector, 208–9
and funding of 'strategic partners', 75, 82–3
and health service markets, 91
and merging of intermediary bodies, 172
shift from contracting to commissioning services, 77–8, 198
and terminology for voluntary sector, 52
see also Conservative governments; Conservative Party
Code of Practice for Community Groups (2003), 32
coercive isomorphism, 128

collective action. *see* campaigning activity; non-bureaucratic organisations; social movements
command-and-control organisations, 102–3, 104, 145, 151
as dominant managerial style, 161–4, 233
marketing approach, 169–71
performance measurement and quality control, 166–9
popularity of mergers, 171–4
and strategic planning, 165–6
commerce
promotion as voluntary action, 184
see also business
Commission for the Compact, 83, 192
Commission on the Future of the Voluntary Sector (Deakin Commission), 37, 38–9, 44, 48, 51, 74, 75, 115, 118, 119
Commission on the Future of Volunteering, 66, 80–2, 116, 157
commissioning services, 77–8, 198, 215
commons and non-bureaucratic model, 225–6
community activity, 184
community care services and market-based approaches, 90
community development, history, 17, 30
Community Development Journal, 30
community groups and community-based organisations
and civil society paradigm, 179
constraints on, 81
exclusion from state support, 74, 77
historical context, 30, 32
and non-bureaucratic model, 222
Community Interest Company (CIC), 195
Community Links, 154, 155
Community Matters, 114
community peacekeeping as voluntary action, 184

community sector, 3, 4
  see also community groups and
    community-based
    organisations; voluntary and
    community sector
Community Sector Coalition, 237–8,
    241
Community Service Volunteers, 55
Compact Voice, 115, 116, 189–90
Compact Working Group, 115
Compacts with voluntary sector,
    48–9, 51–2, 73–7, 113–14,
    115–16, 190
  dismantling by Coalition
    government, 82, 83
Comparative Nonprofit Sector
    Project, 44, 45, 209–10, 237
competition and loss of shared
    resources, 171
compliance model and governance,
    136–7
Conservative governments, 75, 79
  on distinctive features of voluntary
    sector, 207
  and market-based approaches to
    voluntary organisations, 121
  and 'mixed economy of welfare', 46,
    70–3, 88
  privatisation, 88–90
  rise of neo-liberalism, 87–8
  and sectorisation approach, 207
  see also Coalition government
Conservative Party
  on distinctive nature of voluntary
    sector, 208–9
  on state and voluntary sector, 82
consultants, 113, 125, 126, 127
consumer approach and 'business'
    model, 95
'contract failure' theory, 158–9
contracting. *see* out-sourcing of
    services; sub-contracting of
    services
control and ownership, 141–5,
    146
conventional organisational theory
    and non-bureaucratic model,
    221–2, 238, 241–2

conviviality and voluntary action
  historical context, 16, 30–2, 34
  play and benefits of volunteering,
    157–8
  see also expressive behaviour
Cooper, Cary, 162
co-operative societies, 31
co-operatives and volunteering, 186
co-optation model and governance,
    137
Cornforth, C., 136–7
corporate partners for voluntary
    organisations, 122–3
corporate voluntary agencies, 236
Councils of Social Service, 21, 62
Councils for Voluntary Service (CVSs),
    4, 21, 40–1, 49
  and alternative paradigm, 241
  and management practices and
    training, 50, 114, 120
  and market-based approaches, 95,
    96, 121
  and partnership approach, 114, 116
craft guilds and mutual aid, 21, 22, 34
Cross-Cutting Review of the Voluntary
    Sector, 75–6, 119, 207–8
Crowson, N., 29
cultural capital and volunteering, 156
culture and voluntary action, 184
customers, 95
  as focus of companies, 163–4
  and marketing techniques, 170–1
  see also service users

Dahrendorf, Ralf, 82, 212
data collection as voluntary action,
    184
Davis Smith, Justin, 4, 60, 81–2
  four strands of volunteering, 183,
    186
  historical context, 16, 17, 18, 19, 20,
    22, 24, 27
  Make a Difference scheme, 80
Deakin, Nicholas, 71, 91, 112, 171–2
Deakin Commission, 37, 38–9, 44, 48,
    51, 74, 75, 115, 118, 119
democratic model and governance,
    137
'deserving' and 'undeserving' poor, 20

developmental incentives, 227
DiMaggio, P., 128
Directory of Social Change (DSC), 189, 190, 212–13
disasters and emergency response, 184
dominant paradigm in volunteering, 7, 176–88, 231–2
  alternatives to, 178–88, 216–30, 233–4; 'civil society' paradigm, 178–9, 186; implications of, 235–44; as serious leisure activity, 179–82, 229; three-perspective model, 181–2, 233; typology of, 235–7; UN and typology maps, 182–7
  and Aves Committee, 56, 66
  and pressures from within the voluntary sector, 112–29, 194, 232
donations and Gift Aid scheme, 79

East London University, 211
Economic and Social Research Council (ESRC), 50, 51
economic capital and volunteering, 156
economic justice as voluntary action, 184
education
  and self-improvement, 32, 33
  as voluntary action, 184
  see also training
electoral reform and social movements, 28
Ellis Paine, A., 95
Elsdon, Konrad, 32, 219
emergency response as voluntary action, 184
employer status and governing bodies, 134
employment conditions and bureaucratic model, 100
endowments and development of charities, 19, 134
England Volunteering Development Council (EVDC), 82
'entrenched' hybrid groups, 108, 109, 111, 144, 146, 174, 218, 233, 236, 243

entrepreneur model and governing bodies, 139
environment and voluntary action, 185
Etherington, Sir Stuart, 116
event support and voluntary action, 185
Excellence Model and quality standards, 119
expressive behaviour, 103–4
  and funding, 242
  historical context, 16, 32–3, 34
  and non-bureaucratic organisations, 224
  and unorganised groups, 110
  and voluntary organisations, 147, 148–55, 160, 222
  and volunteering, 156–8
  see also conviviality and voluntary action
expressive organisations, 149–50, 222
expressive-instrumental organisations, 149, 150, 151

faith-based voluntary organisations, 152–3, 155, 187, 227
federated organisations, 23, 236
Filer Commission on Private Philanthropy and Public Needs (US), 36, 42–3
Finlayson, Geoffrey, 24
flexible management practices, 166
formal and informal volunteering, 217
formal rules and bureaucratic model, 100
foundations and US non-profit sector, 44, 45
fraternities
  and ideology, 226
  and mutual aid type volunteering, 186
free markets and economic theory, 87–8
Freedom Corps (USA), 81
Freeman, J., 128
Friedman, Milton, 87–8
friendly societies, 21, 22–3, 24, 26, 33–4, 186
  and conviviality, 31, 149

funding
    and alternative paradigm, 242
    Coalition government and funding
        cuts, 82–3, 117–18, 198
    and conviviality, 30, 31
    cross-funding between voluntary
        sector and state, 26
    giving and Gift Aid scheme, 79
    and governance of voluntary
        organisations, 145
    increase in state funding, 78–9
    and independence of voluntary
        organisations, 69, 83, 190; and
        grant aid, 78, 93, 117, 171, 242;
        Strengthening the Voluntary Sector
        programme, 190–2, 195
    for local intermediary bodies, 42,
        172
    and Local Strategic Partnerships, 49,
        74
    local volunteer bureaux/centres, 62,
        63, 64
    market values and sustainability of
        intermediary bodies, 121–2
    and market-based approach to
        welfare, 93, 96, 117
    New Labour and intermediary
        bodies and 'strategic partners',
        75, 113–14, 115–16
    state harnessing of voluntary
        activity, 47, 62, 115–16, 190;
        Aves Report and organisation of
        volunteers, 61, 62, 64;
        dependence on state funding,
        69, 78, 117, 171; instrumental
        approach and targeted support,
        72, 74, 76, 79, 80–1, 242
FutureBuilders initiative, 76

Gaskin, K., 81
Gerard, David, 153–4
Gershon, Sir Peter, 92
Gilchrist, A., 30
Gingerbread groups, 23
giving and Gift Aid scheme, 79
Glennerster, H., 108, 142, 159, 238
goal-oriented organisations, 152
Goodwin, M., 220
Gordon, Lord George, 28

Goschen Minute, 21
Gosden, P., 21, 23, 31
governance, 1, 133–46, 232–3
    alternative approaches, 138–40;
        non-bureaucratic organisations,
        228
    formal rules and bureaucratic
        model, 100
    functions of governing bodies,
        134–6, 178; criticisms of
        effectiveness, 135–6, 145
    and independence of voluntary
        sector, 192, 193
    and market-based approach to
        welfare, 93–4, 96
    models and theories of, 136–8,
        139–41
    and ownership, 133, 140–5, 146
Governance Hub, 136
Governance Work-stream, 136
government. *see* Coalition
        government; Conservative
        governments; New Labour
        governments; partnership
        approaches; state and voluntary
        action
'government volunteerism', 81
grant aid, 78, 93, 117, 171, 242
    Strengthening the Voluntary Sector
        programme, 190–2, 195
grassroots associations, 3, 219, 224
    and academic research, 5
    and civil society paradigm, 179
    as driven by values, 155
    as expressive organisations, 151, 222
    ideology and guidance, 226, 229
    involvement of volunteers, 228, 229
    see also non-bureaucratic
        organisations
Griffiths, Sir Roy, 92
Grotz, Jurgen, 186–7
'Guardians' and governance, 133, 139,
        144
guidance of non-bureaucratic
        organisations, 226–7
guilds and mutual aid, 21, 22, 34
Gummer, B., 224
Guthrie, M., 173

Hall, Peter Dobkin, 43
Hampton, Philip, 92
Handy, Charles, 50, 118, 164, 174
Hannan, M., 128
Hansmann, Henry, 141, 143, 158–9, 238
Harlan, S., 140
Harlock, J., 52
Harris, B., 26
Harris, Margaret, 50, 213, 238
    associations, 106, 151, 224
    governing bodies and governance, 133, 134–5, 138–40
    invention of voluntary sector, 46–7, 96
Hatch, Stephen, 38
health care and voluntary action, 185
Hedley, Rodney, 4, 60
'help-ales', 22, 31
Hemming, Henry, 157, 158
hierarchy
    and associations, 105–6, 109
    and bureaucratic model, 100, 102–3, 109, 145; alternatives to, 163–4
    and micro voluntary agencies, 220
Hilton, M., 29
Hinton, Nicholas, 38
history of voluntary action, 4, 15–35, 231–2
    cavalier attitude towards archives, 15
    invention of voluntary sector, 36–52, 113, 232
    invention of voluntary work, 53–66, 232; boom in 1960s, 54–5
    management of, 15–16; Aves Report recommendations, 59–62, 65
hobbies. *see* interests; leisure
Hodgson, Lord, 92
holidays, voluntary organisation of, 33
Home Office
    Efficiency Scrutiny of Government Funding of the Voluntary Sector, 47, 65, 207
    encouragement of volunteers, 56, 71–2

'home-grown' management style, 65, 125, 164, 242
homelessness and faith-based charities, 153
'horizontal' policies, 46
'horizontal volunteering', 179
housing and privatisation, 89
Howlett, Steven, 6
human capital and volunteering, 156
human resources as model, 65, 167, 177, 239
human rights and voluntary action, 185
Hunter, A., 166
hybridisation and voluntary organisations, 219–20, 235–7, 241–3
    'entrenched' hybrid groups, 108, 109, 111, 144, 146, 174, 218, 233, 236, 243
    'shallow' hybrid groups, 108–9, 110–11, 144, 146, 218, 233, 242–3

identity and voluntary action, 2
    distinctive identity, 159, 207–12, 238
    diversity of organisations, 7, 51, 111, 207, 209–12
    and hybridisation of voluntary organisations, 108–9
    market-based approaches and loss of identity, 86, 96, 232, 234; and corporate partners, 123; and treatment of volunteers, 94–5
    volunteers and inclusiveness, 60, 65, 94–5
ideology, 155, 226–7, 229
incentives
    and non-bureaucratic groups, 226, 227–8
    see also motivations for volunteering
independence of voluntary sector, 1–2, 232
    and ability to act with confidence, 191
    and democratic state, 82

independence of voluntary
    sector – *continued*
  and funding, 69, 78, 83, 93, 117,
    171, 190, 193; support from
    Strengthening the Voluntary Sector
    programme, 190–2, 195
  industry initiatives to strengthen,
    189–202, 234
  and legitimacy, 191
  pressures from within the sector,
    112–29, 194, 232
Independence Summit (2009), 192–3
Independent Commission
    on the Future of Volunteering, 66,
    80–2
Independent Order of Oddfellows,
    23, 31
'independent sector' and funding in
    UK, 72–3, 90
Independent Sector (IS), 43–4
'informal associations', 109
informal groups. *see* unorganised
    groups
informal social care, 39, 106–7
informational incentives, 227
infrastructure organisations. *see*
    intermediary
    bodies/infrastructure
    organisations
Institute for Fundraising, 125
Institute for Volunteering Research,
    IVR Impact Assessment Toolkit, 156
institutional isomorphism, 128
instrumental approach, 147–8
  and bureaucratic model, 103–4, 148,
    221
  and expressive dimensions, 148–55,
    160, 222, 224, 233; and
    volunteering, 156–8
  and non-bureaucratic model, 224
  state harnessing of voluntary
    activity, 72, 74, 76, 79, 80–1,
    190
instrumental organisations, 149, 151,
    221
instrumental-expressive organisations,
    149, 150–1
interests and voluntary action, 32–3,
    148–9, 149–50, 158, 180

intermediary bodies/infrastructure
    organisations, 39–42
  and alternative paradigm, 241
  historical context, 20
  key functions, 41–2
  and management practices and
    training, 50, 51, 84, 125;
    promotion of managerialism,
    118–20, 124
  and market-based approaches
    and values, 95–6, 117, 120–3,
    214
  merging of bodies, 172
  and narrowing of perspective on
    voluntary action, 112, 113–23,
    127; and Coalition cuts and
    welfare reforms, 117–18; and
    managerialism, 118–20, 124;
    and market values, 120–3;
    promotion of partnership and
    service delivery, 114–18, 122–3
  New Labour and funding of, 75,
    113–14, 115–16
  in USA, 43–4
  see also local intermediary bodies;
    national intermediary bodies
internal markets in NHS, 90–1
International Monetary Fund (IMF), 87
International Society for Third Sector
    Research (ISTR), 45
International Year of Volunteers (IYV),
    81, 183, 186
isomorphic processes, 128

Jeavons, T., 103, 152
Jochum, V., 74
Johns Hopkins University,
    Comparative Nonprofit Sector
    Project, 44, 45, 209–10, 237
Jones, S., 33
Joseph Rowntree Foundation, 192

Kanter, R., 224
Kay, R., 174–5
Kearney, J., 81
Kendall, Jeremy, 46, 51, 206, 212
  and Comparative Nonprofit Sector
    Project, 44, 209, 210, 237
  on historical context, 17, 18, 22, 27, 32

Keynes, John Maynard, 87, 88
Knapp, M., 44, 51, 206, 209, 210, 212, 237, 238
Knight, Barry, 212
knowledge
  acquisition, 227
  dissemination, 185
  of experienced practitioners, 242
Koinonia, 225
Kramer, R., 138
Krugman, Paul, 87

Labour. *see* New Labour governments
Landry, C., 164
law and legal services and voluntary action, 185
leadership for voluntary organisations, 25–6, 174–5
  non-bureaucratic groups, 223, 226–7, 228, 229
Leat, Diana, 37, 38, 39, 43, 45, 77, 238
leisure
  event support and voluntary action, 185
  and history of voluntary action, 17; clubs and societies, 30–3, 34, 148–9, 149–50
  leisure type volunteering, 187
  play and benefits of volunteering, 157–8
  volunteering as serious leisure, 179–82, 229
less formal groupings, 219
  degrees of formality, 223–4
  see also non-bureaucratic organisations
Lewis, D., 126
life-span of non-bureaucratic organisations, 222, 223
Little, A., 126, 127
livery companies and mutual aid, 21, 22
Lloyd George, David, 70
lobbying incentives, 227
local activism and NCIA, 199–200, 201
local authorities
  Aves Report and funding of volunteer bureaux/centres, 62, 63, 64

Compacts with voluntary sector, 48–9, 73–7, 82, 83; prescriptive approach, 74, 190
funding: constraints of commissioning services, 78; and cuts under Coalition government, 83; market-based approach and privatisation, 89–90; and 'mixed economy of welfare', 72–3
lack of enthusiasm for volunteers, 56–7
local intermediary bodies, 40–2, 50–1, 95, 112, 114, 116
  funding of local volunteer bureaux/centres, 62, 63, 64
  'rationalisation', 172
Local Strategic Partnerships, 49, 74, 116
local volunteer centres, 241
Lohmann, Roger, 5, 151, 224, 225–6, 240–1
London School of Economics (LSE), 50, 211
  Centre for Voluntary Organisation, 4, 206
London South Bank University, 211
Lyons, M., 177, 178, 179, 186

McKay, J., 29
Macmillan, Harold, 89
Major, John, 75, 80, 88
Make a Difference scheme, 80
Management Development Network, 125
management practices
  absence of critical analysis, 51, 125–6, 239
  applicability and alternatives for voluntary organisations, 161, 164–75, 233–4, 241–2; 'home-grown' style, 65, 125, 164, 242; marketing practices, 169–71; measurement of performance and quality, 166–9; mergers and alliances, 171–4; strategic planning, 164–6

management practices – *continued*
  Aves Report recommendations,
    59–62; preparation and training
    of volunteers, 60–2, 65;
    recruitment and selection of
    volunteers, 59–60, 65;
    volunteering infrastructure,
    61–2
  bureaucratic model and challenge of
    voluntary organisations, 102–4,
    161–4, 215, 239
  domination of command and
    control in corporate sector,
    161–4, 233
  and invention of voluntary sector,
    49–52; lack of academic critical
    analysis, 51, 125–6
  leadership: and cross-sector
    personnel, 25–6;
    non-bureaucratic organisations,
    223, 226–7, 228, 229;
    requirements, 174–5
  and market-based approaches, 91–2;
    generic not specialised
    managers, 94, 124
  New Labour and capacity building,
    75–7, 84, 119–20
  rise of chief executive role, 112, 114,
    115, 123–4, 127
  volunteer management profession,
    5, 55, 59, 65, 73, 125, 239
  see also managerialism
managerial hegemony theory and
    governance, 137
managerialism
  and Aves Report recommendations,
    65
  and changing practices in voluntary
    organisations, 4–5, 51, 112,
    126; intermediary bodies and
    championing of, 118–20, 124
  and New Labour, 65, 76
  and voluntary organisations,
    161–75, 233; domination of
    command and control
    approach, 161–4, 233
  see also New Public Management
'market economy' and 'market
    society', 96–7

market-based approach to welfare, 71,
    85–98
  commissioning of services, 77–8,
    198, 215
  impact on voluntary action, 92–6,
    120–3, 232
  limitations of 'market society', 96–7
  and national intermediary bodies,
    95–6, 117
  privatisation, 88–90, 214; NCIA's
    anti-privatisation campaign,
    198–9
  public sector reform and market
    model, 89, 90–2, 122–3
  rise of neo-liberalism, 87–8
  see also 'business' model and
    voluntary organisations
marketing practices, 169–71
Marshall, Tony, 159, 160
Marx, Karl, 15
Mason, David, 5, 103–4, 148–51, 157,
    158, 222
mediating institutions, 159–60
  see also intermediary
    bodies/infrastructure
    organisations
membership association model, 99,
    104–5, 124, 143–4, 218, 219, 222,
    229, 234–5
membership model and governing
    bodies, 139
  membership association model,
    143–4, 218, 222
Mencap, 23, 37–8
mergers and alliances, 171–4
micro voluntary agencies, 219–20,
    229, 236
Milofsky, Carl, 110, 166, 219, 222,
    223, 241
mimetic isomorphism, 128
Ministry of Health, encouragement of
    volunteers, 56
'mixed economy of welfare', 46, 70–3,
    88, 96
  and role of voluntary sector, 159
monasteries and poor relief,
    18, 22
monetarism, 87

motivations for volunteering, 7
  and civil society paradigm, 178
  and dominant paradigm, 176, 177;
    alternatives to, 178–88
  and instrumental-expressive
    organisations, 150–1
  and organisations driven by values,
    152–5
  research on, 238–9, 240
  and serious leisure paradigm, 180,
    229
  unmanaged volunteers, 227–9
mutual aid
  and civil society paradigm, 178, 186
  and conviviality, 31
  exclusion from policy agenda, 70,
    77
  and expressive organisations, 150
  historical context, 16, 17, 21–3, 26,
    33–4
  and UN global typology, 183;
    mutual aid type volunteering,
    186

National Association of Community
  Associations, 114
National Association of Councils for
  Voluntary Service (NACVS), 114,
  116
National Association for Voluntary
  and Community Action (NAVCA),
  114, 115, 116, 117, 118, 120
National Centre for Volunteering, 63
National Coalition for Independent
  Action (NCIA), 1, 118, 189,
  193–201, 214
  anti-privatisation campaign, 198–9
  composition and origins, 194–6
  critique of exisiting system and
    manifesto, 196–201, 202, 234
National Council for Social Service
  (NCSS), 3, 21, 38, 39–40, 55, 62,
  113
National Council for Voluntary
  Organisations (NCVO), 1, 21, 38,
  39, 48, 63, 114, 160, 214
  and alternative paradigm, 241
  Civil Society Almanac, 83
  civil society organisations, 219

and Coalition funding cuts, 82–3,
    118, 198
  'Improving Effectiveness in
    Voluntary Organisation', 49–50
  managerialism and Management
    Development Unit, 50, 118–19,
    120, 164
  and market-based approaches, 95–6,
    120–1
  and partnership approaches, 115
  Quality Standards Task Group, 75,
    119
  and service delivery role, 116
  and sub-contracting of services,
    122–3
National Health Service (NHS)
  and 'mixed economy' funding, 72–3
  out-sourcing of services, 89, 90–1
  and volunteers, 54, 56
National Institute for Social Work
    Training, 55, 61
national intermediary bodies, 39–40
  and alternative paradigm, 241
  Independent Sector in USA, 43–4
  and management practices and
    training, 50, 51, 84, 125; Aves
    Report recommendations, 61–2,
    63; promotion of
    managerialism, 118–20, 124
  and market-based approaches and
    values, 95–6, 117, 120–3
  merging of bodies, 172
  and narrowing perspective on
    voluntary action, 112, 113–23,
    127; and Coalition cuts and
    welfare reforms, 117–18;
    promotion of partnership,
    114–15, 122–3
  New Labour and funding, 75,
    113–14, 115–16
  problem of representation, 113
National Occupational Standards, 65
National Support Services, 120
need
  personal need and volunteering,
    103–4
  see also social need
neo-liberalism, 87–8

Neuberger, Julia, Commission on the Future of Volunteering, 80–1, 82, 116, 157
Neuhaus, R., 159
New Economics Foundation (NEF), 194–5
New Labour governments
  and 'boundary crossers', 126
  and distinctive features of voluntary sector, 207–8
  funding of intermediary bodies and 'strategic partners', 75, 113–14, 115–16
  and governing bodies, 136
  and invention of voluntary sector: Compacts with voluntary sector, 48–9, 51–2, 73–7, 82, 83, 113–14, 115–16; investment in training and research, 50–1; and 'mixed economy of welfare', 46, 70–3, 88
  managerialism and voluntary sector, 65, 76, 119–20
  and neo-liberalism, 88
  partnership approaches, 73–7, 84, 198; and focus on service delivery, 74–5, 76–7, 213–14; intermediary bodies and promotion of, 114–16
  promotion of voluntary sector, 79–80
  and terminology for voluntary sector, 52
  'third sector' ideology, 36–7
'new philanthropy', 21
New Public Management, 5, 91, 97
  and 'product champions', 112
  see also managerialism
'Next Steps' programme and Civil Service, 91
NGOs (non-governmental organisations), 29–30
NHS and Community Care Act (1990), 72, 78, 90
non-bureaucratic organisations, 216, 218–30, 234–5
  degrees of formality, 223–4
  implications of, 235–44

organisation and guidance, 226–7
  positive definition, 224–6
non-governmental organisations (NGOs), 29–30
'non-profit paradigm', 177–8, 186
  see also dominant paradigm in volunteering
non-profit sector, 2
  in USA, 36, 42–6, 126, 209–10, 211
  see also voluntary and community sector
normative isomorphism, 128
Nunn, Thomas Hancock, 21

occupational support type volunteering, 187
Office for Civil Society, 48, 160
Office for the Third Sector, 48, 115, 192, 214
older people as volunteers and Aves Report, 60
Open University, Voluntary Sector Management Programme, 50, 125
Opportunities for Volunteering Fund, 63
organisational ecology, 128
organisational forms, 34–5
  and civil society paradigm, 178–9
  diversity of voluntary sector, 209–12
  historical context: 'business' model, 26, 50, 51, 70, 77, 85–6, 94, 95, 119; charities, 19–20, 139
  institutional isomorphism and organisational ecology, 128
  invention of voluntary sector, 38–9; drawbacks of, 205–15
  and market imperatives, 93–4, 120–2
  non-bureaucratic forms, 216, 218–30, 234–5; implications of, 235–44; and limitations of conventional organisational theory, 221–3, 238, 241–2
  organisational context and volunteering, 217–18
  typology of, 235–7
  and volunteering as serious leisure, 181, 229

see also bureaucratic model and organisational form; 'business' model and voluntary organisations; governance; voluntary organisations
out-sourcing of services, 89
  corporate partnerships and sub-contracting, 122–3
  and funding, 93
ownership and governance, 133, 140–5, 232–3
  of government agencies, 142–3
  levels of ownership, 143
  non-bureaucratic organisations, 222–3, 242–3
  and voluntary organisations, 141–5, 146

paid staff in voluntary organisations, 94–5
  ambiguous voluntary agencies, 107–8, 109
  and hybridisation of voluntary agencies, 109, 219–20
  and power, 144–5
  see also professional staff in voluntary organisations
Paine, Angela Ellis, 6
Panel on the Independence of the Voluntary Sector, 2, 193–4, 202
paradigms of voluntary action, 2
  alternative perspectives, 133–202, 216–30, 233–4; governance issues, 133–46, 228, 232–3; implications of, 235–44; non-bureaucratic organisations and action, 216, 218–30, 234–44; unmanaged volunteering, 216–18, 227–9, 240
  narrow paradigms, 6–7, 66, 216, 231–2; and pressures from within the sector, 112–29, 194, 232
  see also dominant paradigm in volunteering
participation and UN global typology, 183

partnership approaches, 5, 73–7, 112, 198
  and boundary crossers, 127
  Compacts between state and voluntary sector, 48–9, 51–2, 73–7; dismantling by Coalition government, 82, 83; and funding, 75, 113–14, 115–16, 190
  corporate partners for voluntary organisations, 122–3
  focus on service delivery, 74–5, 76–7, 93, 116–18
  Local Strategic Partnerships, 49, 74, 116
  state appropriation of voluntary activity, 47; and narrowing of perspective on voluntary action, 114–16; and objectives of state and voluntary organisations, 76–7, 84, 114–15
partnership model and governance, 137
Paton, R., 154, 167, 168, 169
peacekeeping as voluntary activity, 184
Pearce, Jone, 239
Penn, Alison, 26, 70
performance measurement, 166–9
performing and volunteering, 150, 158, 160, 180, 184
personal assistance and voluntary action, 185
personal need and volunteering, 103–4
personal world and social needs, 106–7, 109–10, 111
Pharoah, C., 191, 192
philanthropy
  and conviviality, 31, 149
  historical development, 16, 17, 18–21, 31, 33, 34; and organisational form, 70, 139; and role of state, 24, 26
  and UN global typology, 183
  see also non-profit sector, in USA
physical activity. *see* sports and physical activity
physical capital and volunteering, 156

play and benefits of volunteering, 157–8
playgroups movement, 23
pluralistic welfare model, 38, 41, 159
policy setting and governing bodies, 134
policy sub-elites, 39, 52, 77
political protest
  historical context, 16, 17, 29–30
  and voluntary action, 185
  see also campaigning activity
political and social engagement type volunteering, 186–7
politics of volunteering, 79–82
  political role of voluntary sector, 159–60
'polymorphic' groups, 223–4, 226–7
Poor Law (1834), 21
Popple, K., 30
poverty relief
  'deserving' and 'undeserving' poor, 20
  as focus of texts on voluntary action, 16, 17
  and history of voluntary action, 18–19
  see also social need
Powell, W., 128
power
  and bureaucracy, 99
  and non-bureaucratic groups, 229
  in voluntary agencies, 138–9, 144–5, 146
Prather, J., 150, 158
pre-school playgroups movement, 23
prestige as incentive, 227
principal owners, 133, 143, 144, 145, 146, 232–3, 243
principal–agency theory and governance, 136–7
private sector
  and commissioning of services, 198, 215
  see also 'business' model and voluntary organisations; market-based approach to welfare; privatisation

privatisation, 88–90, 214
  NCIA's anti-privatisation campaign, 198–9
Probation Service and volunteers, 54
professional staff in voluntary organisations, 3, 5
  chief executives, 112, 114, 115, 123–4, 127
  and governance and power, 144–5, 146
  historical origins in Aves Committee, 55, 59, 65
  and 'mixed economy of welfare', 73
  public sector services, 54
profit-making
  and intermediary bodies, 120–1
  and ownership of organisations, 141–2, 143
project-based volunteering, 180
promotion of commerce as voluntary action, 184
Public Administration Select Committee, 117
public goods, 142–3
public sector reform and market model, 89, 90–2, 122–3, 214
purchasing of services in 'mixed economy', 72–3, 90–1, 93
purposive incentives, 227

quality control, 166–9
Quality Standards Task Group (QSTG), 75, 119

rational-legal authority structures, 100, 103–4
Reading Committee, 54
recreation. *see* leisure
recruitment and selection
  and bureaucratic model, 100, 136
  of volunteers: and Aves Report, 58, 59–60, 65; and dominant paradigm, 177–8; and market-based approaches, 94–5; non-bureaucratic organisations, 228; and research, 238–9
Reform Act (1832), 28

regulation
    and constraints on voluntary
        organisations, 81, 83
    historical context, 19
    and New Labour managerialism,
        65, 76
religion
    and expressive organisations,
        150
    and organisations driven by values,
        152–3, 155
    and voluntary action, 185–6;
        religiosity type volunteering,
        187
religious fraternities and mutual
    aid, 22
representation. *see* intermediary
    bodies/infrastructure
    organisations
reputation and corporate partners,
    123
research. *see* academic research and
    teaching
resource dependency theory and
    governance, 137
resources
    and affiliated non-bureaucratic
        groups, 225
    competition and loss of shared
        resources, 171
    and governing bodies, 134
    see also funding
retention of volunteers, 238
Richardson, A., 220
Ridley, Nicholas, 90
Robb, Campbell, 115
Rochester, Colin, 15, 50, 60, 65, 96,
    187–8, 217, 228
    'boundary crossers', 126, 127
    checklist of voluntary activity,
        183–6
    and 'civil society' paradigm,
        178–9
    dominant paradigm, 6, 66
    New Labour and voluntary
        sector, 74
    Total Activities Analysis, 138
    tripartite conceptual map, 176,
        186

Roehampton University, 211
    Centre for the Study of Voluntary
        and Community Activity, 4, 6
    'round earth' map of volunteering,
        176–88
    suggestions for alternative
        paradigm, 216–30, 233–4
    'rubber stamp' model and governance,
        137
rural community councils (RCCs), 40
Russell, L., 94

Saidel, J., 140
Salamon, Lester, 45–6, 218–19,
    237
salaried workers
    and bureaucratic model, 100
    see also paid staff in voluntary
        organisations
Sandel, Michael J., 97
Sargent, A., 169
'scientific philanthropy', 20
Scott, D., 94
second-tier organisations. *see*
    intermediary
    bodies/infrastructure
    organisations
sectorisation paradox, 205–15, 234
Seebohm Committee and Report, 54,
    59–60
selection. *see* recruitment and
    selection
self-help activity
    and civil society paradigm, 178,
        179
    exclusion from policy agenda, 73,
        77
    and expressive organisations, 150
    historical context, 21–2, 23
    and mutual aid type volunteering,
        186
    and UN global typology, 183
self-help groups, 219, 220, 229, 236
    and incentives, 227
Selznick, Philip, 133, 140
SERCO, 122–3
service delivery. *see* voluntary
    organisations, service delivery role
service incentives, 227

service users
  as clients in 'business' model, 95
  and marketing practices, 170–1
  and power in voluntary
    organisations, 139
  user involvement, 95, 191
  see also customers
settlements movement, 31, 166
'shallow' hybrid groups, 108–9,
    110–11, 144, 146, 218, 233, 242–3
shareholders and ownership, 141–2
Sheard, J., 54–5
Simey, Margaret, 26
6, Perri, 37, 38, 39, 43, 45, 77
size and non-bureaucratic groups, 224
Smerdon, Matthew, 190, 191, 192
Smith, David Horton, 176, 210
  associational form, 104, 106, 151
  expressive behaviour and play, 157,
    158
  grassroots associations, 3, 5, 155,
    213
  non-bureaucratic groups and
    associations, 219, 223–4, 226–8,
    240
sociability incentive, 227, 229
  see also conviviality and voluntary
    action
social activities for children and
  young people, 33
social assistance and voluntary action,
  186
social capital and volunteering, 147,
  156
social change, historical context, 16,
  27–30
social enterprises, 86, 97, 236
  state support for, 74, 214
social housing and privatisation, 89
social justice, historical context, 16,
  27–30
social movements, 27–9, 34, 226–7
social need
  identification, 96
  organisational flexibility and
    response to, 103
  and personal world, 106–7, 109–10,
    111
social security system, 23, 108

Social Services Departments
  and 'mixed economy' funding, 72–3
  and volunteers, 54, 56
social welfare
  and commissioning of services, 78
  historical focus on, 16, 24, 177
  and levels of voluntary action, 53–4
  and 'mixed economy' funding, 72–3
  and out-sourcing of services, 89–90,
    93
  and paradigms of voluntary action,
    6, 7, 40–1
social work
  historical origins and volunteering,
    20, 53–4
  and 'mixed economy' funding, 72–3
  and use of volunteers, 54; Aves
    Committee and volunteers in
    social services, 55–66;
    reservations of social workers,
    57; skills and functions of
    volunteers, 57–8
socialising. *see* conviviality and
  voluntary action
societies. *see* clubs and societies
'specified sphere of competence' and
  bureaucratic model, 100, 103
sports and physical activity
  and clubs and societies, 33, 149, 150
  event support and voluntary action,
    185
  and volunteering as serious leisure,
    180
staff
  and power in voluntary agencies,
    138–9, 144–5, 146
  see also chief executives; paid staff
    in voluntary organisations;
    professional staff in voluntary
    organisations
stakeholder model and governance,
  137, 142
state and voluntary action, 69–84, 232
  argument for independence of
    voluntary sector, 82, 189–202,
    234
  Aves Committee and
    encouragement of volunteers,
    54, 55–66

'boundary crossers', 115, 126–7
complementary services, 93, 108, 159
historical context, 16, 17–18, 20–1; affiliated orders and social security, 23; and alternative forms of voluntary action, 34; cross-sector personnel and leadership, 25–6; 'mixed economy of welfare', 46, 70–3; and 'moving frontier', 24–6, 34; supply of complementary services, 93
and invention of voluntary sector, 37–8, 44–5, 46–9; Compacts and partnership approach, 48–9, 51–2, 73–7, 82, 83, 113–14, 115–16, 190; drawbacks of, 205–15
managerialism and government bodies, 161, 162
negative impacts on voluntary action, 80–2, 83–4; critique of NCIA, 196–9, 202; and market-based approach to welfare, 92–3, 214–15
ownership and government agencies, 142–3
political role of voluntary sector, 159–60
see also market-based approach to welfare; partnership approaches; social work
Stebbins, R., 179, 180
stewardship theory and governance, 137
'Stop the Rot' campaign, 194–5
'strategic partners', 49, 51, 75, 82–3, 113–14, 115
strategic planning, 164–6
Strengthening the Voluntary Sector (STVS) programme, 189, 190–2, 194, 195
structural-operational definition of voluntary organisation, 209–10
sub-contracting of services, 122–3

Tarrow, S., 28
Task Force, 55

Taylor, Marilyn, 3, 17, 18, 22, 27, 30, 32
tenants' movements, historical context, 30
Thatcher, Margaret, 70, 87, 88
third sector, 2, 36–7, 43, 52
association as ideal organisational form, 105, 110, 218, 234–5
New Labour's focus on service delivery, 74–5, 76–7, 213–14
see also voluntary and community sector
Third Sector Research Centre (TSRC), 51, 125, 237
Thomas, B., 169
Tilly, Charles, 28–9
Times, The, 19
top-down bureaucratic organisations, 102–3
Total Activities Analysis (TAA), 138
Toynbee Hall, London, 31, 166
Trades Union Congress, 3
trades unions, 3, 31
traditional authority structures, 100
traditional model and governing bodies, 139
traditional service type volunteering, 186
training
Aves Report and training of volunteers, 58, 60–2, 65
of managers, 113, 125
Transforming Local Infrastructure Fund, 172
'transorganizations', 109
Tudor Trust, 196, 197
typologies
alternatives to dominant paradigm, 235–7
typology mapping and volunteering, 182–7

UN International Year of Volunteers, 81, 183, 186
'undeserving' poor distinction, 20
United Nations Volunteers (UNV), 182–7

United States
   and expressive-instrumental
      organisations, 150
   invention of non-profit sector, 36,
      42–6; and academic research,
      45–6, 126, 209–10, 211
   and monetarism, 87
   non-bureaucratic organisations,
      219, 228
universities settlements movement,
      31, 166
unmanaged volunteering, 216–18,
      240
   motivation, 227–9
unorganised groups, 104, 107,
      109–10, 111, 209–10, 219, 229,
      235
   see also non-bureaucratic
      organisations
unpaid work
   and benefits conditionality, 81
   view of volunteering as, 7, 60–1,
      64–5, 94–5, 231; and alternative
      perspectives, 181, 182, 216–18,
      233–4; and dominant
      paradigm, 66, 177, 216; and
      economic capital, 156
user involvement, 95, 191
users. *see* customers; service users
utilitarian incentives, 227

values and voluntary organisations,
      97, 152–5, 158
   religious and faith-based
      organisations, 152–3, 155
'virtual councils', 90
voluntary action
   account of personal experiences,
      2–6
   analysis of role and purpose,
      147–60; voluntary
      organisations, 147–55, 160;
      voluntary sector, 158–60;
      volunteering, 156–8, 160, 233
   changes in attitudes and
      approaches, 1–8; and pressures
      from within the sector, 112–29,
      194, 232
   description, 2

   invention of 'voluntary work',
      53–66, 232; and boom in 1960s,
      54–5
   see also history of voluntary action;
      paradigms of voluntary action
Voluntary Action History Society, 4
voluntary agencies, 2
voluntary and community sector, 2
   analysis of role and purpose, 158–60
   distinctive identity, 159, 207–12,
      238; diversity of organisations,
      7, 51, 111, 207, 209–12; loss of
      distinctive identity, 86, 96, 232,
      234
   drawbacks of sectorisation
      approach, 205–15, 234;
      commonalities and
      sectorisation approach, 205–6;
      distinctions and diversity of
      organisations, 207–12, 234;
      incompatible elements, 212,
      215; paradox of sectorisation,
      214–15
   invention as concept and entity,
      36–52, 232; broader and
      narrower definitions, 44, 210;
      and changing relationship with
      state, 37–8, 44–5, 46–9; and
      development of voluntary
      organisations, 49–52; in UK, 36,
      37–42, 43–6; in USA, 36, 42–6
   New Labour and capacity building,
      75–7, 84, 119–20
   pressures from within the sector,
      112–29, 194, 232
   problems of representation, 113
   typology of sector, 235–7
   and voluntary sector paradigm, 6
   see also independence of voluntary
      sector; third sector
voluntary, community and social
      enterprise (VCSE) sector, 52
voluntary organisations, 2
   analysis of role and purpose, 147–55
   and civil society paradigm, 178–9
   development and management:
      changing practices and
      managerialism, 4–5, 65, 76,
      118–20, 124, 126, 161–75, 233,

241–2; and invention of voluntary sector, 49–52; and market-based approaches, 85–98, 117, 120–3, 214–15

distribution of power in, 138–9, 144–5, 146

diversity, 7, 51, 111, 207, 209–12

and dominant paradigm of volunteering, 177–8, 216, 231–2; emphasis on minority 'corporate' agencies, 212–14, 237–8; non-bureaucratic alternatives, 216, 218–30, 234–44

and expressive and instrumental dimensions, 149–55, 160, 222, 224, 233, 242

and historical archives, 15

impact of New Labour policies and goals of voluntary action, 76–7

and managerialism and management practices, 161–75, 233

and ownership, 141–5, 146, 222–3, 242–3

representation. *see* intermediary bodies/infrastructure organisations

and sectorisation approach, 205–15, 234; shared challenges facing, 206–7; shared features, 205–6; structural-operational definition, 209–10

service delivery role: corporate partners and sub-contracting of services, 122–3; and funding streams, 47, 78, 190; market-based approach and focus on, 86, 93, 117, 121; and mixed economy, 46–7, 70–3, 96, 159; and narrowing of perspective on voluntary action, 116–18, 120, 231–2; partnership working and capacity building, 73–7, 84, 119–20; shift from contracting to commissioning, 77–8, 198, 215; and types of voluntary sector organisations, 213–14

and voluntary sector paradigm, 6; and pressures from within voluntary sector, 112–29, 194, 232

see also funding; governance; management practices; organisational forms; partnership approaches; staff

voluntary sector paradigm, 6
drawbacks of, 205–15
and pressures from within the sector, 112–29, 194, 232
see also dominant paradigm in volunteering; voluntary and community sector

Voluntary Sector Review (journal), 125

Voluntary Sector Studies Network, 50, 125

Voluntary Services Unit (VSU), 47, 48

Voluntary Studies Sector Network, 86

'voluntary work', invention of, 53–66

volunteer bureaux, 62, 63

Volunteer Centre UK, 63, 114

volunteer centres, 63–4, 82
core functions, 64

Volunteer Development England, 63

volunteer management profession, 5, 73, 125, 239
and Aves Report recommendations, 55, 59, 65

Volunteer Management Programme, 65

volunteering
benefits of, 156–8, 160
and organisational context, 217–18
as serious leisure, 179–82, 229
see also dominant paradigm in volunteering; motivations for volunteering; volunteers

Volunteering Code, 116

Volunteering England (VE), 39, 115, 120, 121, 157
creation through merger, 63, 172, 173
and volunteer bureaux/centres, 63–4, 82, 114
and Volunteering Code, 116

Volunteering Foundation, 61–2

'volunteering industry', 176
volunteers
  and civil society paradigm, 179
  identity and inclusiveness, 60, 65;
    and 'business' model, 94–5
  recruitment strategies, 59–60,
    65, 136; and dominant
    paradigm, 177–8; and
    market-based approaches,
    94–5; non-bureaucratic
    organisations, 228
  research on, 238–9, 240
  retention, 238
  and serious leisure paradigm, 181,
    229
  unmanaged volunteers, 216–18,
    227–9, 240
  see also volunteering

Wanless, Derek, 92
Warriner, C., 150, 158
Waterhouse, Penny, 194, 197, 198,
    200–1
Weber, Max, 99–101, 104, 148
Weisbrod, B., 238
welfare pluralism, 38, 41
  'mixed economy of welfare', 46,
    70–3, 88, 159
welfare services
  growing role of state, 24–5
  voluntary sector and service
    delivery: focus of partnership
    approach, 74–5, 76–7, 93,
    116–18; and funding streams,
    47, 78, 190; market-based
    approach and focus on, 86, 93,
    117, 121; in mixed economy,
    46–7, 70–3, 96, 159; supply of
    mainstream not
    complementary services, 93
  see also voluntary organisations:
    service delivery role

welfare state, 24, 29
  'crisis' in 1970s, 70–1
  and levels of volunteering, 53–4
'whole life' ownership and
    governance, 133, 140, 145, 232
Wilkes, John, 28
Wittenberg, B., 213–14
Wolfenden Committee and Report,
    36, 37, 38, 39–42, 44, 75, 113–14,
    119, 159, 164
women
  clubs and societies for, 33
  lady visitors and philanthropy,
    20, 31
  and social movements, 28
'word of mouth' and recruitment, 59,
    60, 228
Workers' Educational Association
    (WEA), 3
Working Group on Government
    Relations, 48, 113–14, 115
working men's clubs and conviviality,
    31–2
workplace model and voluntary
    sector, 65
'worlds' theory and organisational
    form, 106–7, 109–11, 238
written records
  archives of voluntary organisations,
    15
  and bureaucratic model, 100

Yale, Program on Nonprofit
    Organizations, 45
young people and voluntary action,
    54–5, 183
  youth movements, 227
Young Volunteer Force Foundation, 55

Zimmeck, M., 65, 74, 115, 125, 164,
    242
Zurcher, L., 224

Printed and bound by CPI Group (UK) Ltd, Croydon, CR0 4YY